Between Europe and America

BETWEEN EUROPE
and
AMERICA

THE CANADIAN TRADITION IN FICTION

T.D. MacLulich

ECW PRESS

Canadian Cataloguing in Publication Data

MacLulich, Thomas Donald.
Between Europe and America

Includes index.
ISBN 0-920763-96-0 (bound). –
ISBN 0-920763-95-2 (pbk.).

1. Canadian fiction (English) – 20th century –
History and criticism.* I. Title.

PS8187.M33 1988   C813.509   C87-093318-3
PR9192.5.M33 1988

56,677

Between Europe and America was published with the
assistance of the Canadian Federation for the
Humanities using funds provided by the Social Sci-
ences and Humanities Research Council of Canada.
Additional grants have been provided by the Ontario
Arts Council and The Canada Council.

Typeset by ECW Production Services, Oakville.
Printed and bound by University of Toronto Press.
Cover design by Bette Davies.

Contents

Acknowledgements

This book was completed with the help of a Kaypro computer and Murchie's coffee. Its writing was made possible by a Research Stipend awarded by the Social Sciences and the Humanities Research Council of Canada. Larry Mathews and Margery Fee read the manuscript and made useful comments. Clara Thomas provided timely encouragement. Publication was assisted by a grant from the Canadian Federation for the Humanities, using funds provided by the Social Sciences and Humanities Research Council of Canada.

Some portions of the book are based on previously published materials. Chapter Five is a revised version of "Our Place on the Map: The Canadian Tradition in Fiction," *University of Toronto Quarterly*, 52, No. 2 (Winter 1982/83), 191–208; Chapter Eight is based on "Colloquial Style and the Tory Mode," *Canadian Literature*, No. 89 (Summer 1981), pp. 7–21; Chapter Nine and the Epilogue contain material from"What Was Canadian Literature? Taking Stock of the Canlit Industry," *Essays on Canadian Writing*, No. 30 (Winter 1984–85), pp. 17–34. Short portions of the following articles have been incorporated into the manuscript: "Fiction and Canadian Society, 1890–1940," *Studies in Canadian Literature*, 3, No. 2 (Summer 1978), 211–31; " 'Anne of Green Gables' and the Regional Idyll," *Dalhousie Review*, 63 (Autumn 1983), 488–501; "L. M. Montgomery and the Literary Heroine: Jo, Rebecca, Anne, and Emily," *Canadian Children's Literature*, No. 37 (1985), pp. 5–17; "L. M. Montgomery's Portraits of the Artist: Realism, Idealism and the Domestic Imagination," *English Studies in Canada*, 11 (Dec. 1985), 459–73.

for Orleen

The Canadian Tradition in Fiction

Speech, for the Englishman, does not exist in order to express ideas, but in order to denote *class*. That must never be forgotten.

– Wyndham Lewis, *America, I Presume*

My books are water; those of the great geniuses are wine. Everybody drinks water.

– Mark Twain

Is there a "tradition" of Canadian fiction? If there is such a tradition, when did it begin to take on clearly discernible features? And exactly what are those features? Whatever the more sanguine members of the Canlit fraternity may think, these questions are far from being settled. In the recently published *Oxford Companion to Canadian Literature*, W.J. Keith says of the fiction written from 1940 to 1960:

English-Canadian fiction in this period shows few signs of forming a coherent literary pattern. There is no sense of a national movement, of predominant themes and approaches, of an accepted novelistic technique, or even of a concerted attempt to express Canadian or mid-twentieth-century consciousness.[1]

In another recent book David Stouck insists: "until very recently there has been no sense of a developing tradition among Canadian fiction writers. In discussing the Canadian novel one moves from one isolated instance of achievement to another, with great gaps in between."[2] Neither of these critics, then, acknowledges the existence of a well-established Canadian tradition in fiction.

My own view is quite different. I think that an identifiable tradition of Canadian fiction has existed for a considerable time. Whatever critics such as Keith and Stouck may say, I think that the members of the so-called "thematic" school of criticism have already recognized and described many of the leading features of the Canadian tradition in fiction.[3] Like many of the thematic critics, I date the first full

---

[1] W.J. Keith, "Novels in English: 1940 to 1960," in William Toye, gen. ed., *The Oxford Companion to Canadian Literature* (Toronto: Oxford Univ. Press, 1983), p. 573. In the introduction to his recent book, *Canadian Literature in English* (London: Longman, 1985), Keith does apply the word "tradition" to Canadian writing. But he also writes that in the Canadian fiction of the 1940s and 1950s, "no easily discernible, cumulative pattern emerges. Instead, individual novelists are best seen as writing what they wanted to write without any conspicuous sense of belonging to a recognizable group or movement" (p. 138).

[2] David Stouck, *Major Canadian Authors: A Critical Introduction* (Lincoln: Univ. of Nebraska Press, 1984), p. 241.

[3] The leading examples of thematic criticism are: Warren Tallman, "Wolf in the Snow," *Canadian Literature*, No. 5 (Summer 1960), pp. 7-20 and *Canadian Literature*, No. 6 (Autumn 1960), pp. 41-48, rpt. in Eli Mandel, ed., *Contexts of Canadian Criticism* (Chicago: Univ. of Chicago Press, 1971), pp. 232-53; Henry Kreisel, "The Prairie: A State of Mind," in Mandel, ed., *Contexts of Canadian Criticism*, pp. 254-66; Northrop Frye, "Conclusion," in Carl F. Klinck, gen. ed., *Literary History of Canada: Canadian Literature in English* (Toronto: Univ. of Toronto Press, 1965), pp. 821-49, and *The Bush Garden: Essays on the Canadian Imagination* (Toronto: Anansi, 1971); D.G. Jones, *Butterfly on Rock: A Study of Themes and Images in Canadian Literature* (Toronto: Univ. of Toronto Press, 1970); Ronald Sutherland, *Second Image: Comparative Studies in Québec/Canadian Literature* (Toronto: New, 1971), and *The New Hero: Essays in Comparative Quebec/Cana-*

flowering of the Canadian novel from the work of the literary generation that includes Frederick Philip Grove, Morley Callaghan, Ernest Buckler, Hugh MacLennan, Robertson Davies, Ethel Wilson, Sinclair Ross, and W.O. Mitchell. In the years between the two great wars, a few other writers such as Martha Ostenso, Robert Stead, and Raymond Knister also contributed notable single novels to the emerging fictional consensus. In the chapters that follow, I will argue that the work of these authors constitutes a tradition in two senses. In the first place, their books exhibit family resemblances – similar characters, similar settings, similar conflicts, and upon occasion similar stylistic features. In the second place, after these Canadian authors began to create a distinctive body of fiction, their work was used by subsequent writers as a point of departure.

Once the existence of a Canadian tradition in fiction is acknowledged, some additional questions that go beyond the explication and evaluation of individual texts immediately present themselves. When and why did the Canadian tradition begin to take shape? What is the relationship of the Canadian tradition to the older tradition of Europe and the new tradition of the United States? Answers to these questions must take into account both Canada's historical debt to European culture, and the cultural implications of its geographical position at the top of the North American map. I think it is inevitable that any historical examination of the Canadian tradition in fiction will trace a movement away from the emulation of British writers and towards an increasing awareness of the work being done by American writers. Yet Canadian critics have paid surprisingly little attention to the process by which a colonial literature that was overwhelmingly class-conscious or aristocratic in spirit was transformed into a branch of the democratic North American literary mainstream.

---

dian Literature (Toronto: Macmillan, 1977); Margaret Atwood, Survival: A Thematic Guide to Canadian Literature (Toronto: Anansi, 1972); John Moss, Patterns of Isolation in English Canadian Fiction (Toronto: McClelland and Stewart, 1974).

One of the few critics who has directly acknowledged this change in the underlying outlook of Canadian fiction is Warren Tallman, in his idiosyncratic essay "Wolf in the Snow." Tallman's article considers five major Canadian novels: Sinclair Ross's *As for Me and My House* (1941), Hugh MacLennan's *Each Man's Son* (1951), Ernest Buckler's *The Mountain and the Valley* (1952), W.O. Mitchell's *Who Has Seen the Wind* (1947), and Mordecai Richler's *The Apprenticeship of Duddy Kravitz* (1959). Tallman doesn't like the first four of these books very much. He finds their protagonists to be inhibited and self-defeating. Whether the reader encounters Philip Bentley, Dr. Daniel Ainslie, David Canaan, or Brian O'Connal, Tallman contends, "the initial impression gained is that of his isolation," and in each character "the isolation is ingrained, inherent, indwelling."[1] Tallman argues that these characters, like too many Canadians, adhere to values that are out-of-place in the new world. They "adopt European disguises having little or nothing to do with the self beneath, the source of vital energy" (p. 243). The underlying premise of Tallman's argument is clear: he thinks that the central values of North American culture differ from the central values of European culture – in fact, he argues that some of the fundamental values of European culture have been overturned in the new world. In North America, he contends, "finer is relatively crude, because frequently untrue, and crude can be relatively fine" (p. 252).

In effect, Tallman treats Canadian literature as an extension of American letters. He looks at Canadian literature through dogmatically American eyes, and he imposes an outlook that he has transferred unchanged from his romantic and primitivistic reading of American literature. Tallman's American outlook is most apparent when he turns to his last exhibit, Richler's *The Apprenticeship of Duddy Kravitz*. It quickly becomes apparent that Tallman sides with Duddy against a society that views Duddy only as "a *pusherke*. A little Jew-boy on the make."[2] Tallman contends that Duddy

---

[1] Tallman, "Wolf in the Snow," pp. 232, 247. All further references to this work appear in the text.

[2] Mordecai Richler, *The Apprenticeship of Duddy Kravitz* (Harmondsworth: Penguin, 1964), p. 242.

exemplifies the transformation of conventional European values that has taken place in North America, and he admires the unabashed directness and the single-minded intensity with which Duddy pursues his dream. I shall argue later that Tallman is so fascinated by Duddy's vitality that he neglects the clear signals that Richler gives us concerning Duddy's moral failure. But given Tallman's initial premises, his misreading of Richler's novel is almost predictable. Despite its eccentricities, Tallman's article remains a landmark in the criticism of Canadian fiction because it is one of the first attempts to view Canadian fiction against a cultural background that is North American rather than British.

But the Canadian literary tradition is not simply a lesser echo of American literature, as Tallman seems to think. Canadian writers have been much slower to create a distinctive national tradition than have their American counterparts. In cultural terms, nineteenth-century Canada did not develop an identity of its own, but remained poised uncertainly between Europe and America. Only during the early years of this century do a significant number of Canadian authors start to free themselves from a highly class-conscious or European view of literature, and begin to create a body of fiction that is thoroughly North American in spirit. And not until nearly mid-century does there appear a generation of Canadian writers whose accomplishment in defining a Canadian tradition can be compared to the achievement of "classic" nineteenth-century American writers. In other words, not until well into the present century do the best Canadian novelists begin, as Hugo McPherson puts it, "to 'create' Canada in the way that Hawthorne, a century earlier, helped to create New England."[1]

Before I examine twentieth-century Canadian fiction, I will look at the nineteenth-century literary context out of which the Canadian tradition in fiction eventually emerged. A basic premise of my argument will be the contention that the very notion of literature has undergone a considerable change during the more than two centuries since Frances Brooke published *The History of Emily Montague* (1769), the

---

[1] Hugo McPherson, "Fiction 1940-1960," in Klinck, ed., *Literary History of Canada*, p. 694.

book from which the beginnings of Canadian fiction are usually dated. It is now a commonplace of literary history that during the eighteenth and nineteenth centuries a new kind of prose fiction gained a striking prominence. As Ian Watt has argued, the rise of the novel in eighteenth-century England was closely linked with the rise of the commercial middle class.[1] During the nineteenth century, the continued expansion of the middle classes together with the spread of at least a rudimentary level of literacy among an increasingly large proportion of the total population created a new kind of reading public: the popular or mass readership. As a result, the bourgeois novel of social realism, which describes the everyday life of characters who are predominantly drawn from the middle classes, increasingly supplanted the older romance, which describes the adventures of characters who are members of the gentry or the aristocracy.

In Canada, the aristocratic view of literature remained dominant much longer than it did in the United States. Many of the important literary figures in pre-Confederation Canada shared a sense of cultural exile. They thought that a truly cultured and sophisticated society existed only among the genteel classes of the old world, and they thought of literature as something that was written by members of the social elite and was aimed at members of the same class. Consequently, in much of their work they wrote for a cultivated and class-conscious readership that simply did not exist in great numbers in Canada. As J.P. Matthews remarks in *Tradition in Exile*, throughout most of the nineteenth century "Canadian letters were influenced by the English tradition and relatively uninfluenced by the American."[2]

The work of several nineteenth-century historical romancers clearly illustrates the difficulties that early Canadian authors encounter when they try to adapt the European literary tradition to a new world social environment. During

---

[1] Ian Watt, *The Rise of the Novel: Studies in Defoe, Richardson and Fielding* (Harmondsworth: Penguin, 1974).

[2] John Pengwerne Matthews, *Tradition in Exile: A Comparative Study of Social Influences on the Development of Australian and Canadian Poetry during the Nineteenth Century*, Univ. of Toronto Department of English Studies and Texts, No. 10 (Toronto: Univ. of Toronto Press, 1962), p. 8.

much of the nineteenth century, Canadian authors treat the North American setting of their historical tales merely as a kind of exotic decor or picturesque stage setting for stories that are thoroughly European in conception. Instead of creating identifiably North American characters and social settings, they habitually imitate the refined manners and the rigidly stratified society that they found in European aristocratic romances. In the majority of Canadian historical novels, the authors do make some attempt to situate their protagonists against a North American background, but the impact of the North American environment on their fiction is minimal: only a few of the lesser stage properties are altered, and the minor characters are given a new provenance. The central patterns of plot and characterization are still borrowed directly from European literature. The overwhelmingly European flavour of this early fiction is lessened only slightly in several stories inspired by the fiction of James Fenimore Cooper.

A more democratic or North American conception of literature first becomes prominent in the work of turn-of-the-century writers such as Ralph Connor and L.M. Montgomery. The commercial success of these writers has often led critics to dismiss their work as merely "popular" fiction. I will argue that the appearance of these popular writers actually represents an important and salutary shift in the social affiliation of our literature, a movement towards a view of literature that is based on values shared by the majority of Canadian society. In fact, these popular writers begin to create the outlines of a truly native literary tradition, and their immediate successors finish the process of adapting Canadian fiction to the democratic view of literature that prevails in North America.

Two main impulses guide the novelists and story writers in whose work the Canadian tradition in fiction reaches maturity. One impulse is documentary. These writers deliberately build their fiction around characters and situations that are recognizably drawn from their own society. At the same time, these writers also have a more purely literary goal. They want to move Canadian fiction into the mainstream of twentieth-century writing, and they want their novels and stories to be judged by the same standards that are being applied to contemporary British and American fiction. In their fiction, they try to adopt the methods and attitudes that characterize the "serious" fiction of their age. That is, they adopt what they take to be the conventions of modernist fiction.

The resulting fiction is less formally innovative than modernist fiction elsewhere, and is closely tied to the social conditions under which Canadian writers have lived and worked. In North America the dominant cultural values are overwhelmingly set by the largest social grouping, the middle classes or bourgeoisie. It was natural, therefore, that during the later nineteenth century the bourgeois novel of social realism emerged as indisputably the most important form of American literature. In Canada, however, this development occurs much later. The bourgeois novel does not become an important part of our fiction until nearly the turn of the century, and it is only after the First World War that a majority of our novelists adopt social realism as their habitual fictional mode. Consequently, the emergence of the bourgeois novel in Canada has been fused with the arrival of modernism. As a result, Canadian modernism has been extremely cautious and traditional, for most Canadian novelists have never lost touch with the social realism that is the hallmark of the nineteenth-century novel.

The Canadian literary tradition, when it declared itself, was recognizably North American in emphasis, but it was not identical with the work of American writers. In order to clarify the differences between the Canadian and American traditions, it is useful to have at hand a sort of literary map of the continent, against which both national literatures may be measured. I will take my chart of North American fiction from the opening pages of Leslie Fiedler's *The Return of the Vanishing American*, in which Fiedler observes: "American writers have tended to define their own country ... in terms of the four cardinal directions: a mythicized North, South, East, and West."[1] Fiedler identifies four "topological subgenres" of the American novel that correspond to these four mental regions, and he calls these forms – naturally enough –

---

[1] Leslie Fiedler, *The Return of the Vanishing American* (New York: Stein and Day, 1968), p. 16.

Northerns, Southerns, Easterns, and Westerns. Put simply, my argument will be that whereas Westerns dominate the American literary tradition, the predominant form in the Canadian tradition is – appropriately enough – the sort of fiction Fiedler calls the Northern.

No simplistic theory of political and economic determinism can account for all the features that mark off the work of Canadian writers from the work of writers in Great Britain or in the United States; nonetheless, it seems clear that Canada's colonial origins and its subsequent existence in the shadow of a vastly more populous and more powerful neighbour have profoundly influenced the shaping of the country's literary tradition. The success of the American Revolution, for example, gave nineteenth-century American writers an option that was not open to Canadian writers: they could consciously decide to be "American" writers. That is, American writers could adopt a vocabulary and a set of attitudes that asserted their belief in one of several readily available conceptions of what it meant to be an American. In nineteenth-century Canada, such a choice was impossible, for no-one knew yet what it meant to be a "Canadian" author. To some extent, this difficulty has persisted to the present day. As a result, most assertions of the Canadian identity are still comparative rather than absolute: Canadians habitually define their country's identity by contrasting it with the United States.

Throughout most of their country's history, Canadians have been aware of living just north of the nation that has confidently laid claim to being the most important and powerful in the world. Consequently, as Rick Salutin argues, the attention of many Canadians "focuses southward more often than northward – or inward. We feel ourselves at the edge of something vast, teeming, variegated and contentedly self-absorbed, something that expects to be the object of attention from the outside. We are to it as the margin to a densely printed page."[1] Nonetheless, a significant number of Canadian writers have tried to oppose the powerful assimilative pressure of American culture. The forces encouraging

---

[1] Rick Salutin, *Marginal Notes: Challenges to the Mainstream* (Toronto: Lester and Orpen Dennys, 1984), p. 1.

Canadian writers to dissent from American values were succinctly outlined by George Woodcock to an audience at Harvard University, when he said: "Canadians, faced with the wilderness on one side and a dangerously powerful neighbor on the other, had little doubt as to the actual nature of their predicament; what they needed was the combination of mythology and ideology that would enable them to emerge from mere escapism and present a countervision more real than actuality."[1] The Canadian "countervision" to the American way of seeing things does not emphasize a Huckleberry Finn-like search for innocence but rather describes the obtaining of an experience that brings increased wisdom and perhaps even spiritual insight. In an individualistic age and on an individualistic continent, Canadian authors have often upheld the value of the community and the value of traditional religious and ethical perspectives. The formal conservatism of their writing is consistent with the conservative outlook their fiction has habitually expressed.

In Canada, some of the traditional subjects of fiction have seemed to be closed off to writers. Feeling themselves to be removed from the real centres of authority in North American, Canadians have seldom written fiction that deals with political power in the usual sense. And only infrequently have they tried to work on a broad canvas of historical or social events. Instead, our novelists and short story writers have located their most characteristic work within an intimate domestic framework, where the politics of the family are the main source of conflict. Or they have set their fiction in small communities that are experienced by their inhabitants virtually as extended families. Thus, lack of power in the larger sense is an important covert theme of much Canadian fiction, just as petty tyranny within a domestic setting is one of its most common overt themes. This helps to explain the special prominence of women in our literary tradition. In Canada, both male and female authors have

---

[1] George Woodcock, "Possessing the Land: Notes on Canadian Fiction," in David Staines, ed., *The Canadian Imagination: Dimensions of a Literary Culture* (Cambridge, Mass.: Harvard Univ. Press, 1977), p. 73.

14

been preoccupied with two subjects that are traditionally prominent in women's fiction: domestic tyranny, and the feeling of being powerless in someone else's world.

Many of the leading characteristics of the Canadian tradition in fiction are apparent in the work of Frederick Philip Grove, the first Canadian novelist who can justly be described as a "major" literary figure. More clearly than any other writer of his generation, Grove saw that in Canada the task of the writer was still a documentary one. Accordingly, Grove deliberately set out to provide a "realistic" portrait of a particular stage in the development of his adopted nation. He saw his task as the chronicling of the life of representative men and women in the new world. Above all, he wanted to tell the story of the prairie settlers and their descendants. In his novels, he creates a sweeping panorama of Canadian life, capturing in fictional form the settlement of the prairies and the transition from a rural to an urban way of life. But in form and technique most of Grove's fiction remains close to the nineteenth-century British and continental fiction that provided his primary literary models. And the language of Grove's fiction remains the language of an outsider, an immigrant. Despite occasional attempts at creating vernacular speech, Grove never achieves the colloquial ease that later writers such as Morley Callaghan, Mordecai Richler, and Margaret Laurence bring to their fiction.

Thanks to the research of D.O. Spettigue, the story Grove tells in his autobiographical memoir, *In Search of Myself* (1946), is now known to be largely a fabrication. Spettigue has shown that Grove quite literally killed off his European literary identity as Felix Paul Greve in order to be reborn as the North American writer Frederick Philip Grove.[1] Nonetheless, we may be able to learn something about Grove's outlook, if not about the facts of his life, by examining his purported autobiography. In this book Grove invents the personal history he thinks most appropriate for a European who has assumed the role of a new world author. As Felix Paul Greve, Grove had lived a shabby existence on the fringes of the European literary world. He was poor, he was a chronic liar, and he was financially unreliable, perhaps

---

[1] See D.O. Spettigue, *FPG: The European Years* (Ottawa: Oberon, 1973).

criminally dishonest. When he creates a new European past for himself, however, Grove makes himself a gentleman's son, a member of the squirearchy. Apparently Grove feels that his credibility as a writer will be enhanced if he gives himself an upper-class background. But Grove associates literature in North America with the common man, not with the leisured upper classes. Therefore, once Grove's autobiographical persona moves to North America, he quickly starts to associate with ordinary working men, and undertakes a number of menial jobs. In his fictional autobiography, then, Grove is trying to have things both ways. He is trying to be at once a cultured European man of letters and a self-taught North American proletarian writer.

This awkward attempt to achieve a compromise between Europe and America helps to explain why Grove remains in some respects the paradigmatic Canadian writer. For there is a parallel, albeit a loose and imprecise one, between the situation of the uneasy immigrant writer and the situation of those English-speaking writers who collaborated in creating the Canadian tradition in fiction. The fiction of our immigrant writers, from Grove and his contemporary Laura Goodman Salverson to later authors such as John Marlyn, Adele Wiseman, and Mordecai Richler, represents a compromise between ethnic separatism and assimilation to the English-speaking mainstream. By choosing to write in English, these authors have addressed their books to the majority social group, but they have used their English-language stories to celebrate the experiences and the values of a non-English-speaking ethnic minority. I think that English-speaking Canadian writers are also trying to articulate the experience of a group that feels itself to be marginal within the larger North American social context.

For quite a long time, the documentary impulse and the literary impulse worked harmoniously together in our fiction; but in recent years the two impulses have begun to pull our writers in opposing directions. In fact, we are witnessing another far-reaching shift in the prevalent conception of literature. This change is occurring because some writers in both Europe and the United States have always found the popularity of the bourgeois novel a source of embarrassment. A literary form that has a predominantly middle-class readership and that deals with middle-class experience, they feel, cannot really be a legitimate branch of high culture. As a result, during the present century the novel has undergone a transformation that is rather surprising, in view of its historical role as the literary genre that incorporates elements of "real life" into literature. The twentieth-century novel has become acutely self-conscious of its status as a literary artifact. Many of the novel's leading exponents have come to think of the novel as an artform that is as subtle, as sophisticated, and as much a form of pure art as painting or music. Consequently, the predominant form of serious fiction in our century is what has been called the art novel.[1]

At the present time, Canadian writing is poised between tradition and innovation, between old-fashioned certainties about the world and the self and the disconcerting openness of postmodern art and philosophy. Many of our best authors appear to find this unsettled literary climate greatly to their liking. But there are also some disturbing aspects to the current literary scene. Writers and critics today are being forced to declare their allegiance either to the traditional notion of fiction as mimesis or to the new notion of fiction as pure verbal invention. In contemporary writing the bourgeois novel that has been the staple product of our novelists has increasingly been replaced by what is called metafiction, experimental writing, or simply postmodernism. As a result, contemporary fiction is coming to be dominated by a specialized kind of writing that appeals primarily to a quite small group of academically trained readers. It may even be true that the bourgeois tradition in Canadian fiction is nearing an end.

Today, wherever the reader looks in the landscape of recent Canadian fiction, whether at the later novels of older authors or at the many excellent books by younger authors, there is evidence that our literature has achieved the awakening called for so memorably in the "Invocation" of James Reaney's *A Suit of Nettles*. Today, our writers are creating

---

[1] Leslie Fiedler uses this term in *What Was Literature? Class Culture and Mass Society* (New York: Simon and Schuster, 1982), pp. 64-72.

a land of upturned privies with occupants inside
them
Crawling out through new tops like astonished moths
Bursting from their unusual, foul and dark cocoons.[1]

In this new literary climate, many younger university-based
critics – and perforce their students – are turning insistently
to the latest books by the newest authors. In itself, this
interest in the innovative, the experimental, and the postmodern cannot be faulted. Unfortunately, however, the
infatuation with new writers and their works often means
that the pioneers of the Canadian tradition in fiction are in
danger of being pushed aside. Surely these writers deserve a
better fate. We should not forget that the liberation achieved
by today's writers was made possible only by the lonely and
arduous efforts of those novelists out of whose work the
current literary ferment has emerged.

---

[1] James Reaney, *A Suit of Nettles* (Erin, Ont.: Porcépic, 1975), p. xxii.

CHAPTER ONE

The Aristocratic View of Literature

Where men are free as they should be,
And Jack's as good's his master.

> – Alexander McLachlan

Nineteenth-century American literature constitutes an emphatic declaration of literary independence. Early in the century, the works of Cooper and Irving staked out a tentative claim on a literary terrain that was recognizably American rather than European. The territorial claim was solidified at mid-century by the masterpieces of Hawthorne, Melville, Thoreau, and Whitman. Later in the century, the vernacular artistry of Mark Twain proclaimed to the world the birth of a distinctively American literary voice. In the early part of the century, however, many American writers remained caught between an aristocratic vision of literature and a more democratic outlook. They found it difficult to reconcile their reverence for Europe with their residence in North America.

As a result, although Cooper, Hawthorne, and Melville adopt American subjects, they remain deferential towards the style of their European forerunners. In the battle to assert the value of emotion, refinement, and sentiment, they enlist the old world tradition as an ally. They do not locate their adversaries among their literary predecessors, but among the unliterary citizens of a pragmatic and materialistic society. Only Melville, through the Shakespearean rhetoric of *Moby-Dick*, has the audacity to match himself against a truly major European writer. Nonetheless, Cooper, Hawthorne, and Melville all contributed significantly to the shaping of a literature that was North American in form and substance. In the Leatherstocking tales Cooper creates a famous embodiment of an American archetype, the frontiersman. Hawthorne writes his best fiction about recognizable New England types. Melville sets his greatest book on a ship manned by rough New England mariners, leavened by a sprinkling of savages from the far corners of the globe.

At the time Melville was writing *Moby-Dick*, however, America's "official" culture was still in the grip of a fading gentility that refused to acknowledge its own decline. At that time, according to Alfred Kazin, "American literature was still captive to 'high culture,' was self-consciously genteel, and, in the fading of authentic belief, was replacing religion with moralism. The literary class was still homogeneous and unaware that it lacked muscle. Social power was in other hands."[1] In the second half of the century, the proponents of gentility lost the upper hand. American writers became unabashedly proud of using native materials. As if in obedience to Emerson's preachments on self-reliance, Thoreau, Whitman, and Twain not only used American subjects but also repudiated the genteel and educated style of the old world. They no longer wrote as gentlemen, but spoke with a Yankee twang and flaunted the brash self-assurance of the egalitarian new world.

In nineteenth-century Canada, on the other hand, the situation was quite different. Our early writers did not show the urge towards national self-definition that is so evident in their American counterparts. They were conspicuously reluctant to follow American writers in creating works of literature that were aggressively North American in subject, outlook, and language. In both Canada and the United States, the North American scene was gradually rendered habitable for the literary artist by a succession of developments that included the historical romance, local colour fiction, and fiction with a social purpose. In Canada, howev-

---

[1] Alfred Kazin, *An American Procession* (New York: Knopf, 1984), p. 141.

er, all of these developments took place at a considerably later date than they did in the United States.

Why did our writers continue to defer to the British example, long after a more immediate and useful standard of comparison might have been found in American letters? The best short account of the social forces that affected – and for the most part retarded – the emergence of an autonomous Canadian literary tradition is still the first chapter of E.K. Brown's *On Canadian Poetry* – "The Problem of a Canadian Literature."[1] As Brown succinctly points out, a small, widely scattered, and largely agricultural population, most of whom existed under conditions but little removed from the early stages of settlement, would naturally have little time and little incentive to produce polite literature. In fact, Brown maintains that the colonialism, puritanism, and materialism of the frontier era shaped social attitudes that were still discernible well into the twentieth century.

The anti-literary forces that Brown describes arise from a society in which workers, tradesmen, and businessmen are the dominant figures. Despite what Brown implies, these people did not oppose all literature. Although they had little use for the kind of literature Brown admires, they willingly supported a literature that catered to their own standards, as the emergence at the turn of the century of writers such as Ralph Connor, L.M. Montgomery, and Robert Service demonstrates. The commercial success of these best-selling authors, however, affronts Brown's very conception of literature. Connor, Montgomery, and Service, he comments disdainfully, "were all more or less aggressively unliterary; and their only significance for our inquiry is the proof they offered that for the author who was satisfied to truckle to mediocre taste, living in Canada and writing about Canadian subjects, was perfectly compatible with making an abundant living by one's pen" (p. 4).

Brown's conception of literature is thoroughly Arnoldian. According to Brown, the best literature transcends the conditions of its origin; it embodies themes and values that are timeless and universal. Like Arnold, Brown does not

---

[1] E.K. Brown, *On Canadian Poetry*, rev. ed. (1944; Ottawa: Tecumseh, 1977), pp. 1-27. All further references to this work appear in the text.

acknowledge that a culture's understanding of literature reflects the outlook of a particular social group, and may change in response to changing historical or social forces. (For example, Arnold's own view of literature is not timeless and universal, but expresses the outlook prevalent in the educational arm of the English ruling classes during the nineteenth century.) As a result, Brown's analysis, astute though it is, does not do justice to the way in which certain cultural attitudes shaped the thinking of most of the writers who lived in nineteenth-century Canada. Specifically, he ignores the very considerable extent to which the slow development of a Canadian literary tradition is explained by the adherence of nineteenth-century Canadian writers to a class-conscious or aristocratic notion of literature that was poorly matched to the actual conditions of society in North America. Only towards the very end of the century did a majority of our writers adopt a view of literature that was more in keeping with the egalitarian outlook that actually prevails in North American society.

The History of Emily Montague (1769), the book that is sometimes described as "the first Canadian novel," was actually written by a temporary visitor, someone to whom Canada was literally a foreign place, a colony where she resided only briefly as part of an occupying garrison. In this novel, Frances Brooke shows Canada as a world of picturesque scenery, quaint French-Canadian customs, and spectacularly cold winters. The main action of Brooke's novel involves two love stories, one between the coquettish Arabella Fermor and the dashing Captain Fitzgerald, the other between Emily Montague and Edward Rivers. Brooke's lovers take occasional excursions into the town or the countryside, and report on the native inhabitants with the detached amusement of world travellers describing a primitive tribe. Quebec merely provides Brooke with an exotic setting for her description of two courtships that obey all the social rituals that prevail among well-bred members of the British gentry.

A dismissive view of Canada's literary potential is apparent even in the work of authors who committed themselves to life in the new world. For example, there is a striking absence of fiction that portrays the life of ordinary settlers. This is strange, because poems on the settlement theme are quite common; leading examples include Oliver Goldsmith's *The Rising Village* (1825), Standish O'Grady's *The Emigrant* (1842), Alexander McLachlan's poem of the same name (1861), and Joseph Howe's *Acadia* (1874). The central themes of these poems are the severing of ties with family and friends, and the struggle to create a new home in the wilderness. These would also seem to be natural themes for fiction. But no important novel by a nineteenth-century Canadian writer deals with the process of settlement. Until quite late in the century, only the Scottish novelist John Galt, who resided in Upper Canada from 1826 to 1829, wrote fiction that looks closely at the tribulations of a settler's life. Why did our nineteenth-century fiction writers avoid a subject our poets found so attractive?

The explanation may lie in the fact that the poems of settlement are all descended from one of the most famous of all eighteenth-century poems, Oliver Goldsmith's *The Deserted Village* (the Canadian Goldsmith was a grand-nephew of the British writer). Although the Canadian poems can be read as new world rebuttals of the elegaic sadness of *The Deserted Village*, in form and diction most of them borrow heavily from Goldsmith's original. Above all, the authors of these colonial poems rely on the respectability of Goldsmith's poem to guarantee the merit of their own efforts. But apparently Galt's name did not carry enough prestige to prompt our fiction writers to imitate his two novels of settlement, *Lawrie Todd* (1830) and *Bogle Corbet* (1831). Instead of transmuting the settlement experience into fiction, most writers chose to present their stories as direct autobiography. That is, they justified writing about the settler's life on pragmatic rather than aesthetic grounds, asserting that they wished their books to be useful as guides to prospective emigrants. As a result, the most interesting accounts of early settlement in the Canadas are found in nonfictional works by genteel settlers, such as Mrs. Traill's *The Backwoods of Canada* (1836) and Mrs. Moodie's *Roughing It in the Bush* (1852).

Mrs. Moodie and Mrs. Traill, however, still identify themselves as part of European polite society. They often draw attention to new world customs and attitudes that differ from the habits of the old world; but they do so largely in order to demonstrate that the old ways are superior. Their genteel pretensions prevent them from becoming deeply perceptive observers of the North American scene. Even the adaptable Mrs. Traill can remark with satisfaction that most of her Rice Lake neighbours have a social background similar to her own: "Our society is mostly military or naval; so that we meet on equal grounds, and are, or course, well acquainted with the rules of good breeding and polite life; too much so to allow any deviation from those laws that good taste, good sense, and good feeling have established among persons of our class."[1]

Many early Canadian authors provided unpretentious and lively accounts of their personal experiences; however, when they wrote fiction these authors felt compelled to don the spectacles of European literary gentility. As a result, during much of the nineteenth century, our native writers built their novels around established European fictional patterns, however poorly those patterns might fit conditions in the new world. In their fiction they made a minimal effort to record conditions in their immediate environment. For literary purposes Canada was as foreign to them as it was to any European author. In fact, it is interesting to examine the images of Canada that were created by non-Canadian writers, for our own writers shared many of the attitudes that outsiders brought to bear on their portrayals of Canadian settings and people.

John Galt had at least witnessed in person the conditions he wrote about in his accounts of North American settlement. Other British writers were not so scrupulous about becoming familiar with their subjects. For example, Frederick Marryat's novel for children, *The Settlers in Canada* (1844), tells of a British family who, when their family fortune is abruptly reduced to a mere £1700, can do nothing to escape penury in England save emigrating to Canada.

---

[1] Catharine Parr Traill, *The Backwoods of Canada*, New Canadian Library, No. 51 (Toronto: McClelland and Stewart, 1966), p. 98.

Once arrived in the backwoods, they soon begin to turn their wilderness lands into the new world equivalent of an old world landed estate. They have servants, and they employ details of men provided by the commander of a nearby fort. Even a forest fire that briefly threatens their newly-built establishment turns out to be a providential blessing, for it clears the trees from a substantial portion of their lands. But the novel concludes with the return of the family to England, when they unexpectedly regain the lands they previously had lost. This renewed inheritance seems to come as a reward for the patience with which the family submitted to their exile in the Canadian wilderness. Another unlikely image of Canada is provided in Mary Bennett's *The Canadian Girl* (1838), an outrageous farrago of piratical adventures and romantic love-making in what purports to be a backwoods setting. Bennett shares with Marryat the idea that important fictional characters must belong to the gentry or to the upper classes. In her novel, as in Marryat's book, the pioneering family quickly turn their wilderness acres into a good imitation of an English country estate.

The American writer Robert Traill Spence Lowell had actually lived in Newfoundland for over three years before he wrote *The New Priest in Conception Bay* (1858). Patrick O'Flaherty has claimed: "Newfoundland in Lowell's work is no mere backdrop for the action but a setting that is almost as fully realized and as important to the plot as Wessex is in the novels of Hardy."[1] Certainly, Lowell's portrayal of a Newfoundland fishing village is vigorous and colourful, and his fishermen utter some pungent Newfoundland dialect. But O'Flaherty's claim is a gross exaggeration. The Newfoundlanders play only a secondary role in Lowell's novel. In choosing the main characters of his novel, Lowell demonstrates that he shares the literary class prejudices of his day. Moreover, *The New Priest in Conception Bay* is actually built around an incongruous transposition of a Gothic plot into a Newfoundland setting. The story revolves around a girl who is held captive by an evil priest in a house that serves as the local equivalent of both a convent and a monastery. The

---

[1] Patrick O'Flaherty, *The Rock Observed: Studies in the Literature of Newfoundland* (Toronto: Univ. of Toronto Press, 1979), p. 93.

overall result is a wildly implausible anti-Catholic tract – *The Awful Disclosures of Maria Monk* transferred to a Newfoundland outport.

For much of the nineteenth century our writers remained faithful to social and literary paradigms that were increasingly inappropriate to North American conditions. In consequence, our writers produced fictional pictures of Canada that were only slightly less incongruous than the pictures contained in the books of Marryat, Bennett, and Lowell. The principal exceptions to this statement are Thomas McCulloch's *The Stepsure Letters* (1821) and Thomas Chandler Haliburton's stories about the shrewd Yankee pedlar Sam Slick, starting with the first series of *The Clockmaker* (1836). But these works do not undermine my main thesis. McCulloch and Haliburton did not set out to write polite literature: they were producing satirical newspaper sketches, aimed at ordinary readers rather than an educated elite. Their lapses from polite decorum, their informality and irreverence, are sanctioned by the conventions of the genre in which they write.

Along with Haliburton, the leading prose writers of pre-Confederation Canada are Major John Richardson and Susanna Moodie. At first glance, the works of these three writers look quite different. But a closer examination reveals some important shared characteristics. Richardson and Moodie, for example, started their literary careers with the assumption that the only proper setting for genteel fiction was a European one. Richardson only began to feature North American settings in his novels after Cooper had conclusively demonstrated the literary possibilities – and financial rewards – of North American frontier materials. Mrs. Moodie, on the other hand, completely refused to soil her fiction with North American settings. In her fiction, the closest approach to North America occurs in *Flora Lyndsay* (1854), which tells the story of a couple who prepare to emigrate to Canada. That is, the fictional *Flora Lyndsay* ends where the autobiographical *Roughing It in the Bush* begins. The fiction of both writers depicts a highly stratified society; both writers draw their leading characters from the educated ruling classes; and they both include members of other social classes only as secondary characters – often as comic characters or, in

Richardson's case, as villains. Moreover, in their autobiographical writings both Moodie and Richardson show little sympathy for ordinary members of North American society, and they agree that the class structure of the old world is an entirely appropriate way of arranging society in the new world. In addition, Richardson and Moodie share with Haliburton a tendency to belittle the faults of colonial society. And in the best-known works of all three authors, the writer's anxiety over his or her status as a colonial is visible.

Take the case of Major Richardson. At the time he wrote his best-known novel, *Wacousta; or, The Prophecy* (1832), Richardson had already attempted to establish himself in two professions in Europe, but neither as a soldier nor as a writer had he prospered to any great extent. Understandably, Richardson came to distrust European society and he strikingly projected his personal feelings into his novel. *Wacousta* therefore provides an interesting glimpse into the insecurities that can beset a colonial when he tries to assert his equality with the citizens of the imperial centre. For the novel reveals Richardson's uncertainty both about his own status and about the cultural status of North America. In the preface to an 1851 edition of the book he remarks that Wacousta "is not alone in his bitter hatred and contempt for the base among those who, like spaniels, crawl and kiss the dust at the instigation of their superiors, and yet arrogate to themselves a claim to be considered gentlemen and men of honor and independence."[1] In this passage Richardson is, in fact, talking about himself, for he cherished the same animus against his British enemies as his hero feels towards Colonel De Haldimar. The novel's movement towards the revelation of Wacousta's true identity mirrors Richardson's wish that British polite society would discover his own "true" identity as an officer and a gentleman.

Richardson equated his literary ability with his own gentility. When his efforts to build a career in the British Army proved ineffective, he tried to use literature to support his claim to be recognized as a gentleman. His early literary

---

[1] John Richardson, *Wacousta*, New Canadian Library, No. 58 (Toronto: McClelland and Stewart, 1967), p. xviii.

efforts, however, failed to bring him the approval he sought from British readers. As a result, he projected some of the indignation of a slighted colonial into his best-known novel. In *Wacousta* Richardson created a story that criticized the rigidly structured European society represented in the novel by Colonel De Haldimar. Richardson also strikingly embodied his personal grievances against European society in his protagonist Wacousta, the half-savage rebel whose pursuit of revenge against the De Haldimar family reflects Richardson's own resentment against the society that had not accorded him the status he felt he deserved.

Unlike Richardson, Thomas Chandler Haliburton does portray the everyday life of his fellow colonials. But Haliburton's attitude towards his fellow Nova Scotians is complicated. In *The Clockmaker* Haliburton distances himself from Nova Scotian society by viewing it through the eyes of the shrewd clockmaker Sam Slick. Moreover, Haliburton makes his fellow citizens the butt of his humour, as he portrays them being victimized, outwitted, and lectured by the calculating Yankee pedlar. When Sam berates the Bluenoses for their lack of drive and ambition, while Squire Poker listens with amiable amusement, we may be pardoned for thinking that Haliburton endorses Sam's scorn for the unenterprising Nova Scotians. But Haliburton's private sentiments are actually quite different from Sam's outlook. We can obtain a more accurate picture of Haliburton's own viewpoint if we examine a later volume in the Sam Slick series, *The Attaché* (1843), in which Haliburton sends Sam to England in company with Squire Poker and the Reverend Mr. Hopewell, formerly of Slickville.

At the start of *The Attaché*, as Haliburton briefly introduces his main characters for the benefit of new readers, he makes the Squire give this revealing account of his first encounter with Sam:

> I first became acquainted with him while travelling in Nova Scotia. He was then a manufacturer and vendor of wooden clocks. My first impression of him was by no means favourable. He forced himself most unceremoniously into my company and conversation. I was disposed to shake him off, but could not. Talk

he would, and as his talk was of that kind, which did not require much reply on my part, he took my silence for acquiescence, and talked on. I soon found that he was a character; and, as he knew every part of the lower colonies, and every body in them, I employed him as my guide.[1]

The passage, I think, is not simply a reprise of the first chapter of *The Clockmaker*. In addition, it describes Haliburton's uneasy relationship with his fictional alter ego. Haliburton is intimating how, once he had created Sam, that ingenious Yankee trickster quickly took control of the books in which he was the major character. In *The Attaché* Haliburton struggles – although not quite successfully – to regain the upper hand over his most famous creation.

In *The Attaché*, then, Haliburton attempts to tone down Sam's republican sentiments and to gain a hearing for his own Tory viewpoint. This is harder than it sounds, for Haliburton knows that Sam must continue to express an extravagant pride in the merits of his free and enlightened countrymen, and the squire must continue to act as Sam's dutiful Boswell. Haliburton's solution is to make Mr. Hopewell the spokesman for Toryism. Thus, if Sam argues that "England is a stupid country compared to our 'n'" (I, 259), then Mr. Hopewell counters with a speech in praise of English society:

"I think it the most refined, the most agreeable, and the most instructive in the world. Whatever your favourite study or pursuit may be, here you are sure to find well-informed and enthusiastic associates. If you have merit, it is appreciated; and for an aristocratic country, that merit places you on a level with your superiors in rank in a manner that is quite incomprehensible to a republican. Money is the great leveller of distinctions with us; here, it is talent. (II, 2)

---

[1] Thomas Chandler Haliburton, *The Attaché; or, Sam Slick in England*, (London: Bentley, 1843), I, 10-11. All further references to this work appear in the text.

In fact, in a concluding chapter in which his own voice blends with Squire Poker's, Haliburton explicitly dissociates himself from Sam's ideas. "I have not the most remote idea of putting Mr. Slick forward," he tells his readers, "as a representative of any opinions, but his own individual ones. They are peculiar to himself" (II, 286). "Loyal myself," Haliburton adds, "a great admirer of the monarchical form of government; attached to British Institutions, and a devoted advocate for the permanent connexion between the parent State, and its transatlantic possessions, I have not hesitated to give utterance to these opinions" (II, 287-88). Haliburton's true attitude is perhaps most clearly revealed by his eventual decision to retire to England, where his books had made him a familiar name, and where he even became for a time a Member of Parliament.

Haliburton and Richardson were the first native-born Canadian authors to write fiction about their visits to the old world. In *Ecarté; or, The Salons of Paris* (1829) and *Frascati's; or, Scenes in Paris* (1830), Richardson simply makes his colonial protagonists adopt the standards of the European upper classes. In the first series of *The Attaché* (1843), however, Haliburton does announce his intention of comparing English and American "national traits" (I, 13). Unfortunately, Sam's account of British society never goes much beyond caricature and cliché. The main burden of Sam's complaint is that English society lacks "natur": that is, lacks vitality and spontaneity. Every aspect of life, from clothing and social behaviour to ideas and economic relations, is governed by fixed rules or customs. Even the landscape has been forced to submit to man's control. "There is nothin' here to take hold on," Sam complains, "It's so plaguy smooth and high polished, the hands slip off; you can't get a grip of it" (I, 229). *The Attaché* represents a distinct falling off from *The Clockmaker*, probably because Haliburton did not personally endorse Sam's democratic perspective on English society. As a result, he felt compelled to make either the Reverend Mr. Hopewell or Squire Poker dispute most of Sam's extravagantly republican pronouncements. Neither of these characters, however, can match Sam's wit and verbal energy.

Like Major Richardson, Susanna Moodie thinks of litera-

ture as something that is produced by and for a social elite –
to which, of course, she herself belongs. As Michael Peterman
points out: "Throughout her life, Susanna Moodie thought of
herself, not as a Canadian, but as an Englishwoman."[1]
Throughout *Roughing It in the Bush*, Mrs. Moodie makes it
clear that she feels superior to her backwoods neighbours,
and that she views her literary abilities as one more proof of
her gentility. Near the end of her book, Mrs. Moodie explains
that she views the story of her misadventures in Canada as a
cautionary tale, a warning addressed to British readers of
good family who may be thinking of emigrating. Her intention, she announces, is to discourage these genteel readers
from "sinking their property, and shipwrecking all their
hopes, by going to reside in the backwoods of Canada."[2] She
explains:

> To the poor, industrious working man it [Canada]
> presents many advantages; to the poor gentleman,
> *none*! The former works hard, puts up with coarse,
> scanty fare, and submits, with a good grace, to
> hardships that would kill a domesticated animal at
> home. Thus he becomes independent, inasmuch as
> the land that he has cleared finds him in the common
> necessaries of life; but it seldom, if ever, in remote
> situations, accomplishes more than this. The gentle-
> man can neither work so hard, live so coarsely, nor
> endure so many privations as his poorer but more
> fortunate neighbour. (p. 236)

Two things emerge clearly from this passage. One is that
Mrs. Moodie is deliberately addressing a restricted public,
composed of readers who share her own educational and
social background. The other is that she views Canada as
being beyond the pale of civilization, a cultural desert fit only

---

[1] Michael A. Peterman, "Susanna Moodie," in *Canadian Writers and
Their Works*, ed. Robert Lecker, Jack David, and Ellen Quigley, Fiction
Series, I (Downsview, Ont.: ECW, 1983), 67.

[2] Susanna Moodie, *Roughing It in the Bush*, New Canadian Library, No.
31 (Toronto: McClelland and Stewart, 1962), p. 237. All further
references to this work appear in the text.

for the barbarous lower orders of society.

Mrs. Moodie's social outlook is quite clearly expressed in *The Victoria Magazine*, a periodical she and her husband edited for a year soon after they moved from the backwoods to the comparative civilization of Belleville. In the final issue of the periodical, they explained: "The hope of inducing a taste for polite literature among the working classes ... first stimulated us to accept the editorship of the Magazine."[1] That is, they wanted to raise the cultural level of "that most numerous and not least respected class of our fellow-Colonists, – the rural population of the Province" (p. 2). Although Mrs. Moodie occasionally issues democratic-sounding pronouncements, such as her statement that "the only *real* barrier that exists between the different classes of men" (pp. 89-90) was their differing educational levels, she is no radical. Far from it. She makes this clear when she rebukes her fellow immigrant, the poet Thomas McQueen, for expressing dangerous republican ideas: "Mr. McQueen, in his hatred of kings, seems to forget that certain distinctions of rank, are necessary to the well-being of society" (p. 71). It turns out that she advocates education for the working man only because he will then be more willing to remain in his place on the social scale. "The man that knows his duty," she writes, "is more likely to perform it, and perform it well, than the ignorant man whose services are compulsory" (p. 90). *The Victoria Magazine* contains a good deal of fiction, but most of its stories are set in Europe and deal with characters who are at least members of the gentry, if not of the aristocracy.

Most of our pre-Confederation novelists, I am arguing, based their cultural frame of reference on an idealized picture of traditional British society. For them, the pyramid of authority and prestige was clearly defined. Social climbing was done by aping the manners of one's betters, not by asserting one's own democratic merits. Even after mid-century, Canadian authors were reluctant to use the humbler among their own countrymen as the basis of their fiction. The work of Mrs. Rosanna Leprohon provides a case in point.

---

[1] *The Victoria Magazine*, ed. William. H. New (Vancouver: Univ. of British Columbia Press, 1968), p. 287. All further references to this work appear in the text.

Before she wrote the Canadian novels for which she is best remembered, Mrs. Leprohon had produced six tales that were serialized in Canadian magazines. Like Mrs. Moodie's fiction, all of these stories used British settings and British characters. When she decided to set her later fiction in Canada, Mrs. Leprohon was deliberately taking a step towards creating a literary tradition that would be, in her own words, "Canadian in origin, subject, and sympathies."[1] But she took this step quite tentatively, for her characters were still drawn from a cultivated social elite. Another sign of Canada's literary conservatism is provided by the favourable reception of William Kirby's *The Golden Dog* (1877), a historical romance in the manner of Sir Walter Scott. The gap between Canadian and American attitudes is suggested by the fact that Kirby's novel appeared only six years before Mark Twain, in *Life on the Mississippi*, published his sweeping indictment of Scott's fiction as the source of the South's mistaken chivalric idealism.

The clash between aristocratic and democratic society is clearly evident in a little-known novel by Mary Leslie (who wrote as "James Thomas Jones"). *The Cromaboo Mail Carrier* (1878) begins with one of the most striking paragraphs to be found anywhere in our early fiction:

> Cromaboo is the most blackguard village in Canada, and is settled by the lowest class of Irish, Highland Scotch and Dutch. It consists of seven taverns, six churches, and about one hundred shabby frame houses build on little gravelly mounds. Fights are frequent, drunkenness flourishes, vice abounds; more tobacco is smoked there than in any village of the same size in the Dominion; swearing is so common

---

[1] Rosanna Leprohon, *Antoinette de Mirecourt; or, Secret Marrying and Secret Sorrowing*, New Canadian Library, No. 89 (Toronto: McClelland and Stewart, 1973), p. 17.

that it passes unnoticed, and there is an illegitimate child in nearly every house – in some two, in others three, in one six, – and the people think it no sin.[1]

After this lively opening, the rest of the novel is a disappointment. The story turns out to revolve around the few painfully virtuous characters whose lives redeem this den of iniquity. Moreover, after two chapters that deal mainly with the poor but virtuous young villager who is the novel's hero, the author steps in to reassure the reader that the social refinements expected of polite fiction will, despite initial appearances, be introduced into this story:

Do not be discouraged, my reader, and give up the story. I promise you a *bon bouche* for desert, though you have begun your repast with simple bacon and beans. I promise to introduce you to the most fashionable people. I promise you romance, adventures, love-making, in galore, and finally orange blossoms and wedding favours; kisses – blessings – only have patience. (p. 14)

And the rest of the novel does concern itself mainly with the romantic affairs of the genteel characters. Whatever the author knew about the realities of Canadian life (and she is franker about drunkenness and illegitimacy than many of her contemporaries), she could not bring herself to make them central features of her fiction. Moreover, she felt compelled to build the main plot of her story around characters whose birth, education, and wealth entitled them to claim membership in the "better" classes of society.

There is, however, a sop thrown to democratic values in one of the twists taken by the novel's central plot. The heroine's most devoted admirer is the virtuous working man referred to previously – the Cromaboo mail carrier, Robert Hardacre Smith. Near the end of the novel, one of the

---

[1]James Thomas Jones, *The Cromaboo Mail Carrier: A Canadian Love Story*, Toronto Reprint Library of Canadian Prose and Poetry (1878; Toronto: Univ. of Toronto Press, 1973), p. 3. All further references to this work appear in the text.

characters remarks about Robert: "I fear I underrated him because of his low birth; he is *a gentleman* .... In my prejudice of class I forgot that God, who makes all good and noble things, makes gentlemen; that a man without a pedigree may have the highest character, the greatest worth" (pp. 277-78). For modern readers, however, the force of this judgment is undermined by the previous disclosure of Robert's parentage. For the principal surprise in the plot is the revelation that this young man is in fact the natural son of a wandering British peer, Sir Robert Hardacre. That is, the virtues of the Cromaboo mail carrier are explained by assigning him an aristocratic father. Apparently the author cannot imagine true gentility arising from wholly proletarian stock.

I have dwelt on this novel, not to extol its intrinsic merits, but rather to illustrate an attitude that our turn-of-the-century fiction was leaving behind. Our early fiction writers made a minimal effort to record conditions in their immediate environment. Instead, they built their stories around European characters and European social patterns, which they transplanted into settings that were North American in name only. After Confederation, however, it became apparent to most observers that in Canada, as in the United States, farmers, workers, and merchants were building a society in which prestige and power could be attained by anyone with the force of character to seize them. Canada is a North American nation, in which class distinctions are less clear-cut than they are in the old world. Social status is more a matter of money, less a matter of inherited status and polished manners. The leaders of this new society were not members of a traditional ruling class; they were not trained in the social graces and were not familiar with the higher reaches of the arts. Instead, they forced their fellow citizens to respect the manners, speech patterns, and social standards that had previously been associated with the middle and lower levels of society. In response to this change in their society, our authors gradually ceased to write for an audience that held aristocratic values.

By the end of the century, books like *The Cromaboo Mail Carrier* had become the exception rather than the rule. Only a few unfashionably conservative writers, such as Clara H.

Mountcastle (who used the pen name "Caris Sima") in *A Mystery* (1886) and Lily Dougall in *What Necessity Knows* (1893) – and later on Mazo de la Roche and perhaps Ethel Wilson – continued to describe Canadian society in terms that would be more appropriate for describing the society of a provincial English town. Most of our turn-of-the-century writers no longer saw themselves as aspiring gentlefolk, but instead identified themselves as members of the rising Canadian bourgeoisie. Taking their cue from a number of highly popular American and British writers, they started to write for and about the middle levels of society. Thus, by the time the century drew to a close, the majority of our fiction writers were creating stories and novels that dealt directly with the ordinary people and scenes of their native country. Before examining their work, however, I want to look at the form of nineteenth-century fiction in which the aristocratic view of literature was most strongly apparent, namely the historical romance.

CHAPTER TWO

Romances of the New World

Canada, from its position on the map, its hardy climate, its grand natural scenery, its dramatic and stirring historical associations should be the Scotland of America .... It should produce the great historical novelist; the Sir Walter Scott of the New World.

— Robert Barr

The appearance in 1814 of Sir Walter Scott's *Waverley* touched off a series of echoes that eventually affected the literatures of most of the European nations. Dickens, Thackeray, and Bulwer-Lytton in England; Hugo, Dumas, and Balzac in France; Manzoni in Italy; Gogol and Tolstoy in Russia – these are only some of the many writers who contributed to the torrent of historical fiction that appeared during the nineteenth century. The editor of a modern edition of Scott's first novel asserts: "The historical novel properly speaking did not exist before Scott wrote *Waverley*. After *Waverley* it quickly became one of the most common and popular modes of the novel."[1] But the popularity of historical fiction throughout the nineteenth century cannot be laid exclusively at Scott's door. Like most literary innovators, Scott was responding to changes in the society around him. *Waverley* fell on ground that had been well prepared.

The rise of historical fiction owed a great deal to the

---

[1] Andrew Hook, "Introduction," in Sir Walter Scott, *Waverley* (Harmondsworth: Penguin, 1972), pp. 9-10.

romantic nationalism that furnished the cultural context within which most nineteenth-century theorizing about literature took place. Towards the end of the eighteenth century, a dramatic transformation swept through European civilization, when the cosmopolitan rationalism of the Enlightenment gave way to the more volatile intellectual climate fostered by Romanticism. The political expression of Romantic thought was nationalism, a doctrine that replaced the Enlightenment's belief that human nature was everywhere the same with the belief that humanity could be grouped into separate communities or nations, each nation possessing its own language and its own heritage of customs, religion, and history. This conception of the nation as an organic community, comprising all the members of a particular "folk," replaced earlier – and less emotionally charged – conceptions of the state.[1]

The Romantic theory of the nation held that one of the most important attributes of nationhood was the possession of a richly storied past. It was logical, therefore, that writers should turn to historical subjects, especially to subjects drawn from the history of their own nations. Of course, earlier novelists had sometimes set their fiction in bygone days. But these pre-Romantic story-tellers had treated the past merely as a temporal analogue of the geographical arcadias in which most romances are set. In *Waverley* and in his subsequent books, Scott brought a different approach to bear on the literary presentation of the past. As George Lukács has emphasized, Scott had a highly developed awareness of how historical forces imposed themselves on the individual.[2] This acute historical sense was in turn supported by a detailed knowledge of the customs and conditions that prevailed in the settings about which he wrote. In short, Scott introduced what has been called the "historicist"

---

[1] The argument advanced in this paragraph is indebted to K.R. Minogue, *Nationalism* (London: Batsford, 1967), and to Margery Fee, "English-Canadian Literary Criticism, 1890-1950: Defining and Establishing a National Literature," Diss. Toronto 1981.

[2] George Lukács, *The Historical Novel*, trans. Hannah and Stanley Mitchell (London: Merlin, 1962), p. 34.

viewpoint into historical fiction.[1]

The vogue for historical fiction quickly spread to North America. Americans were eager to demonstrate that their country also possessed all the characteristics of a true national community, including that essential attribute possessed by every self-respecting European nation, a dignified and dramatic history. In their eagerness to give their country a colourful history, nineteenth-century Americans took part in an extensive exercise in collective myth-building. In effect, they deliberately invented many of the trappings of nationality that Europeans seemed to acquire without effort, as part of their national birthright.[2] One of the most important ways in which American writers contributed to this process was through the writing of historical fiction. By setting their stories in the American past, writers were helping to repudiate the charge, levelled by many European observers and echoed by not a few native Americans, that the new world lacked a significant history. Writers such as James Fenimore Cooper and William Gilmore Simms – and even Nathaniel Hawthorne, despite his criticisms of New England society – were supporting the claims of their homeland to be recognized as a fully-developed society, a place where civilization had taken firm root.

Cooper, though not the first American author to treat native historical subjects, was the first author who succeeded in making such materials both popular and respectable. Cooper created a distinctly North American variation on the pattern that had been laid down by Scott. Above all, Cooper replaced Scott's "hero of middle rank" – someone who holds a specific social position in a hierarchically structured society – with the democratic frontiersman Natty Bumppo. Natty Bumppo is one of the earliest literary examples of the figure

---

[1] Avrom Fleishman, *The English Historical Novel: Walter Scott to Virginia Woolf* (Baltimore: Johns Hopkins Press, 1971), p. 19.

[2] The process is summarized in Henry Steele Commager, "The Search for a Usable Past," *American Heritage*, 16 (Feb. 1965), 4-9, 90-96. This article is reprinted in Commager's *The Search for a Usable Past and Other Essays in Historiography* (New York: Knopf, 1967).

that has been called "the American Adam."[1] The companion-
ship of Natty Bumppo and Chingachgook makes Cooper's
Leatherstocking tales one of the fountainheads of the American myth of the frontiersman. Cooper's fiction thus supports
the claim by Americans that their society is equal to –
although in some respects it may differ from – European
society. Consequently, when Canadian authors turned to
historical fiction, they had two principal models available to
them: they could emulate Scott or they could emulate
Cooper. We can therefore trace the main features in the
development of our nineteenth-century historical fiction by
examining the influence of these two writers.

In 1838 Major John Richardson described himself as "the
first and only writer of historical fiction the country has yet
produced."[2] His boast was almost correct. Only one significant book of historical fiction predates the publication of
Richardson's *Wacousta* (1832). That book is Julia Catherine
Hart's *St. Ursula's Convent; or, The Nun of Canada* (1824).
Hart's story, however, is important more for its chronological
priority than for its intrinsic merits. *St. Ursula's Convent* is
not historical fiction in the modern sense. Despite the claim
made in the book's subtitle to present "scenes from real life,"
there is no attempt to reconstruct the texture of life in the
era of the British Conquest, which provides the temporal
setting for the book's action. Hart's use of an eighteenth-century setting is not prompted by her knowledge of history, but
is rather an act of literary homage to the eighteenth-century
sentimental fiction on which her tale is modelled.

The plot of *St. Ursula's Convent* is an energetic but
implausible combination of many of the favorite motifs of
sentimental fiction. There are interchanged babies, bereave-
ments, reunions of long-separated family members, tearful
return-to-life scenes after mistaken presumptions of death,
and a narrowly averted brother-sister marriage. In the end
all comes right, and the novel concludes with a flurry of
marriages. Throughout the book stress falls on the salutary

---

[1] R.W.B. Lewis, *The American Adam: Innocence, Tragedy and Tradition
in the Nineteenth Century* (Chicago: Univ. of Chicago Press, 1955).

[2] Quoted by H. Pearson Gundy, "Literary Publishing," in Klinck, ed.,
Literary History of Canada, p. 181.

consequences of the emotional sufferings undergone by the characters, who are reminded not to place their reliance on this "sublunary world" (a seventeenth-century phrase recurrent in the book) as a source of enduring satisfaction, but to place their faith in the deity. That is, the novel is a moral fable, not a study of character or manners. The characters learn that God "has indeed forbidden all violent attachments to terrestrial objects, which might interfere with our love to him."[1]

Despite the geographical promise implicit in the title of Hart's novel, much of the book's action takes place in Europe. The Canadian setting enters the story only because, when the son of the Chevalier De St. Louis offended his father, he "was, as too frequently happened under the ancient regime, by a Letter de Cachet banished to Canada" (p. 1). Like Mrs. Brooke in *The History of Emily Montague*, Hart treats Quebec only as a picturesque setting for a conventional romantic plot. Her view of the French Canadian farmers is especially patronizing. She refers to them as "peasantry," and calls them "an honest, peaceful, and contented people, paying their rents with great exactness, and their tythes to the clergy" (p. 56). The most favourable reference to North American customs occurs during the double wedding with which the novel concludes. At the celebration that follows their marriage to British noblemen, the two Canadian brides cause a momentary stir when, in democratic Canadian fashion, they join in the dance of the English villagers. But Hart's story ends with all the characters happily established in Europe; moreover, the son of the banished man regains his ancestral title and property. Canada, in Hart's fiction at any rate, is at best a place of purgatorial suffering. True felicity can only be found in Europe.

When we move from *St. Ursula's Convent* to *Wacousta*, we move from a world of morality to a world of feeling. The misfortunes of Hart's characters take place in accordance with the inscrutable workings of divine providence. Richard-

---

[1] Julia Catherine Beckwith [Hart], *St. Ursula's Convent; or, The Nun of Canada*, Maritime Literature Reprint Series, No. 2 (Sackville, N.B.: R.P. Bell Library, 1978), pp. 64-65. All further references to this work appear in the text.

son's characters undergo as many difficulties as Hart's characters, but his emphasis falls not on the moral significance of these experiences but on their power to evoke a strong emotional response in the reader. In other words, *Wacousta* brings Canadian fiction into the world of Romanticism. Yet the shift from one literary mode to another is not absolute. In some respects *Wacousta* still resembles the fiction of an earlier era, for Richardson does not display the historical awareness that Scott introduces into his novels. Instead, Richardson treats the historical events that form the backdrop of his fiction as merely exotic or exciting settings for his tales of romance, betrayal, and revenge.

With its wilderness setting and its Indian characters, *Wacousta* is clearly in some respects a deliberately North American novel. In fact, Richardson has acknowledged that Cooper's *The Last of the Mohicans* provided a model for his own story. In the preface to a later edition of *Wacousta*, Richardson states that he has "absolutely devoured" Cooper's novel three times, and he admits that his story is one "of which I have certainly robbed that first of vigorous American novelists – the 'Last of the Mohicans' Cooper."[1] Like Cooper, Richardson has created a tale of flight, capture, and rescue in the North American forest. Also like Cooper, Richardson has set his story against the unrest created by the American struggle for independence, and has given Indian treachery a prominent place in the action. However, Richardson creates no frontiersmen, no northern counterparts of Cooper's Natty Bumppo. In fact, Richardson does not even make North Americans the protagonists of *Wacousta*. All of his principal actors are British; the French-Canadian settlers and the Indians play only supporting roles.

Wacousta opens with an extended portrayal of an isolated British garrison, which is threatened by the "surrounding hordes"[2] of Indians led by the crafty native leader Pontiac. The beleaguered garrison at first appears to present an image of European civilization at war with the North American wilderness; however, the conflict between savagery

---

[1] Quoted in Leslie Monkman, "Richardson's Indians," *Canadian Literature*, No. 81 (Summer 1979), p. 87.

[2] Richardson, *Wacousta*, p. 2.

and civilization is not the fundamental theme of Richardson's story. The native antagonism towards the garrison emanates principally from the vengeful renegade Wacousta (and when Wacousta dies, the Indians make peace). Moreover, in the third volume of the novel, as Wacousta narrates the story of Colonel De Haldimar's past treachery, he becomes to some extent a sympathetic character. In fact, Wacousta turns into an example of that central Romantic figure, a self-doomed Byronic rebel. Wacousta is motivated by the desire to take revenge on Colonel De Haldimar, his deceitful former friend. Richardson portrays Colonel De Haldimar as an unattractive figure, a heartless martinet who is prepared to execute his own men for the smallest breach of regulations. Wacousta's account of the Colonel's past conduct reveals De Haldimar as a hypocrite and a self-serving schemer. Colonel De Haldimar gained Clara Beverley's love only by betraying his one-time friend, Sir Reginald Morton, latterly known as Wacousta. In short, De Haldimar is revealed as a man without personal honour, someone who embodies the worst characteristics of the European elite. And in Richardson's eyes, a gentleman should above all other things be honourable.

In *The Canadian Brothers; or, The Prophecy Fulfilled* (1840), the sequel to *Wacousta*, Richardson does make North Americans his principal actors, and he does include a North American frontiersman among his characters. Yet even in this novel, Richardson never totally commits his fiction to a new world outlook, for the European characters still set the standards by which the colonial characters are judged. Richardson carefully distinguishes between cultivated and genteel North Americans, and the half-savage denizens of the backwoods. Some North Americans, such as the Grantham brothers after whom the book is named, are worthy by birth and education to rank as equals with the European characters. The merits of Gerald Grantham, for example, are guaranteed by the approving comments of General Isaac Brock. On the other hand, the crude frontiersman Jeremiah Desborough is clearly a lesser sort of being than the Granthams. Desborough is a cold-blooded murderer, perhaps a smuggler, certainly a spy, and on one occasion a cannibal. His crimes entirely outweigh any wrong that has been done to him, and unlike Wacousta he receives no sympathy from the reader.

Richardson was not the only writer who imitated Cooper's best-known wilderness romance. In *Argimou: A Legend of the Micmac* (1847),[4] D.S. Huyghue takes his basic plot pattern from *The Last of the Mohicans*, and he tells a story of capture and pursuit through the New Brunswick wilderness. Huyghue sets his story against an incident in the struggle between Britain and France for North America. But European politics are not his main concern. In Huyghue's tale, as in Cooper's novel, a wilderness neophyte is guided by experienced woodsmen. In the course of the journey, Huyghue's hero learns to value the humanity as well as the woodcraft of his native guides. Unfortunately, Huyghue's literary skills are minimal. He inserts his native legends at improbable points, and he cannot create suspense. His Indian characters are noble savages rather than fully individualized human beings. His concern with racial extinction is not integrated into his main plot, but emerges only in authorial digressions. Yet the novel remains of interest because Huyghue confronts the cultural decline of the Indian more directly than any other Canadian novelist before Rudy Wiebe. Huyghue's novel is really an elegy for a people who have all but vanished. He includes among his characters an aged Indian who sees the inevitability of the European triumph. Pansaway's stories retell historical incidents from the native perspective, and give the Indian's perspective on the arrival of the white man in North America. Like Wiebe in *The Temptations of Big Bear*, Huyghue wants his readers to recognize that there is a native perspective on North American history.

Another book that shows the influence of Cooper's forest romance is *The Last of the Eries* (1849), whose author is identified only by the initials "H.H.B." The title betrays an indebtedness to Cooper, but the author has imperfectly

---

[1] This novel has recently been made accessible by the publication of a modern reprint. See "Eugene" [Douglas S. Huyghue], *Argimou: A Legend of the Micmac*, Maritime Literature Reprint Series, No. 1 (Sackville, N.B.: R.P. Bell Library, 1977).

learned the lessons about creating a North American fiction that are embodied in Cooper's wilderness tales. In *The Last of the Eries* the author's concessions to the North American setting are quite minimal. In his preface the author announces that he has tried both to entertain and "to give the reader some information regarding the principle tribes of Western Canada, and those people generally known as Five or Six Nations."[1] But the novel's ethnography, along with the purported history of the Erie tribe that gives the novel its title, is almost completely imaginary. The author's romantic view of the Indians is indicated when one of his characters remarks: "I think a certain degree of similarity exists between these Indians in their picturesque costumes, and the wild men of the Highlands" (p. 132). The Indians, then, simply fulfill an established literary role: they are a North American equivalent for the exotic or picturesque lower-class characters who lend colour to tales of European historical adventures. *The Last of the Eries* is really a sentimental novel rigged out with a wilderness decor.

In the middle years of the century, the Cooperesque forest romance lost favour with our writers. Increasingly our writers preferred to locate their stories closer to events that they perceived as the political centre of their community's past. This preference was encouraged by the rapid political maturation of the scattered British colonies in North America. In the years leading up to Confederation, as the colonies developed an increasingly vigorous political life, their inhabitants began to think of themselves as belonging to a new collective entity – a nation in spirit, if not in sober legal fact. In consequence, British North Americans began to inspect their own history for the marks of nationhood, and after mid-century our writers tentatively began to aid in the systematic creation of a collective mythology that would give Canadian history something of the dignity and significance associated with European history. Both French-Canadians and English-Canadians realized that the most distinctive feature of their history was the British Conquest of New France, followed by the accommodation that allowed both

---

[1] H.H.B., *The Last of the Eries* (Simcoe: J. Gundry, 1849). All further references to this work appear in the text.

linguistic groups to live in comparative harmony. After mid-century, therefore, Canadian authors chose increasingly often to set their historical tales against the last years of the *ancien régime*, or against the turmoil of the immediate post-Conquest years.

Consequently, after mid-century Canadian authors turned away from Cooper's fiction and increasingly modelled their tales on the work of Cooper's British exemplar, Sir Walter Scott. Scott's fiction appealed to Canadians of both linguistic groups. French Canadians could admire Scott because he was respectful of the past, and was sympathetic to those who were losers in the historical struggles he described. English-speaking readers could note that Scott did not endorse an uncritical glorification of the past; if anything, he favoured the new forces that were altering the traditional way of life. Both cultural groups could take satisfaction in the way Scott portrayed historical struggle as leading to a reconciliation of the contending groups, and could readily apply this optimistic vision of the historical process to their own history.

Soon after mid-century, sympathetic and informed portrayals of the last years of the *ancien régime* appeared almost simultaneously in French-Canadian and English-Canadian letters. In this respect, if in no other, the literatures of the two linguistic groups are hard to separate. The speedy appearance of an English translation of Philippe Aubert de Gaspé's *Les anciens canadiens* (1863) gives that book a place in the story of English-Canadian letters; and the three Canadian novels of Mrs. Rosanna Leprohon, which were quickly translated into French, belong as much, or more, to the history of French-Canadian letters as to the English-Canadian tradition. Indeed, one of Mrs. Leprohon's historical romances, *Le Manoir de Villerai* (1861), has only been published in a French translation.

Aubert de Gaspé's *Les anciens canadiens* combines a historical tale with antiquarian lore in what the author took to be the manner of Sir Walter Scott. Just as Scott had recorded the traditions of the Scottish people, Aubert de Gaspé attempted to preserve the cultural traditions of New France. In composing his book, Aubert de Gaspé was obeying the injunctions of friends, including the historian

François-Xavier Garneau, who urged him "to leave out nothing which could illustrate the manners and customs of the early Canadians."[5] That is, by attempting to preserve the cultural traditions of New France, Aubert de Gaspé was responding to the French Canadian nationalism that had been growing at least since the Conquest. However, the resulting book was more a collection of folktales, anecdotes, and customs than a conventional work of historical fiction. Only in the last one-third or so does the minimal story-line predominate over the digressive material.

Aubert de Gaspé's familiarity with the historical fiction of Sir Walter Scott probably lies behind several passages that appear to draw a parallel between Scottish history and the history of the French in North America. The major similarity, of course, lies in the fact that both the Scots and the French-Canadians have been conquered by the English. One of Aubert de Gaspé's major characters, Archibald Cameron of Lochiel, is an exiled Scot whose father died at Culloden. Archie, as he is commonly known, warns his French-Canadian friends that England is determined to secure her Empire: "If the conquest of Canada is necessary to her she will never swerve from her purpose or count the sacrifice. Witness my own unhappy country" (p. 156). But *Les anciens canadiens* also seeks to rationalize the occurrence of the Conquest. The book's action spans the fall of New France, which is attributed to the fact that "the mother country, a veritable step-mother, had abandoned her Canadian children" (p. 167). Therefore, in conformity with an idea that was commonly held in both English and French Canada, Aubert de Gaspé could suggest that the Conquest was a providential event, saving Quebec from the terrible excesses of the French Revolution. Thus, the references to Archibald Cameron's background foreshadow not only the French defeat, but also the harmony that will ensue in Canada once active hostilities have ceased.

Mrs. Leprohon's three Canadian stories – *Le Manoir de Villerai* (1861), *Antoinette de Mirecourt* (1864), and *Armand*

---

[1] Philippe Aubert de Gaspé, *Canadians of Old*, trans. Charles G.D. Roberts, New Canadian Library, No. 106 (Toronto: McClelland and Stewart, 1974), p. 11. All further references to this work appear in the text.

47

Durand (1868) – were set in the traditional society of New France before the Conquest. Mrs. Leprohon chose to write about this society because it offered the most appropriate North American setting for plots that turn upon the existence of a strongly defined class structure. Only in the upper strata of society would the delicate emotional susceptibilities of her heroines have a natural place. As in Mrs. Brooke's *The History of Emily Montague*, the women are preoccupied with romantic intrigue, and the men – even though most of them are officers – are more concerned with social matters than with military or commercial affairs. In short, Mrs. Leprohon sets her fiction in the same world of upper-class females as did the authors of the eighteenth-century fiction that was still her chief model.

The manor house is an important image in all three of Mrs. Leprohon's Canadian stories. For Mrs. Leprohon, the seigneurial way of life embodies an admirable attitude towards duty and tradition; it represents values that she feels ought to be given greater prominence in her own time. At any rate, such is the interpretation of her work offered by Henry J. Morgan, in his *Bibliotheca Canadensis* (1867). Morgan writes: "by her often graphic descriptions of the refinement and chivalry of that period [the immediate pre- and post-Conquest period], [she] has sought to exert a salutary influence over the present matter of fact and 'hard money' world in which we live."[4] Although Mrs. Leprohon sets her fiction in the past, she is not especially interested in the way historical events impinge on the lives of her characters. She locates her characters in seventeenth-century Quebec primarily in order to remove them from the moral standards prevalent in her own society.

When Mrs. Leprohon does refer to the historical events that were taking place around her characters, she interprets them in moral terms. In *Antoinette de Mirecourt*, for example, Mrs. Leprohon is primarily concerned with exposing the immorality of the secret marriage contracted between the heroine and her scheming suitor, Major Audley Sternfield. But the novel's central love story also functions as a kind of

---

[1] Henry J. Morgan, *Bibliotheca Canadensis: or, A Manual of Canadian Literature* (Ottawa: Desbarats, 1867), p. 224.

48

political allegory. At one point Mrs. Leprohon tells her readers that the Conquest brought "a host of strangers, among whom unfortunately were many needy adventurers, who sought to build themselves positions on the ruined fortunes of the vanquished people."[1] Mrs. Leprohon's heroine is taken in by one such adventurer, who covets her inheritance more than he admires her beauty and her character. Collectively, then, the British are rather like Antoinette's suitor: they are "aliens alike to our race, creed, and tongue" (p. 82). And Antoinette's vulnerability to the schemes of Major Sternfield seems to evoke the powerlessness of the French Canadians in the face of their new British rulers.

Mrs. Leprohon, however, appears to argue that French Canadians need not be corrupted if they will only remain true to the best aspects of their own tradition. The true strength of French Canadian society, she feels, stems from a religious faith and a sense of community solidarity that are shared by the best members of all social classes. Mrs. D'Aulnay, who gives Antoinette the unfortunate advice that leads to her disastrous secret marriage with Audley Sternfield, seems to represent the decadence of "the old French *noblesse*" (p. 19). Antoinette, on the other hand, represents the new French Canada that is emerging after the Conquest. At the novel's conclusion Antoinette is united with the "good" English soldier, Colonel Evelyn, who is polite and considerate where Sternfield is rude and self-centred. Moreover, Colonel Evelyn is willing to defend a humble *habitant* against the cupidity of an English opportunist. Colonel Evelyn's marriage to Antoinette is therefore an early version of the rapprochement between the two solitudes that Hugh MacLennan would later depict in the marriage of Heather Methuen and Paul Tallard in *Two Solitudes*.

Like Hart and Richardson, Mrs. Leprohon is loyal to the view that society is based on the existence of clearly-defined distinctions between the various social classes. *Le Manoir de Villerai* revolves around the betrothal, arranged by their parents, between Blanche de Villerai and Gustave de Montarville. Despite a long-standing mutual respect, they are not

---

[1] Leprohon, *Antoinette de Mirecourt*, p. 40. All further references to this work appear in the text.

in love; yet they have great difficulty in deciding to follow their own inclinations. The eventual marriage between Gustave de Montarville and Rose Lauzon may seem to argue against the rigidity of class barriers. But the exception is only a partial one. Mrs. Leprohon has carefully depicted Rose as an unusual member of the *habitant* class. Rose is beautiful; she is animated by the highest moral principles; and she possesses an education suited to someone far above her nominal social status. In other words, she is an aristocrat in spirit long before she marries into the seigneurial class. The European basis of Mrs. Leprohon's vision of society is underlined when the two lovers choose to live in France after their marriage, rather than remain in a Quebec that has fallen under British rule.

The shadow of Europe also falls across Charles Heavysege's only work of fiction, *The Advocate* (1865). The novel, as Kenneth Hughes points out, is a rewriting of Shakespeare's *The Tempest*, with additional borrowings from *Romeo and Juliet*.[1] The story is nominally set in 1800, but there is little feeling that a particular historical period is being recreated. Fundamentally, Heavysege is trying to produce a piece of "literature." The inflated rhetoric in which Heavysege's characters speak is prompted by a desire to emulate the richness of Elizabethan dramatic rhetoric. As a result, Heavysege buries his fictional Montreal under an implausible impasto of theatrical plot machinery and Shakespearean language.

Hughes argues for the existence of a political allegory in Heavysege's novel. There is some basis for this contention, for the advocate apparently preys on girls of French-Canadian or part-French parentage. Moreover, when the dissolute sons of a French-Canadian seigneur kidnap the advocate's ward, they revile her as a representative of the oppressive English. But Heavysege's principal emphasis is moral rather than political. The novel's title character is a licentious lawyer, who has fathered two illegitimate children. In the end, morality is reasserted when the advocate kills the evil and deformed product of one of his illicit affairs, then repents

---

[1] Kenneth J. Hughes, "Heavysege's *The Advocate*: The Art of Failure," *Journal of Canadian Fiction*, 2 (Summer 1973), 95-98.

his action and before dying acknowledges his other illegitimate child, a daughter who has up to this time lived as his "ward." This conclusion does not predict a reconciliation of French and English, but rather shows the triumph of virtue over vice.

A closer attention to historical atmosphere is evident in the only historical novel written by William Kirby, whose romance *The Golden Dog* (1877) is undoubtedly both the best-known and the most ambitious of all nineteenth-century Canadian historical fictions. Kirby habitually worked in close imitation of British literary models. Before he wrote *The Golden Dog*, he patterned his long poem *The U.E.* after Goldsmith's verse; subsequently, he published the Tennysonian *Canadian Idylls*. When he wrote *The Golden Dog*, Kirby certainly had Sir Walter Scott's fiction in mind. In creating his minor characters, he emulated the garrulousness of Scott's secondary characters. He incorporated large doses of historical detail, imitating what he took to be Scott's manner. But Kirby lacked Scott's gift for creating engaging and varied characters; his characters are standard fictional types, and are too obviously symbolic counters in Kirby's didactic system. Perhaps Kirby could construct a plot that smoothly incorporated his view of New France's history, as John Sorfleet has argued.[1] But he could not create an appealing narrative persona through which events and characters can be filtered.

Yet Kirby's novel represents a significant development in our fiction's assimilation of North American materials. Not until *The Golden Dog* does a novel tell a story from the Canadian past primarily in order to illustrate its historical meaning. Hart turns the past into a morality play. Richardson uses the North American settings to create images that powerfully project his own disturbed state of mind. Mrs. Leprohon focuses on the love stories of her protagonists, and keeps historical events very much in the background. *Les anciens canadiens* is closer to the modern conception of historical fiction as a reconstruction of a past age as seen

---

[1]John Robert Sorfleet, "Fiction and the Fall of New France: William Kirby vs. Gilbert Parker," *Journal of Canadian Fiction*, 2 (Summer 1973), 132-46.

from within, but Aubert de Gaspé's novel is as much an anthology of folklore as a work of fiction. Kirby retains a moral viewpoint, but he employs it in the service of his interpretation of Canadian history. Admittedly, his view of history is simple; but it is no simpler than the ideas expressed by some of the leading historians of his day.

Kirby took over from French-Canadian historians such as François- Xavier Garneau a viewpoint that blamed the fall of New France on the dissoluteness of the French court, and on the corruption of French officials in the new world. His vision of the proper political order is embodied in his portrayal of the happy, near-feudal life at Tully Manor. But this ideal order is overturned by the corrupt machinations of the French Court and its agents in New France. Kirby explains: "The fall of Quebec, and the capitulation of Montreal were less owing to the power of the English than to the corrupt misgovernment of Bigot and Vaudreuil, and the neglect by the court of France of her ancient and devoted colony."[1] In his concluding chapter Kirby looks forward to the period of the American Revolution, and explains that the French Canadians remained loyal to England because they knew they had been abandoned by revolutionary France. His book ends by suggesting that the Conquest has made possible a fusion of the best features of the French and English peoples. Ultimately, Kirby's book becomes a hymn to the political status quo, a celebration of Britain's right to rule in the northern portion of the continent.

The Golden Dog was quickly recognized by critics and writers alike as a major landmark in the growth of Canada's fledgling literature. Indeed, during the later years of the nineteenth century, it was Kirby's novel, together with the historical narratives of Francis Parkman, that fully awakened Canadian authors to the heroic and epic literary potential inherent in their own past.

Parkman's history of the French in North America was an enormously ambitious undertaking. Although the first volume of Parkman's saga was published in 1865, the project was not completed until the publication in 1892 of *A Half-Century of Conflict*. But long before that date Canadi-

---

[1] William Kirby, *The Golden Dog* (Boston: Page, 1897), p. 618.

ans had recognized that Parkman's narratives revealed an unsuspected richness in their past. Canadians learned from Parkman to see the history of New France as an epic series of romantic journeys into the unknown. For example, John George Bourinot in 1893 told the Royal Society of Canada that "the days of the French regime were in a sense days of heroic endeavour." He leaned openly on Parkman's account of the *ancien régime* when he went on to say: "The pen of Francis Parkman has given a vivid picture of those days when bold adventurers unlocked the secrets of this Canadian Dominion, pushed into the western wilderness, followed unknown rivers, and at last found a way to the waters of that southern gulf where Spain had long before, in the days of Grijalva, Cortez and Pineda, planted her flag and won treasures of gold and silver. . . ."[1]

Parkman's version of the history of New France satisfied the desire of both writers and readers to witness heroic individuals engaged in conflicts of far-reaching significance. Consequently, a great many turn-of-the-century Canadian historical romances – and some later tales of historical adventure, for that matter – take place in a romantic region that could most properly be described as Parkman's Canada. Bourinot, for example, sees far greater potential for fiction in the history of Quebec than in that of Ontario, and speaks disparagingly of "prosaic Ontario, whose history is only a century old – a history of stern materialism as a rule, rarely picturesque or romantic, and hardly ever heroic except in some episodes of the war of 1812-15. . ." (p. 24). Bourinot ignores the Loyalist myth that historians such as Egerton Ryerson had already begun to elaborate, and the Loyalists were likewise ignored by most of our nineteenth-century novelists.[2] Not until the early twentieth century, in books such as Wilfred Campbell's *A Beautiful Rebel* (1909) and Jean McIlwraith's *Kinsmen at War* (1927), did writers build historical tales around episodes from Ontario's past.

---

[1] John George Bourinot, *Our Intellectual Strength and Weakness* (Montreal: Foster Brown, 1893), pp. 4-5. All further references to this work appear in the text.

[2] A study of the literary impact of Loyalism can be found in Dennis Duffy, *Gardens, Covenants, Exiles: Loyalism in the Literature of Upper Canada / Ontario* (Toronto: Univ. of Toronto Press, 1982).

Encouraged by Kirby's example and fortified by Parkman's view of history, our writers turned out a considerable stream of historical novels during the turn-of-the-century period. Not all of these books dealt with the history of French Canada, but all of them presented a romantic view of the past. The authors looked for heroes and villains among our historic personages, and tried to discover uplifting examples of individual achievements. Although historical fiction increasingly shared the spotlight with other kinds of fiction, the historical novel remained popular among Canadian authors, and most of the writers who contributed to the outpouring of fiction that appeared at that time wrote one or more stories that used a historical background.

Although it was Kirby who established once and for all the feasibility of historical fiction with a Canadian setting, it was Gilbert Parker who demonstrated that the fall of New France could be turned into a highly marketable literary commodity. Parker first gained attention through his stories of the French-Canadian wanderer he called Pretty Pierre. The stories collected in *Pierre and His People* and in two subsequent volumes about Pierre are nominally set in the Canadian Northwest, but most of the protagonists in these stories are actually European wanderers, unhappy exiles far from their native land. In fact, of Parker's main characters, only Pretty Pierre himself is a North American; and usually Pierre plays a supporting role in someone else's adventures. That is, Parker's outlook is British rather than North American. Typically the stories in the Pierre books tell how a European protagonist undergoes a process of self-discovery, after which he returns home – that is, returns to England.

Parker built his literary career principally in England, where he even briefly served as a Member of Parliament. But he continued to use Canadian settings for much of his writing. In addition to the Pretty Pierre stories, he published novels set in rural Quebec and historical romances set during the last days of New France. It was a historical romance, *The Seats of the Mighty* (1896), that brought Parker his greatest success. A few critics have attempted to elevate this novel to a high place among our nineteenth-century classics, but the novel itself works against them.[1] *The Seats of the Mighty* is an unsavoury piece of work. The narrator and hero, Captain Robert Moray, is a adventurer of dubious principles, who unfolds his tale with an offensive self-righteousness. Moray's self-justifications, however, cannot disguise the story's real appeal, which is its pervasive atmosphere of thinly veiled sadism and sensuality. Certainly *The Seats of the Mighty* is no worse than many other best-selling novels that have attained an ephemeral celebrity. But neither is it any better.

Parker took the germ of his novel from the story of Major Robert Stobo, who was a prisoner at Quebec from 1757 to 1759. He learned of Stobo from the Quebec antiquarian James Macpherson Lemoine, but he had the ambition to write a novel about the *ancien régime* even before he went looking for a historical incident on which to hang his tale. In forming this ambition, it seems likely that he was influenced in no small measure by Kirby's example. Indeed, shortly after his novel appeared, Parker told an interviewer that to the present Canada had produced "only one really notable work of fiction – William Kirby's 'Le Chien d'Or.' " He found it "singular" that only Kirby had made use of the abundant literary possibilities offered by Canadian history. "There was," Parker continued, "the Hudson Bay Company, with a history extending back to the time of Charles II., with Prince Rupert for its first Governor, with all the series of adventures and moving incidents which fell to the lot of the argonauts of the far north; there was the city of Quebec, the point of conflict of the two races in the hemisphere, with all its brilliant and romantic life under the ancient regime, and that all was left untouched save by this man I admire – William Kirby."[2]

Despite Parker's professed admiration for Kirby's novel, however, his own historical fiction is quite different – racier, more superficial, and more sensational. Parker treats the

---

[1] See Elizabeth Waterston, "Introduction," in Gilbert Parker, *The Seats of the Mighty*, New Canadian Library, No. 75 (Toronto: McClelland and Stewart, 1971), pp. iv-ix; see also John Coldwell Adams, *Seated With the Mighty: A Biography of Sir Gilbert Parker* (Ottawa: Borealis, 1979), p. 157.

[2] "Mr. Gilbert Parker," *The Globe*, 31 Oct. 1896, p. 13.

French-Canadian past as a romantic scrapbook full of picturesque scenes and exciting adventures. As a result, he trivializes his historical setting, making events turn on petty personal quarrels between selfish individuals. For example, it is the premise of *The Seats of the Mighty* that the war between France and England in North America was fought not for political or economic advantage but in order that Madame Pompadour might regain some potentially compromising love letters held by Captain Moray.

Like Parker, Charles G.D. Roberts incorporates a rather sensationalized and shallow view of Canadian history into his historical tales. Although Roberts is better known for his poetry and his realistic animal stories than for his novels, he produced a considerable body of fiction, including several novels that drew upon the history of his own Maritimes region. Roberts' attitude to the historical settings of his fiction is explained in a 1923 reissue of *The Forge in the Forest*. In a tacit acknowledgement of the contribution made by another American writer in shaping the popular image of Nova Scotia's past, Roberts calls his homeland the "land of Evangeline." He claims that the story of Acadia "with its background of untamed wilderness, is not less crowded with romantic incident and gallant adventures that are the annals of old world courts and kings." In his own Acadian books, Roberts says, he has "tried to capture and fix the romantic colour of the period, while following closely the outlines of historic record."[1] In Roberts' fiction the impulse to create "romantic colour" clearly overshadows any attempt at historical accuracy.

The Forge in the Forest is a typical example of Roberts' historical fiction. In that novel Roberts creates a sensational tale of wilderness captivity, pursuit, and rescue, in which he pits his hero against a villainous antagonist, and weaves into the plot several mysterious encounters with the half-mad prophet Grûl. Roberts sets this tale of adventure and love against a well-known historical background, the expulsion of the Acadians from Nova Scotia. The book shows strong traces of a Maritime folk tradition that makes Le Loutre, the black

---

[1] Charles G.D. Roberts, "Author's Note," *The Forge in the Forest* (London: Dent, 1923), p. vii.

Abbé, into a devil incarnate, inciting treachery among the Micmacs. The novel also perpetuates tales of the brave resistance of the Acadians, and the self-serving schemes of the imperial officials at Quebec.

In his account of the fictional possibilities offered by the Canadian past, Parker laid considerable stress on the history of the fur trade. But with the exception of the British writer R.M. Ballantyne, who set a number of his stories for young readers in the far north, no nineteenth-century novelist made much use of the fur trade as a setting for fiction. The first author to make literary capital out of the history of the fur trade was an early twentieth-century figure, Agnes C. Laut. Laut eventually produced a number of quite respectable popular histories of North American discovery and exploration. But before she found her true *métier*, she published several dashing adventure stories that embellished well known episodes of Canadian history.

In *Lords of the North* (1900) Laut portrays the climactic events of the struggle between the North-West Company and the Hudson Bay Company, and in *Heralds of Empire* (1902) she looks to an earlier historical era, when England gained control of the Hudson Bay territory with the aid of the French adventurers, Pierre Esprit Radisson and Chouarte des Groseilliers. Laut decided to write her historical romances in order to counteract the dullness with which North American history was usually presented to students. Her abilities as a novelist, however, do not match her historical knowledge. Laut's writing is both derivative and overly emotional. Her fiction is marred by exaggerated and implausible plots, which are inspired not so much by historical events as by formulas derived from sensational popular fiction. She could not match the unsentimental vision achieved by Duncan Campbell Scott in his powerful short stories depicting the everyday life of fur traders. In *Lords of the North* she awkwardly grafts a Gothic plot of revenge and kidnapping onto the story of Lord Selkirk's Red River Settlement. In *Heralds of Empire* she makes Radisson a dashing swordsman typical of the Dumas school of historical adventures.

In both of these novels, Laut's purpose is to celebrate the triumph of European civilization over a chaotic wilderness and its savage inhabitants. Laut's attitude is clearly evident in the introduction to *Lords of the North*, where her narrator boasts of working for the North-West Company, "which ruled over an empire broader than Europe in the beginning of this century."[1] Laut's narrator presents the fur traders as heroic figures, carrying out a virtual mission of conquest on behalf of European civilization. The narrator describes the present Canadian Northwest, which he says the fur traders "reclaimed from savagery for civilization," as "the best monument to the unheralded forerunners of empire" (p. 5). In *Heralds of Empire* Laut is also committed to a view of her white protagonists as the agents of a superior order. In one particularly effusive passage, which is also used as the book's epigraph, she likens the pioneers of the new world to Homeric heroes.

Parker, Roberts, and Laut did not write for an educated elite but for a large, middle class readership, who thought of fiction as entertainment rather than as art. As a result, these three authors wrote historical fiction that was glib, fast-paced, and full of lively incident. They also appealed to their middle-class readers in another important way: they treated social class as a relatively unimportant matter. Roberts does not stress the social rank of the Acadian seigneurs who are his protagonists. The hero of *The Forge in the Forest*, for example, is more of a bush-ranger than a colonial nobleman. In the Pretty Pierre stories Parker brings upper-class Englishmen into the egalitarian society of the early West. And in *The Seats of the Mighty*, though Robert Moray is a gentleman, he is not someone of exalted rank. Nor does Moray acknowledge the villainous Doltaire as his social superior, despite Doltaire's royal paternity. Admittedly, Laut looks above the true *coureurs de bois* for the protagonists of her stories of the fur trade. But she stresses the adventures in which her characters are involved, not their refined manners or their social rank.

This shift in our historical fiction reflects the overall movement of our literature at this time towards a less class-conscious and more democratic kind of fiction. Earlier

---

[1] Agnes C. Laut, *Lords of the North* (Toronto: Briggs, 1900), p. 3. All further references to this work appear in the text.

historical fiction had been preoccupied with social rank. Richardson can perhaps be dismissed as merely a compulsive social climber, even in his fiction. Leprohon and Kirby, however, were trying to establish a social claim that was collective rather than personal. Their fiction was intended to demonstrate their country's right to be admitted into the society of the best European nations. Kirby, in particular, wanted to create a novel that, in magnitude and significance, would match the highly respected work of Sir Walter Scott. Parker and Roberts, on the other hand, were not trying to thrust their books among the highest ranks of literature. They were, first and foremost, trying to write fiction that would sell. This commercialization of our literature could be viewed as a regrettable lowering of standards. There is, however, another way of looking at the development.

The historical novel, as it emerged in the early nineteenth-century, had a built-in bias towards aristocratic protagonists, for the history it depicted was understood to consist largely of the deeds of heroic individuals, usually drawn from the upper reaches of society. Such a view of history was particularly inappropriate in North America, and it may be no cause for regret that towards the end of the century our historical tales gradually acquired a less aristocratic flavour. At that time our writers turned away from the patterns established by Scott and Cooper, and instead began to emulate the swiftly-paced, incident-filled historical tales written by the popular writers of that era. Writers such as Anthony Hope and Robert Louis Stevenson usually drew their protagonists from the middle ranks of society, not from the upper classes. They stressed the action of their stories, and did not dwell minutely on the conversational habits and the manners of their characters. By emulating this kind of historical fiction, our authors were moving away from an exclusively aristocratic conception of literature.

It remained true, of course, that the majority of historical fictions continued to deal with military leaders, or with those characters who were swept up in the clash of rival armies. But the claims of other levels of society were increasingly acknowledged. In the early years of the new century, some historical novelists even began to espouse – albeit tentatively – the democratic values that had come to dominate society in the new world. Wilfred Campbell's *A Beautiful Rebel* provides a good illustration. Campbell ends his tale by forcing his hero to make a symbolic choice: he may satisfy his old world desire to know his true lineage, but this knowledge, he is warned, will bring him personal disaster; or he may remain ignorant of his origins, and make a new life in the democratic new world, where a man's status is determined by his individual achievements and not by his birth. Campbell's hero chooses the way of the new world, and is accepted by his beloved, who is the beautiful rebel of the novel's title. The couple, whose love crosses ancestral political allegiances, are described as the "emblem of the young nation that was to be."[1] By the turn of the century, then, even historical fiction, which once presented an exclusively aristocratic conception of society, has become a vehicle for expressing the egalitarian viewpoint that prevails in the new world.

---

[1] Wilfred Campbell, *A Beautiful Rebel: A Romance of Upper Canada in Eighteen Hundred and Twelve* (Toronto: Westminster, 1909), p. 317.

CHAPTER THREE

From Kailyard to Canada

Lest on too close sight I miss the darling illusion,
Spy at their task even here the hands of chance and change.
     – Charles G.D. Roberts, "The Tantramar Revisited"

Towards the end of the nineteenth century a substantial number of Canadian authors, most of them novelists and short story writers, began to compete successfully in the international literary market. Writers such as E.W. Thomson, Robert Barr, Charles G.D. Roberts, Robert Service, Bliss Carman, and Gilbert Parker moved to England or the United States, in order to enter fully into the literary life of a well-developed artistic and commercial community. A greater number of writers stayed in Canada, but published their books with British or American publishers. Prominent among this group are R.E. Knowles, Duncan Campbell Scott, Ralph Connor, W.A. Fraser, L.M. Montgomery, and Stephen Leacock. In Canada, too, a more elaborate cultural infrastructure was emerging. Periodicals such as *The Week*, *Canadian Magazine*, and *Rose-Belford's Monthly* gave our writers a number of domestic outlets for their essays, stories, and poems. The average quality of the resulting literature was not high, and in most publications popular work was mixed promiscuously with attempts at more serious writing. Nonetheless, the work of these writers demonstrates the emergence, during the years between Confederation and the end of the century, of a lively, if still precarious, Canadian literary culture.

We can begin to appreciate the extent of the change that swept through our literature at the turn of the century if we examine some striking figures that are cited by Gordon Roper in the *Literary History of Canada*. Roper tells us:

> The remarkable increase in the writing of fiction in Canada during these years can be seen clearly when the figures for publication of fiction in book form up to 1880 are placed against those for the years 1880 to 1920. Up to 1880 about 150 Canadians published over 250 volumes of fiction. Almost two-thirds of these volumes appeared in the sixties and the seventies .... In contrast, during the years 1880 to 1920, more than 400 Canadians published over 1,400 volumes of fiction.[1]

What do these numbers mean? Well, for one thing, the average rate of literary production during the 1860s and 1870s was about eight volumes of fiction per year. From 1880 to 1920 the average was about 35 volumes per year. The increase is dramatic. It marks, I suggest, the attainment of a sort of critical mass, after which the Canadian tradition in fiction became more or less self-sustaining. In fact, elsewhere in the *Literary History of Canada* Roper, together with his collaborators Rupert Schieder and S. Ross Beharriell, suggests: "the Canadian fiction-writers between 1880 and 1920 were read more widely by their contemporaries, inside and outside Canada, than have been the Canadian fiction-writers – collectively – since."[2]

To learn what sort of novels and stories our writers were producing at this time, it is helpful to turn again to the *Literary History of Canada*. In the literature of this period, according to Gordon Roper, Rupert Schieder, and S. Ross Beharriell, "seven or eight kinds of fiction predominate: the local colour story; the historical romance; the action or

---

[1] Gordon Roper, "New Forces: New Fiction 1880-1920," in Klinck, ed., *Literary History of Canada*, p. 261.

[2] Gordon Roper, S. Ross Beharriell, and Rupert Schieder, "Writers of Fiction 1880-1920," in *Klinck, ed., Literary History of Canada*, p. 339.

adventure story; the animal story; the mystery, detective, or crime story; novels of ideas or of social criticism; and the sensational and sentimental society story."[1] Some of these forms owe little or nothing to the writer's regional or national affiliation. Their conventions are a sort of literary *lingua franca*, freely available to writers of any nation. But a few of the forms – and these are the most important to my argument – do show the imprint of their place of origin. The realistic animal story, for example, has for a long time been acknowledged as a specifically Canadian contribution to world literature. But though the animal story is an important feature of Canadian letters, it does not contribute significantly to the development of the fictional mainstream. The novel of social purpose, although seldom highly accomplished in purely literary terms, is significant to the extent that it introduces the modern urban scene into Canadian fiction. But it is the local colour story, a form which by definition deals with the writer's local scene, that is the most significant of these genres. Gordon Roper confirms this judgment. The vogue for local colour fiction, he tells us, "was the fashion that affected more Canadian writers of this period than any other."[2]

Desmond Pacey has described our local colour stories as "regional idylls," and the label is an apt one.[3] The regional idyll recreates a simple rural world, usually a heightened version of the author's childhood environment. Readers were invited to join the author on a sentimental journey into the immediate past of their own country. The resulting blend of sentiment and nostalgia offered a welcome temporary escape from a world that was growing increasingly urban and industrial. Prominent among the writers of this sort of fiction are clergymen such as Ralph Connor and R.E. Knowles and moralizing ladies such as Marian Keith (Mrs. Mary Esther

---

[1] Gordon Roper, Rupert Schieder, and S. Ross Beharriell, "The Kinds of Fiction 1880-1920," in Klinck, ed., *Literary History of Canada*, p. 284.

[2] Roper, "New Forces: New Fiction 1880-1920," in Klinck, ed., *Literary History of Canada*, p. 282.

[3] Desmond Pacey, *Creative Writing in Canada*, rev. ed. (Toronto: Ryerson, 1961), p. 102. All further references to this work appear in the text.

MacGregor) and Nellie McClung. Typical examples are Knowles's *St. Cuthbert's* (1905), Keith's *Duncan Polite* (1905), and McClung's *Sowing Seeds in Danny* (1908).

Unlike writers of historical fiction, such as William Kirby and Gilbert Parker, the authors of regional idylls looked to their own experience to furnish the subjects of their books. There is still a historical aspect to most regional idylls, but usually the authors are looking back to their own childhood and youth, not to an historical era outside their own experience. The use of a North American setting in these books indicated an important change in the outlook of our writers. They were beginning to recognize that literature could be based on the everyday experiences of ordinary people from their own country. In fact, by the turn of the century the authors of the books that have come to be called regional idylls no longer assumed the existence of social classes based on inherited rank and privilege. Instead, they wrote for readers drawn from the commercial and profession-al classes, and they wrote about characters and settings that were familiar to many of their readers. As a result, despite the sentimentality of most of their books, the authors of our turn-of-the-century regional fiction helped to create a sense that their new nation did have a cultural identity of its own.

The importance of the regional idyll in the development of Canadian fiction has never been adequately acknowl-edged. Our critics have tended until recently to agree with E.K. Brown's assessment of regionalism as "another force which tells against the immediate growth of a national literature."[1] Brown's dismissal of our early regional fiction is caused, in fact, by a kind of intellectual snobbery. Conse-quently, Brown offers a scathing dismissal of most of our turn-of-the-century fiction. He speaks scornfully of "a hand-ful of Canadians who at about this time began to make their huge and ephemeral reputations as best-selling writers" (p. 4). Brown's outlook is quite common among academic critics. To put things plainly, Brown is offended because the writers he is considering – he names Gilbert Parker, Ralph Connor, L.M. Montgomery, and Robert Service as the leading

---

[1] Brown, *On Canadian Poetry*, p. 23. All further references to this work appear in the text.

figures – appear so willing to cater to the tastes of a general readership. A similar distrust of popular literature leads Desmond Pacey to describe the turn-of-the-century period as "without doubt the age of brass" succeeding the "golden age" of the Confederation Poets and their contemporaries (p.89).

Like Brown and Pacey, most academic critics have singled out for praise the authors who introduced new modes and new themes into Canadian letters. As a result, they have assigned a high value to the belated and tentative outcroppings of modernism that began to appear in Canadian writing during the twenties and thirties. Certainly, the arrival of modernism is an important chapter in the development of our fiction, but it is far from being the whole story. The upsurge of regional fiction that appeared at the turn of the century also played an important role in laying the groundwork of a native literary tradition.

Considered individually, most of the regional idylls are undistinguished; nonetheless their collective importance is great. By sheer volume, they provided the compost or fertilizer out of which better work could grow. For the writers of the regional idyll were the first who attempted to do what the major figures of a later generation of writers have been praised for accomplishing: the making of serious literature out of materials that are unmistakably and unashamedly Canadian. If they did not fully succeed in attaining their artistic goals, they nonetheless took the first steps down the path their successors have followed. Their discovery of the literary potential of their native regions anticipates similar discoveries that were made by later writers such as Hugh MacLennan and Margaret Laurence. In fact, there are important strands of thematic continuity extending from the early regional idyll to later books that are recognized as Canadian classics.

Today we are far more ready than we once were to look with approval on "regional" art, seeing it as an authentic expression of a particular culture's traditions and attitudes. Nonetheless, we still tend to view the heyday of the regional idyll as simply an embarrassing phase that Canadian writing has outgrown. For a new nation, however, the stages of cultural history may take on a significance that differs from their significance in the cultural history of the parent state, or even in the cultural history of an older neighbouring state. In the history of British fiction, the rise of the regional idyll is properly considered a relatively minor event, important chiefly as an incident in the history of popular taste. In the United States, the emergence of local colour fiction during the latter decades of the nineteenth century is given a greater importance, but the local colourists are still relegated to secondary place in the American tradition. In Canada, however, the literary tradition was still relatively undeveloped in the later years of the nineteenth century. The appearance of the regional idyll had a major effect on our embryonic literature, marking an important step towards the use of local settings and local themes as the basis for fiction.

Models for the regional idyll were available in both British and American fiction. Stories that deal with the life of provincial English towns, as does Mrs. Gaskell's *Cranford*, and stories that deal with the life of the British countryside, as Hardy's novels do, were familiar to Canadian readers. It might be stretching the point to claim our regional idylls as direct descendants of this fiction, but the English example was surely not without an indirect influence. A more direct inspiration for some Canadian authors was probably furnished by American writers of regional fiction. Western writers such as Bret Harte and Mark Twain helped to pioneer a sort of fiction that was far removed from the genteel standards of the Boston Brahmins. A slightly later group of writers, the authors "of local colour" fiction – writers such as Edward Eggleston, Charles Eggbert Craddock (Mary N. Murfee), Hamlin Garland, and Sarah Orne Jewett – probably had a more direct influence on Canadian literary taste.[1] But the single most influential model for the Canadi-

---

[1] William H. Magee links the work of Canadian regional writers to the American local colour tradition in "Local Colour in Canadian Fiction," *University of Toronto Quarterly*, 28 (1959), 176-89.

an regional idyll was the group of late nineteenth-century British writers who quickly became known as the Kailyard School.[1]

The label "Kailyard" applies to most of the early work by J.M. Barrie (later famous as the creator of Peter Pan), and most of the fiction written by S.R. Crockett and Ian Maclaren (the pen-name of the Reverend John Watson). The most famous examples of Kailyard fiction – Barrie's *Auld Licht Idylls* (1888) and *A Window in Thrums* (1889), Maclaren's *Beside the Bonnie Brier Bush* (1894), and Crockett's *The Stickit Minister* (1893) – are collections of loosely related sketches, unified more by a common setting and recurrent characters than by any continuing plot. The actors in these tales are simple people, limited even in their vices, and they adhere staunchly – even picturesquely – to some branch of the Presbyterian church. According to the most careful student of the Kailyard School: "The smiles and tears, the little joys and sorrows of rustic characters speaking slowly and pawkily in an odd variant of English – that was, roughly speaking, the formula."[2]

All of the Kailyard books explore the joys, sorrows, and foibles of characters who adhere to a rural way of life that had vanished some years ago from the real Scottish countryside. That is, the Kailyard authors set their stories in the old days of small farms and hand weaving, before debilitating modern improvements began to be introduced. In *Auld Licht Idylls* Barrie says of Thrums: "Until twenty years ago its every other room, earthen-floored and showing the rafters overhead, had a handloom. . . ."[3] He opens *A Window in Thrums* by telling us: "In the old days the stiff ascent left Thrums behind, and where is now the making of a suburb

---

[1] Elizabeth Waterston has considered the influence of the Kailyard School on Canadian writers in "Canadian Cabbage, Canadian Rose," *Journal of Canadian Fiction*, 2 (Summer 1973), 129-31. Waterston's discussion, however, is limited exclusively to writers of Scottish descent.

[2] George Blake, *Barrie and the Kailyard School* (London: Arthur Barker, 1951), p. 32.

[3] J.M. Barrie, *Auld Licht Idylls* (London: Hodder and Stoughton, 1888), p. 9.

was only a poor row of dwellings and a manse, with Hendry's cot to watch the brae."[1] Maclaren begins *Beside the Bonnie Brier Bush* by contrasting the utilitarian new school of Drumtochty with the more pleasantly situated old schoolhouse, which was set "in the sweet pine-woods at the foot of the cart road to Whinnie Knowe and the upland farms."[2]

What did Canadian authors find so attractive about the Kailyard School's fiction? In part – but in part only – the appeal had an ethnic basis. Elizabeth Waterston points out: "There was hardly a Canadian village throughout the later nineteenth century without its dominating Kirk, its Scottish schoolmaster and its Scottish-trained printer and journalist. The Lowland thread was much more visible and significant in Canadian towns than in those of the United States."[3] The conspicuous success of the Kailyard writers apparently emboldened a number of Presbyterian ministers, such as R.E. Knowles and Ralph Connor (Charles W. Gordon), to write fiction about the Scots who had come to Canada. But the impact of the Kailyard School on our literature goes well beyond encouraging the use of Scots dialect or the portrayal of picturesque religious practices – though these features are conspicuous in some Canadian regional idylls. Rather, the example of the Kailyard writers undoubtedly prompted many Canadian authors to consider the fictional possibilities of native communities that were just as superficially commonplace as the villages the Kailyard writers described. The Kailyard writers treated subjects that were humble and domestic; yet their books had achieved a spectacular success. From the Kailyard writers, our writers learned that successful popular fiction could be episodic in form, local and domestic in subject-matter, and sentimental in mood.

The best-known works of the Kailyard writers collect a number of tales that describe the daily life of a small

---

[1] J.M. Barrie, *A Window in Thrums* (London: Hodder and Stoughton, 1890), p. 1.

[2] Ian Maclaren, *Beside the Bonnie Brier Bush* (London: Hodder and Stoughton, 1894), p. 5.

[3] Elizabeth Waterston, "The Lowland Tradition in Canadian Literature," in W. Stanford Reid, ed., *The Scottish Tradition in Canada* (Toronto: McClelland and Stewart, 1976), p. 221.

community. This form – a loosely connected series of "idylls" or tales, telling of life in the countryside or the market village – appealed to many writers who wished to chronicle the doings of communities in various parts of Canada. Collections of tales set in rural Quebec include Duncan Campbell Scott's *In the Village of Viger* (1896), Cecil Walsh's *Bonhomme* (1899), and James LeRossignol's *Little Stories of Quebec* (1908). E.W. Thomson's *Old Man Savarin and Other Stories* (1895) portrayed both the French-Canadian and the Scotch inhabitants of the lower Ottawa valley, and Connor's *Glengarry School Days* (1902) gives a vivid picture of life in an Ottawa valley lumbering and farming community. Other regions of Canada, locales all the way from Newfoundland to the West, also found their way into this kind of fiction. Norman Duncan's *The Way of the Sea* (1903) deals memorably with the hard life of Newfoundland's outport fishermen. Connor's *Black Rock* (1898) and Nellie McClung's *Sowing Seeds in Danny* (1908), although they join the sentimentality of the regional idyll with the morality of the temperance tract, bring this sort of fiction to a prairie setting.

Of course, not all regional writers confined themselves to the short story form. The Kailyard writers had also written longer tales set in their favorite locales, and Canadian writers did likewise. R.E. Knowles wrote a series of novels set in communities that were dominated by Scottish settlers – though he also admitted an occasional comic Irishman, as he does in *The Handicap* (1910). In *The Lone Furrow* (1907) W.A. Fraser added a melodramatic mystery to his portrayal of a narrowly Presbyterian Ontario town. Marian Keith's *Duncan Polite* (1905) is set in an isolated Ontario settlement that resembles Barrie's Thrums or Maclaren's Drumtochty. Early novels set in small French-Canadian communities include Francis W. Grey's *The Curé of St. Philippe* (1899) and LeRossignol's *Jean Baptiste* (1915).

The most perfect Canadian adaptation of the Kailyard manner, however, is found in Connor's *Glengarry School Days* (1902). When he set the first portion of *The Man from Glengarry* (1901) in the region he knew from his own childhood, Connor had uncovered a rich vein of personal memories, which his readers also found highly appealing. He astutely decided to exploit the same materials in his next book. S. Ross Beharriell remarks that Connor's approach in *Glengarry School Days* "had much in common with the nineteenth century local-colourists,"[1] yet he does not think that Connor was directly influenced by the American regional writers. Beharriell, however, neglects the possibility that Connor was looking eastward across the Atlantic for his literary model, rather than southward. Books by the Kailyard writers would almost certainly have been a feature of Connor's Scottish-Presbyterian home. The likelihood that Connor was familiar with Kailyard fiction becomes a virtual certainty when we consider the striking resemblances between *Glengarry School Days* and the works of the Kailyard writers. Like Barrie's *Auld Licht Idylls* and *A Window in Thrums*, Connor's book is a collection of sketches rather than a novel. Motifs that are prominent in Connor's book – the quirks of staunch Presbyterians, the uplifting influence exercised by a dying mother, amusing schoolroom episodes – are also staples of Kailyard fiction. But the final effect of Connor's book is subtly different from the effect achieved by most Kailyard writers. Like the Kailyard writers, Connor looks back to a vanished world, but he does so in order to explain the vigour and manliness of his own generation of Canadians. His nostalgia does not carry an accompanying sense that the present-day world is diminished and unworthy.

Duncan Campbell Scott's *In the Village of Viger* is another leading example of the Canadian regional idyll. Scott begins by establishing a backward-looking temporal perspective that resembles the outlook of the Kailyard writers. Viger is presented as a pastoral retreat, a peaceful haven in a world of growing cities. But Viger is threatened: "It was too true that the city was growing rapidly. As yet its arms were not long enough to embrace the little village of Viger, but before long they would be, and it was not a time that the inhabitants looked forward to with any pleasure." As yet the village was little changed, and "it seemed impossible that

---

[1] S. Ross Beharriell, "Introduction," in Ralph Connor, *Glengarry School Days*, New Canadian Library, No. 118 (Toronto: McClelland and Stewart, 1975), n. pag.

70

any change could come. The change was coming, however, rapidly enough."[1] In most of the stories in this volume, Scott looks back to life as it was before the city began to impinge on the old ways. Often he echoes the dominant note of the Kailyard writers: wistful resignation leavened with whimsy. One story, "The Tragedy of the Seigneury," can be interpreted as a melodramatic elegy for the vanished seigneurial way of life in the Quebec countryside.

In order to see the works of the Kailyard School as our late nineteenth-century writers saw them, we need to take a quick glance at the cultural environment in which these writers lived and wrote. At least until the First World War, the literary climate in Canada remained overwhelmingly conservative and cautious. Canadian writers were aware of the literary controversies that raged in London or New York, but for the most part they lacked the self-confidence to take a controversial position. Our writers and critics felt their cultural isolation very strongly. To espouse radical new ideas would only remove them further from what they felt to be the centre of civilized society. On the other hand, by echoing the majority outlook – inevitably a conservative and traditional position – they gained a feeling of participating in the mainstream of civilized cultural life.

During the later years of the nineteenth century, then, the literary climate in Canada did not encourage a careful discrimination of literary merit. Our writers and critics were aware of the changes that had occurred in European and American fiction. For the most part, however, they had difficulty in separating work of lasting merit from work that was ephemeral. They did not, for example, distinguish between the harsh naturalism of Zola and the more decorous realism of Howells and James; neither did they always distinguish between serious fiction and popular best-sellers. Viewed from a distant colony, it was all literature. As a result, many writers had no qualms about adopting the sentimental conventions of the Kailyard writers, rather than the sophistication of James or the documentary realism of

---

[1] Duncan Campbell Scott, "The Little Milliner," In *The Village of Viger and Other Stories*, New Canadian Library, No. 92 (Toronto: McClelland and Stewart, 1973), p. 19.

Howells.

For a closer look at the literary climate of the time, we can turn to the pages of the literary periodicals published in Canada during the later years of the century. We can gauge the general tone of literary opinion by examining allusions to a literary controversy that was widespread in Victorian Britain and in post-Civil War America, the debate between "realism" and "idealism" in fiction. Here is how one writer explained what he called "the ordinary and well-understood meanings" of these two terms:

> I take it that ... realism, as applied to fiction, is the doctrine of the superior importance of the real facts of life; that is, the reproduction of actual life utterly devoid of any striving for romance, poetry, or uncommon incidents and situations. Idealism, I take it, is the doctrine of the superiority of ideal creations over the facts of life.[1]

Like most Canadian critics, this writer favoured idealism because it was "filled with a great purpose to benefit mankind," whereas realism degraded both its subjects and its readers.

The supporters of idealism took particular exception to certain French and American writers, though British novelists whose works hinted at naturalistic doctrines, such as Hardy, were not exempt from censure. John George Bourinot hoped that Canadian writers would "not bring the Canadian fiction of the future to that low level to which the school of realism in France, and in a minor degree in England and the United States, would degrade the novel and story of every-day life."[2] Graeme Mercer Adam lamented:

> The good old romantic and imaginative novel of our grandmothers' times seems a creation wholly of the past. What we have in its place is the English melodrama of such books as "Called Back"; the

---

[1] Stuart Livingston, "Bjornstjerne Björnson," *The Canadian Magazine*, April 1893, p. 98.

[2] Bourinot, *Our Intellectual Strength and Weakness*, p. 30.

intellectual vivisection methods of the American schools of James and Howells; or, worse still, the loathsome realism and putridity of the school of Zola and France.[1]

Louisa Murray, in the very title of her polemic against "Democracy in Literature," equated dangerous republican political ideas and immoral literary doctrines in a way that was quite common. She cited with approval the imprisonment of the London bookseller Vizetelly for selling Zola's novels, and she said that Howells' novels "if accepted as true pictures of the best that life can give, could scarcely fail to check all aspirations after the higher possibilities of existence, without which life would certainly not be worth living."[2]

One of the few Canadian writers who welcomed the new fiction with anything approaching an open mind was Sara Jeannette Duncan. Duncan appointed herself as the chief Canadian champion of the fiction of Howells and James, whom she often defended against the attacks of those she viewed as censorious Philistines. She approvingly described Howells and James as "engaged in developing a school of fiction most closely and subtly related to the conditions and progress of our time, of which we all should know something."[3] Yet even Duncan could write: "The modern school of fiction, if it is fairly subject to any reproach, may bear the blame of dealing too exclusively in the corporealities of human life, to the utter and scornful neglect of its idealities."[4] Apologists for both realism and idealism, then, based their arguments on moral grounds. At bottom, they simply disagreed over whether literature could best impart its messages by portraying the world as it is, or by portray-

---

[1] Graeme Mercer Adam, "Some Books of the Past Year. – II," *The Week*, 15 Jan. 1885, p. 103.

[2] Louisa Murray, "Democracy in Literature," *The Week*, 2 Aug. 1889, p. 550.

[3] Sara Jeannette Duncan, "Literary Pabulum," *The Week*, 24 Nov. 1887, p. 831.

[4] Sara Jeannette Duncan, "The Art Gallery of the English Language," *The Week*, 15 July 1886, p. 533.

ing the world as it ought to be.

Highways of Canadian Literature, by John Daniel Logan and Donald G. French, is today generally regarded as one of the weaker of our early literary histories. Most readers today would probably see it as largely a catalogue of authors' names and book titles. Certainly, Logan and French do give a good deal of space to writing that is now summarily dismissed by most academic critics. Whatever the defects of their judgments, however, Logan and French were closer to the spirit of their own time than we are today. Some of their comments may help us to understand how an earlier generation saw our turn-of-the-century literature. For example, Logan and French remark that in the regional idylls our authors "began to realize that life around them was as interesting as Barrie's Thrums or Bret Harte's California."[1] Logan and French do not use the term regional idyll. Instead, astutely recognizing that communal solidarity is a common theme of these stories, they call this sort of fiction "the community novel" (p. 298). Often the characters of such books are shown rallying around shared values and cherished social institutions. Admittedly, there is often a clash between old and new generations, but by the end of these stories the rift in the community has been healed, and harmony reestablished. These clashes frequently revolve around the dogma and ritual of the church. Such disputes occur, for example, in Marian Keith's *Duncan Polite* and in R.E. Knowles's *St. Cuthbert's*.

Logan and French also cite a revealing remark made by Adeline M. Teskey, who told how her reading of Ian MacLaren's *Beside the Bonnie Brier Bush* left her with the feeling: "I know just as interesting people in Canada" (p. 299). The eventual result of this observation was Teskey's first regional idyll, *Where the Sugar Maple Grows* (1901). Teskey followed this book with a second work of the same kind, *The Village Artist* (1905). The latter book also furnishes a particularly clear illustration of literary idealism in action. Serena Slade, the woman known as the "village artist," is not

---

[1] J.D. Logan and Donald G. French, *Highways of Canadian Literature* (Toronto: McClelland and Stewart, 1924), p. 298. All further references to this work appear in the text.

a student of any of the fine arts. Rather, she uses her gift for story-telling to reconcile her fellow townsfolk to their humble place in life, or to reveal a silver lining in circumstances that the narrator – a visitor from the city – views as pitiable or confining. Mrs. Slade justifies her approach by telling the narrator: "when an artist goes to paint a portrait he does not make prominent the warts and blemishes, he just passes them by as though they were not there, and searches for the pretty spots."[1] The beneficial effect of the village artist's work is illustrated in the book's first story, when she assists a woman who finds village life dull and limited. Mrs. Slade explains to the narrator: "I thought I'd paint a little just to cheer her up a bit – bring out the colours of things she could see and hear, or sense in some way, sitting on her own stoop" (p. 11). And the woman responds gratefully: " 'Yes,' she said, 'you're a good neighbour, and you're a great artist too. You've brought out the local colours ... in a way that I shall not soon forget. Mrs. Slade,' says she, 'you've painted the glory of the commonplace' " (pp. 20-21). "Local colours" and "the glory of the commonplace": this is exactly what the regional idyll celebrates.

The influence of the regional idyll is visible in the best work from the turn-of-the-century era, as well as in the lesser-known works I have been dealing with thus far. The two leading works of fiction dating from this era are probably Sara Jeannette Duncan's *The Imperialist* (1904) and Stephen Leacock's *Sunshine Sketches of a Little Town* (1912). Students of children's literature will also be quick to remind us of the merits of L.M. Montgomery's best-known novel, *Anne of Green Gables* (1908). Some commentators apparently rank Leacock's *Arcadian Adventures with the Idle Rich* (1914), the urban companion piece to *Sunshine Sketches*, at the same level as Leacock's masterpiece. A few others might wish to put in a word for Ralph Connor's *The Man from Glengarry* (1901), although Connor's story loses much of its intensity in its second half, after Ranald departs from the Glengarry settlement whose Scottish traditions Connor describes in such affectionate detail. Whatever their individual merits,

---

[1] Adeline M. Teskey, *The Village Artist* (New York: Fleming H. Revell, 1905), p. 59. All further references to this work appear in the text.

most of these books – the single exception is Leacock's *Arcadian Adventures* – belong to the same literary family: they are all versions of the regional idyll. In all of these books, however, the idealism that makes most of our regional fiction so saccharine is tempered by a substantial measure of realism.

Before she wrote about her Prince Edward Island orphan, L.M. Montgomery apparently experienced an insight similar to Adeline Teskey's recognition that interesting people could be found in one's own community. At any rate, she portrayed such a discovery in her fiction on several occasions. In *Anne of Green Gables*, for example, Montgomery first tells how Anne organizes a "story club," whose members must every week compose a far-fetched tale of love or murder, in which, as Anne says, "All the good people are rewarded and all the bad ones suitably punished."[1] As Anne grows up, however, the story club is disbanded, and Anne's implausible story-telling is disciplined. Her new teacher, says Anne, has curbed her pretentious vocabulary and "won't let us write anything but what might happen in Avonlea in our own lives" (p. 271). When she wrote *Anne of Green Gables*, Montgomery was guided by just such a principle – tempered, of course, by a generous dose of idealism.

Montgomery's most autobiographical heroine, the young writer Emily Byrd Starr, also undergoes a similar awakening to the worth of local materials. Emily's early literary career is traced in the three books of the Emily series. Emily, like her creator, learns to eschew the sentimental formulas of popular romantic fiction, and instead looks to her own local community for her subjects. Her first real success comes when she retells an anecdote she has heard in a local farmhouse. She subsequently rejects an opportunity to work on an American magazine, and she tells herself: "as for material – people *live* here just the same as anywhere else – suffer and enjoy and sin and aspire just as they do in New

---

[1]L.M. Montgomery, *Anne of Green Gables* (Toronto: McGraw-Hill Ryerson, 1968), p. 224. All further references to this work appear in the text.

York."[1] She later reflects: "the materials of story weaving are the same in all ages and all places. Births, deaths, marriages, scandals – these are the only really interesting things in the world."[2]

Montgomery's work, however, differs in one important respect from much of the work produced by the lesser regional writers who preceded her. Montgomery assumes a narrative stance that brings her closer to her characters and their community. The narrators of a great deal of regional fiction tend to patronize the characters of their stories; their nostalgia is tempered with a sense of the rustic simplicity of the community they describe. Teskey's narrator, for example, is only an occasional visitor to the town depicted in *Where the Sugar Maple Grows*; and the narrator of *St. Cuthbert's* writes with a sort of proprietorial smugness, proud of being the minister of the strenuously virtuous community he describes. Montgomery's narrator, on the other hand, always speaks as the equal of the characters in her story. She is part of the world of Avonlea. Her knowledge comes from daily familiarity, and she writes in a style that does not set her apart from the interests and educational level of her characters.

Nonetheless, Montgomery's narrator is not above exposing the shortcomings of the characters she describes. Indeed, it is not always recognized that Montgomery smuggles a good deal of muted social criticism into her depictions of hidebound and gossip-ridden rural communities. This critical side of Montgomery's writing is particularly evident in the early pages of *Anne of Green Gables*. In that novel Montgomery clearly paints the stifling, convention-bound atmosphere of Avonlea, which makes the watchful busybody Mrs. Rachel Lynde a figure of power in the community. Consider this paragraph, taken from the opening pages of the novel:

There are plenty of people, in Avonlea and out of it, who can attend closely to their neighbours' business by dint of neglecting their own; but Mrs. Rachel

[1] L. M. Montgomery, *Emily Climbs* (Toronto: McClelland and Stewart, 1925), p. 298. All further references to this work appear in the text.

[2] L.M. Montgomery, *Emily's Quest* (Toronto: McClelland and Stewart, 1927), pp. 2-3.

Lynde was one of those capable creatures who can manage their own concerns and those of other folks into the bargain. She was a notable housewife; her work was always done and well done; she "ran" the Sewing Circle, helped run the Sunday school, and was the strongest prop of the Church Aid Society and Foreign Missions Auxiliary. Yet with all this Mrs. Rachel found abundant time to sit for hours at her kitchen window, knitting "cotton warp" quilts – she had knitted sixteen of them, as Avonlea housekeepers were wont to tell in awed voices – and keeping a sharp eye on the main road that crossed the hollow and wound up the steep red hill beyond. Since Avonlea occupied a little triangular peninsula jutting out into the Gulf of St. Lawrence, with water on two sides of it, anybody who went out of it or into it had to pass over that hill road and so run the unseen gauntlet of Mrs. Rachel's all-seeing eye. (p. 2)

The passage gives an effective introduction to Montgomery's rural world, for Mrs. Lynde's interests define the major preoccupations of Avonlea society – at least the major preoccupations of the feminine half of Avonlea. Life in Avonlea is conducted under the intense scrutiny of sharp-eyed neighbours, such as Mrs. Lynde. Living in this censorious atmosphere has turned Marilla and Matthew Cuthbert into joyless and repressed shadows of their best selves, badly in need of the leavening that Anne's presence brings.

When Anne arrives, Green Gables is the epitome of Avonlea good housekeeping. Even the yard outside Green Gables is swept immaculately clean, in conformity with the community's expectations. "Not a stray stick nor stone was to be seen," we are told, "for Mrs. Rachel would have seen it if there had been" (p. 4). In fact, Green Gables is too clean, betraying the neurotic obsession with housework that arises from Marilla's lack of satisfying human contact. "The kitchen at Green Gables was a cheerful apartment – or would have been cheerful if it had not been so painfully clean as to give it something of the appearance of an unused parlour" (p. 4). And of course Green Gables has a parlour as well, which undoubtedly resembles Mrs. Spencer's intimidating parlour. In this room "a deadly chill struck on them as if the air had been strained so long through dark green, closely drawn blinds that it had lost every particle of warmth it had ever possessed" (p. 49). Marilla is at first a fit representative of this joyless world; she is "always slightly distrustful of sunshine, which seemed to her too dancing and irresponsible a thing for a world which was meant to be taken seriously . . ." (p. 5). Anne's own bedroom, reached through a hall that is "fearsomely clean" (p. 29), is also distressingly spartan. "When Marilla had gone," we are told, "Anne looked around her wistfully. The whitewashed walls were so painfully bare and staring that she thought they must ache over their own bareness" (p. 29). Next morning, Anne's opening of her bedroom window takes on a symbolic meaning: "She pushed up the sash – it went up stiffly and creakily, as if it hadn't been opened for a long time . . ." (p. 33).

The critical dimension of Montgomery's novel is, of course, greatly qualified by her penchant for sentimentality. Everything in the novel – even Matthew's death and Marilla's failing eyesight – must turn out for the best in the end. In arranging her happy ending, Montgomery is true to the principles that are later expressed by her fictional alter ego, Emily Byrd Starr. In *Emily Climbs*, near the end of her literary apprenticeship, Emily defines one of the guiding principles of her art in this way: "But here and now I record this vow, most solemnly, in my diary, *My pen shall heal, not hurt*" (p. 21). Here we have, concisely stated, a fundamental tenet of most of our regional fiction.

Like Montgomery, Ralph Connor in his best novel, *The Man from Glengarry*, goes beyond the limits of the usual regional idyll. In particular, he shows a striking capacity for combining a scathing denunciation of the oppressive orthodoxy of his childhood community with a sentimental idealization of its virtues. It is no exaggeration to say that Reverend Murray's punitive Old Testament religion is weighed in the balance and found wanting. The minister cannot penetrate beneath the moody exterior of Ranald Macdonald and his apparently unregenerate father Black Hugh. It is the minister's wife, the spokesman for a tolerant New Testament gospel of love and forgiveness, who awakens the slumbering religious consciousness of Black Hugh and calls forth the desire for greatness in young Ranald. Mrs. Murray's religion emphasizes doing good in this world. Although she is portrayed as the next thing to a saint, she actually takes the world to come serenely for granted in order to get on with the business of living in this one.

Consider this scene, in which the saintly Mrs. Murray is quizzing her stern husband about his handling of a quarrel that had broken out between Ranald Macdonald and Aleck McRae:

> "Oh, Papa!" said his wife, "what did you say?"
> "Nothing but what was true. I just told him that a boy who would break the Lord's Day by fighting, and in the very shadow of the Lord's house, when Christian people were worshipping God, was acting like a savage, and was not fit for the company of decent folk."
> To this his wife made no reply, but went out of the study, leaving the minister feeling very uncomfortable indeed. But by the end of the second pipe he began to feel that, after all, Ranald had got no more than was good for him, and that he would be none the worse of it; in which comforting conviction he went to rest, and soon fell into the sleep which is supposed to be the right of the just.[1]

The scene exposes the vindictive side of the Minister's conduct, and clearly shows him to be a self-deceiver – almost a hypocrite – in his feeling of self-approval. The barbarity of a religion that dooms a great many of its adherents to feelings of guilt and unworthiness is made apparent when Ranald shortly thereafter appears at the Murray household, convinced that he is "not for decent people" (p. 83). But Connor's sentimental outlook shows when he lets Mrs. Murray change Ranald's mind about leaving the community where he has been treated so unjustly.

---

[1] Ralph Connor, *The Man from Glengarry*, New Canadian Library, No. 14 (Toronto: McClelland and Stewart, 1960), p. 82. All further references to this work appear in the text.

The Man from Glengarry also reveals the intensity of the inner struggle that could be generated when the old religious dogmas came into conflict with natural human impulses. In the first half of the novel, Connor vividly portrays Black Hugh's fearful certainty that he is damned, because he cannot find it in his heart to forgive the French-Canadian lumberjack who has injured him. But Connor cannot let matters rest there. He forces a happy resolution, in which Black Hugh's son Ranald becomes an idealized apostle of muscular Christianity. Thus, Connor's book is typical of the spirit of many turn-of-the-century works. He looks back with nostalgia on a simpler rural world, and tries to insist on the continued vitality of the old moral standards in the more complex urban Canada of the early twentieth century.

Sara Jeannette Duncan's *The Imperialist* and Stephen Leacock's *Sunshine Sketches of a Little Town* are generally ranked as the best books written during the two or three decades immediately preceding the First World War. Neither *The Imperialist* nor *Sunshine Sketches* is a typical example of the regional idyll; nonetheless, Duncan and Leacock were quite aware of the tradition of sentimental local colour fiction that existed in the later years of the nineteenth century. The pre-War regional idyll was emphatically a "popular" form of fiction. But Duncan and Leacock deliberately create ironic variations on the conventions of the regional idyll, so that their best books express critiques of the values on which more orthodox examples of the regional idyll are based. Duncan's novel clearly sets out to be "serious" literature. Indeed, Duncan told a correspondent that she tried very hard to make *The Imperialist* her best book.[1] *Sunshine Sketches*, however, triumphantly straddles the categories of popular and elite literature.

Critics have long debated whether *Sunshine Sketches of a Little Town* is a satire, a novel, or some kind of novel manqué.[2] Most of their efforts, however, have paid insuffi-

---

[1] Thomas E. Tausky, "Duncan, Sara Jeannette," in Toye, ed., *The Oxford Companion to Canadian Literature*, p. 225.

[2] Robertson Davies, *Stephen Leacock*, Canadian Writers, No. 7 (Toronto: McClelland and Stewart, 1970), p. 21; see also Donald Cameron, *Faces of Leacock* (Toronto: Ryerson, 1967), pp. 138-54.

cient attention to the specific literary context from which Leacock's book sprang.[1] *Sunshine Sketches* is both a summation and a critique of the regional fiction that writers such as Teskey, Knowles, and Connor had made popular in Canada. Indeed, it is possible to argue that in *Sunshine Sketches* Leacock has deliberately overturned virtually all the values that are enshrined in the majority of regional idylls. His Mariposans are ignorant, small-minded, and prejudiced; his lovers are absurd and immature; the central figure in his community is a saloonkeeper, not a minister; and Leacock's book is, in effect, an unabashed anti-temperance tract. Many of the values held by the Mariposans are directly contrary to the four-square moral virtues held up for praise in most regional idylls. Yet Leacock manages to present his characters' sins as mere peccadillos, their stupidities as everyday human failings. Above all, the reader sees that the Mariposans instinctively act to protect themselves against forces emanating from the city. For example, after the Anglican church burns down, they display a community spirit that overrides inconvenient legal niceties. Just consider the town's attitude towards those who hint that the fire was not an accident. The narrator tells us:

> Just what the jurisdiction of Judge Pepperleigh's court is I don't know, but I do know that in upholding the rights of a Christian congregation – I am quoting here the text of the decision – against the intrigues of a set of infernal skunks that make too much money, anyway, the Mariposa court is without an equal. Pepperleigh even threatened the plaintiffs with the penitentiary, or worse.[2]

At one point the narrator of *Sunshine Sketches* remarks that "in Mariposa all really important speeches are addressed to an imaginary audience of boys" (p. 34). Leacock's

---

[1] An exception is W.H. Magee, "Stephen Leacock, Local Colourist," *Canadian Literature*, No. 39 (Winter 1969), pp. 34-42.

[2] Stephen Leacock, *Sunshine Sketches of a Little Town*, New Canadian Library, No. 15 (Toronto: McClelland and Stewart, 1960), p. 85. All further references to this work appear in the text.

book, as well, is addressed to such an audience, for Leacock makes his deepest appeal to the child that is buried in each of his readers. Near the end of "L'Envoi" the reader discovers that he has been one of the "boys" whom the narrator is addressing. When the Conductor of Leacock's train calls out " MARIPOSA! MARIPOSA!" the reader is prepared for a literal and sentimental return to take place. The reader is momentarily shocked when the narrator dispels the fictional illusion, and returns the reader to his own equivalent of the Mausoleum Club. Despite their claims to urban sophistication, Leacock's readers are forced to admit that they too have longed, however fleetingly, for a return to the simple life of Mariposa. In *Sunshine Sketches* Leacock presumes that fond memories of a rural or small town childhood lie beneath his readers' veneer of urban sophistication. The book, then, is aimed directly at a newly urbanized society, most of whose members do not come from urban backgrounds.

In *The Imperialist*, Duncan portrays a community that has grown from a rural marketing centre into a small-scale industrial town. She gives the social life of Elgin, Ontario a shading and subtlety that can be found in no other fictional small town of the prewar era. In creating her major characters, she replaces the sentimental caricatures of most regional fiction with real people. Her Scots retain the prodigious appetite for lengthy sermons on the fine points of Presbyterian doctrines that marks the Scots in Connor's *The Man from Glengarry* and Knowles's *St. Cuthbert's*. But Duncan humanizes both ministers and congregation. Her portraits of the two ministers, the calculating Dr. Drummond and the idealistic Hugh Finlay, are particularly striking. Drummond has a shrewdly unclerical eye for the main chance. Finlay is a bit of a fool, deluding himself out of his own happiness until Drummond rescues him from an ill-considered marriage by carrying off the woman himself.

The Imperialist is normally discussed in the context of Duncan's rejection of idealism in favour of the realism she found in the fiction of William Dean Howells and Henry James. Certainly, Duncan shows a Howellsian interest in the social nuances of small-town behaviour, and she exhibits a complexity in her narrative voice that might be considered Jamesian. This a perfectly valid way of looking at *The*

Imperialist. But another perspective helps to shed light on the novel's opening chapters, especially on the first chapter, whose connection with the main action of the book is tenuous at best. Instead of comparing Duncan's novel to the kind of fiction she admired, we can with equal validity compare it with the kind of fiction she was rejecting. For *The Imperialist* deliberately uses the techniques and attitudes of realism to modify the conventional patterns of the turn-of-the-century regional idyll. The arrival of Christie Cameron and Mrs. Kilbannon from the old country provides a direct reminder of the literary ancestry of Duncan's portrait of Scottish-Canadians. Mrs. Kilbannon was "definitely given over to caps and curls as they still wear them in Bross .... She might be something, Mrs Forsyth thought, out of a novel by Mr Crockett."[1] But Duncan's novel takes only this single direct glance at the Kailyard tradition. In fact, after the opening few chapters she almost completely abandons the nostalgic tone and retrospective outlook of the regional idyll in favour of an approach that is more urbane and cosmopolitan.

In her opening chapter, however, Duncan does adopt the habitual narrative stance of the regional idyll, as she looks back to an earlier and simpler era, when eccentric characters such as Mother Beggarlegs were more common. Frequently, in the early chapters of her novel, Duncan adopts a tone of amused familiarity that sounds remarkably like the playful tone that Leacock's narrator will later adopt. In her account of Elgin's main street, for example, the narrator deftly combines local patriotism with satire:

> Its appearance and demeanour would never have suggested that it was now the chief artery of a thriving manufacturing town, with a collegiate institute, eleven churches, two newspapers, and an asylum for the deaf and dumb, to say nothing of a fire department unsurpassed for organization and achievement in the Province of Ontario. Only at twelve noon it might be partly realized, when the

---

[1] Sara Jeannette Duncan, *The Imperialist*, New Canadian Library, No. 20 (Toronto: McClelland and Stewart, 1961), p. 216. All further references to this work appear in the text.

prolonged "toots" of seven factory whistles at once let off, so to speak, the hour. Elgin liked the demonstration; it was held to be cheerful and unmistakable, an indication of "go-ahead" proclivities which spoke for itself. (pp. 25-26)

But Duncan's narrator brings a tartness to her commentary that is present in no previous fictional observer of the Canadian scene. And Duncan gradually makes it plain that an unbridgeable gulf lies between her shrewdly analytical narrator and the unreflective, self-satisfied folk of Elgin.

Leacock and Duncan agree in the main features of their portraits of Canadian small towns. Elgin, says Duncan, "knew two controlling interests – the interest of politics and the interest of religion" (p. 58). And Leacock would agree that religion and local politics – the more local the politics the better – are the staple interests of his townsfolk. In both communities the ministers are well-known public figures, whose doings are scrutinized with proprietorial interest by their parishioners. The two authors also concur about some of the niceties of social ranking in small town society. For example, the bank clerk Peter Pupkin is prominent among the young men of Mariposa, and Duncan remarks: "there was an allure about a young man in a bank as difficult to define as to resist. To say of a certain party-giver that she had 'about every bank clerk in town' was to announce the success of her entertainment in ultimate terms" (p. 46). Like Leacock, Duncan notices the importance of "the boys" in local affairs – especially politics. After he instructs Lorne Murchison to keep well out of town on election day, Bingham explains: "We can't have him upsettin' his own election by any interference with the boys" (p. 237).

Leacock and Duncan stand at the head of a stream of sophisticated fictions with rural settings that has remained a prominent feature of Canadian letters to the present day. Many of the central works of the Canadian tradition, such as Sinclair Ross's *As for Me and My House* (1941), MacLennan's *Each Man's Son* (1951), Ernest Buckler's *The Mountain and the Valley* (1952), Margaret Laurence's *A Bird in the House* (1970) and *The Stone Angel* (1964), and even Robertson Davies' *Fifth Business* (1970), examine the darker side of life

85

in rural, church-centred communities that resemble the rural communities presented so sunnily in many regional idylls. In Montgomery's *Anne of Green Gables*, for example, the young heroine is surrounded by adults who are marked by the same puritanism that MacLennan and Laurence later depict in much bleaker terms. Such societies of emotional reticence are still conspicuous in recent works such as Rudy Wiebe's *Peace Shall Destroy Many* (1962), Percy Janes's *House of Hate* (1970), Harold Horwood's *Tomorrow Will Be Sunday* (1966), and Alden Nowlan's *Various Persons Named Kevin O'Brien* (1973). Moreover, books such as W.O. Mitchell's *Jake and the Kid* (1961) and *Who Has Seen the Wind* (1947), and more recently Dennis T. Patrick Sears's *The Lark in the Clear Air* (1974) demonstrate the persistence of the regional idyll as a feature of our literature. The highly self-conscious and sophisticated exploration of the past in search of collective or personal myths, as in Margaret Laurence's *The Diviners* (1974) and Margaret Atwood's *Surfacing* (1972), is a relatively recent development in our fiction. But the emphasis on acknowledging a Canadian ancestry that is so prominent in recent fiction simply continues the process of self-scrutiny that was begun by the writers of turn-of-the-century regional fiction.

The persistence of regional fiction, in the face of strong literary forces encouraging novels that are urban in subject-matter and symbolic or psychological in mode, must come from circumstances that are intrinsic to Canadian society. Many Canadians have, until quite recently, come from rural origins, or at least from backgrounds they perceived as simpler and more comprehensible than the cities where they now reside. Even today, in the smaller Canadian provinces, some of the major cities feel like small towns to their inhabitants, who can make comparisons between their own cities and larger centres such as Montreal or Toronto or Vancouver. Of course, the literary portrayal of life in smaller communities has been increasingly mediated by our writers' familiarity with the conventions of the twentieth-century novel. But throughout the century social conditions have encouraged our writers to present a remarkable proportion of their best work as a development of the regional novel.

CHAPTER FOUR

The Arrival of Modernism

We must leave the handrails and the Ariadne-threads,
The psychiatrists and all the apron strings
And take a whole new country for our own.
                    – F.R. Scott, "A L'ange avantgardien"

"To Canada," Charles G.D. Roberts wrote in 1931, "modernism has come more slowly and less violently than elsewhere."[1] There is considerable justice in Roberts's remark. Certainly, judged by the standards of the international avant-garde, early literary modernism in Canada was a rather tame affair. At the same time as some European and American writers were espousing a virtually autonomous religion of art, Canadian writers placed comparatively little emphasis on innovations of artistic technique. For example, among the first generation of Canadian modernist novelists, only Callaghan is at all noted as a self-conscious stylist. And in Callaghan's novels of the thirties he returns to using the novel as a vehicle for moral statements, dropping the naturalistic mode of his first novel. Before MacLennan published *Barometer Rising* (1941), he had abandoned his attempt to imitate the styles of Hemingway and Joyce (influences that are evident in the manuscripts of his two unpublished novels from the thirties), and had taken a more

---

[1] Charles G.D. Roberts, "A Note on Modernism," in his *Selected Poetry and Critical Prose*, ed. W.J. Keith, Literature of Canada: Poetry and Prose in Reprint (Toronto: Univ. of Toronto Press, 1974), p. 298.

traditional form of fiction as his model. Nor is Ethel Wilson's deliberate use of symbolism and archetypal patterns typical of the practice of Canadian writers of the forties and fifties. Most of the novelists who participated at mid-century in the creation of the Canadian tradition in fiction made sociological realism a primary goal of their fiction.

There are several reasons why modernism took a long time to make its influence felt on Canadian fiction. In part, the delay is explained by the cultural isolation of Canadian writers living before the full impact of instant world-wide electronic communication was felt. In addition, the tentative early movement of our writers towards modernist fiction was interrupted by two factors that had nothing to do with literature: the Depression and the Second World War. Most of the pioneering Canadian modernists were born between 1900 and 1914. These writers were of an age to begin publishing during the late 1920s or the 1930s. Of the major figures, however, only the precocious Morley Callaghan actually succeeded in publishing a book prior to 1940. Callaghan, fortunately for him, had found a publisher before the Great Crash of 1929. He could continue a career that had been launched in economically sunnier times. Other writers of the Depression generation found publication difficult during the 1930s. Hugh MacLennan, for example, secured a publisher for his first novel in 1933, only to have the publisher go out of business before the novel could be printed.

It was not until the war brought a revival of economic activity that publication became easier. Then books such as MacLennan's *Barometer Rising* and *Two Solitudes* (1945), and Sinclair Ross's *As for Me and My House* (1941) could appear. Ernest Buckler, W.O. Mitchell, and Robertson Davies did not publish their first novels until after the war, when North American society had embarked on a long postwar economic holiday. These authors completed the process that introduced the attitudes and techniques of literary modernism into Canadian fiction. However, our pioneering modernists needed to work quite directly with the materials provided by their society, in a way that has not been required of their successors. Our first generation of modernist writers did not venture very far into the more experimental regions of modernist technique. Instead, the task was to define the principal features of the Canadian social world and to articulate the typical ways in which Canadians were responding to that world. One important result of this fictional scrutiny of society was the creation of a literary consensus about the prevalent attitudes, the most common situations, and the principal conflicts that prevailed in Canadian society. These writers, then, created the first fully developed tradition of Canadian fiction. In recent years, their work has provided a context that later novelists have variously endorsed, modified, or reacted against.

If we wish to understand why modernism came into Canadian fiction in such a tentative and unspectacular fashion, we must examine the conditions under which our writers worked, especially during the 1920s. In Canada the most conspicuous literary debate during the twenties was, in effect, a continuation of the argument between realism and idealism that was so prominent a feature of nineteenth-century critical discussions. As a convenient simplification, we can describe the main parties to the quarrel as being, on the one hand, the members of the Canadian Authors' Association and, on the other hand, a group of young critics whose principal vehicle was the *Canadian Forum*.

The Canadian Authors' Association was founded in 1921, ostensibly to argue for improved Canadian copyright legislation. It also sponsored the annual Canada Book Week, an event that the Association's detractors viewed as a purely commercial exercise, designed to promote the sale of Canadian books irrespective of their merits. The members of the Canadian Authors' Association found their principal public platform in the *Canadian Bookman*, a journal that was for a time the official voice of the Canadian Authors' Association and that remained throughout the twenties virtually an extension of the publicity departments of the major Canadian publishers. Most of the critics who wrote for the *Canadian Bookman* demanded explicit moral uplift from fiction, and favoured fiction that upheld the traditional Christian values, or at worst provided innocent entertainment. They were not all from the older generation, but they did associate themselves with the existing tradition of Canadian literature, whose high points were provided by the poetry of Archibald Lampman, Charles G.D. Roberts, and Bliss Carman, and by the fiction of L.M. Montgomery and Ralph Connor.

Throughout the 1920s contributors to the *Canadian Bookman* kept alive the debate between realism and idealism in fiction. In a 1922 article, Adrian MacDonald took a worried look at the realism that prevailed in recent British fiction. MacDonald introduces himself as "a somewhat romantic Canadian, who was suckled on the usual hero stories, who was nourished through his childhood on Ballantyne, Henty and Jules Verne, and who cut his aesthetic teeth on Stevenson."[1] MacDonald says he finds "the contemporary English novel ... at first a little disconcerting" (p. 234). In particular, he is disturbed by the pessimism that marks so much contemporary English fiction. He laments: "The correct thing in present-day English fiction is ... to recount, not the vain successes of men, but their failures" (p. 234). As a Canadian, MacDonald claims to find this sort of fiction especially upsetting. Canadians, according to MacDonald, "find it very hard to sympathize with the realists' deep sense of the ineffectiveness of man" (p. 234). He contends: "All this dismal sense of failure is quite foreign to the optimistic spirit of our Dominion" (p. 234).

MacDonald does eventually concede that there is considerable artistic merit in some works of realistic fiction. Not so another writer, H. Glynn-Ward, whose article opens with a blunt denunciation of contemporary fiction: "There has come over the literature of the day the foetid breath of decadence. They call it Realism. They call it Truth. They call it anything but what it is: a pandering to the morbidly unwholesome in human nature."[2] It turns out that what Glynn-Ward objects to, above all else, is the emphasis on sexuality that she finds in the books of "such neurotic sensationalists as D.H.

---

[1] Adrian MacDonald, "English Realism to a Canadian," *Canadian Bookman*, Sept. 1922, p. 234. All further references to this work appear in the text.

[2] H. Glynn-Ward, "A Plea for Purity," *Canadian Bookman*, March 1924, p. 64. All further references to this work appear in the text.

Lawrence and Sherwood Anderson, to name two of the best known" (p. 64). Glynn-Ward concludes her article with a nostalgic call for a revival of an old-fashioned puritanism:

> After all, there was something to be said for the strait-laced puritanism of other days. It stood for discipline, and discipline of the mind, or the morals, or the family, or even of the nation, is not at all a bad thing. Perhaps, when the sex-writers have hung themselves with a surfeit of their own rope, when a few more publishers have been arrested, we shall be glad to revert to a little old-fashioned discipline for our morals, and the world will be the cleaner. We sincerely look forward to it. (p. 64)

Most contributors to the *Canadian Bookman* were not this inflammatory and intolerant. In fact, some writers even defended the milder forms of realistic fiction. Francis Dickie, for example, published a rejoinder to Glynn-Ward's article in which he begged leave "to voice my plea against dogmatism and puritanical intolerance."[1] Dickie pointed out that some nineteenth-century writers of acknowledged greatness, such as Flaubert, Hardy, and Shaw, did not confine themselves to "the flub-dub and happy-ever-after school type of literature which is nauseating to a large class of readers" (p. 110). In fact, Dickie went on to announce his allegiance to realism in no uncertain terms:

> As for realism: If there arises in Canada now or in the near future, a writer who can picture the sordidness, the emptiness of the life of some Barnardo or other orphan home boy on the farm of some mean, unsentimental Canadian farmer; if there arises a writer who can picture the life of brothels in Calgary in the wide open days, show the women's sadness, their tragedy, and too their humor, and little deeds of

---

[1] Francis Dickie, "A Plea for Tolerance," *Canadian Bookman*, May 1924, p. 110. All further references to this work appear in the text.

kindness to one another, . . . then I for one will gladly read his book, and give him praise for a work well done. (p. 110)

The next year Dickie also published another defense of realism. His article, however, was accompanied by an editorial notice inviting readers' comments – which suggests that Dickie's ideas were regarded by the editors as potentially controversial.[1]

A particularly extravagant expression of literary idealism occurs in an article titled "A Peter Pan of Literature."[2] The author, the impressively named N. de Bertrand Lugrin, asserts that since the First World War there has been "a general weakening of faith throughout the whole of Christendom" (p. 116). In consequence, Lugrin argues, "all the fine ideals around which novels used to be written not so long ago, seem to have vanished .... According to many of our modern writers, the world's men and women have lost credence of ideals altogether, just as the children in *Peter Pan* had lost their belief in fairies" (pp. 116-17). Lugrin's response to this situation is quixotic to the point of silliness:

What we seem to need just now is a new Peter Pan, a Peter Pan of literature who will restore to us our lost faith.

We venture to suggest that Canada should take upon herself the responsibility of being this sort of Peter Pan .... The reason we claim that this sort of Peter Pan should come out of Canada is that Canada is the child among nations. Young, beautiful, uncontaminated by the evils of effete civilizations, untouched by any but the hand of God, she stands on the last Anglo-Saxon frontier .... (p. 117)

---

[1] Francis Dickie, "Realism in Canadian Fiction," *Canadian Bookman*, Oct. 1925, p. 165.

[2] N. de Bertrand Lugrin, "A Peter Pan of Literature," *Canadian Bookman*, April 1926, pp. 116-17. All further references to this work appear in the text.

This tone of near-hysteria, however, is not typical of the *Canadian Bookman*'s contributors. In fact, the *Canadian Bookman* published a few quite thoughtful and interesting articles, though its general quality does seem to have declined later in the decade, as the periodical became confirmed in its dual roles as the voice of the Canadian Authors' Association and as a semi-official publicity flyer for the Canadian publishing industry. In these years, the *Canadian Bookman* was largely a vehicle for Canadian literary gossip, and for accounts of the doings of the Canadian Authors' Association. For example, each year the promotional events that made up Canada Book Week received considerable coverage. Particularly where Canadian books were concerned, the *Canadian Bookman*'s review policy was unselective: no distinction was made between popular entertainment and books with serious artistic ambitions.

Reviewers in the *Canadian Bookman* habitually saw a great deal of contemporary writing as degenerate or even dangerous. For example, an anonymous review of Theodore Dreiser's *An American Tragedy* petulantly asks: "is the dead level of life in America quite as far below par as his [Dreiser's] novels lead one to believe?"[1] Canadian writers, too, were subjected to a careful moral scrutiny. When Thomas O'Hagan inquires "what is the chief ailment today in Canadian literature?" he answers his own question in this way: "Is it not, truly and really, the lack of literary ideals, and does not this lack arise from the emptiness of the spiritual life around us?"[2] During the later years of the decade, John W. Garvin often made a special point of reprimanding the lax morality of erring Canadian authors. For example, when Garvin reviewed Morley Callaghan's *A Native Argosy* (1929), he objected to what he considered Callaghan's use of immorality and mental imbalance as the principal subjects of his stories. Garvin complains: "Mr. Callaghan must know that the heroic and noble in human conduct is not less common than the opposite. Then why

---

[1] "Dreiser's Double Decker," *Canadian Bookman*, Jan. 1926, p. 17.

[2] Thomas O'Hagan, "What Ails Canadian Literature," *Canadian Bookman*, Dec. 1924, p. 257.

keep on paddling in a pool of putridity?"[1] And Garvin responded to Frederick Philip Grove's *The Yoke of Life* (1930) by remarking: "It seems to me regrettable that so talented a novelist can see in the life of a pioneer, drudgery and tragedy only. Such a depiction is unhealthy morbidity."[2]

Some of the most vigorous attacks on the Canadian Authors' Association and on Canada Book Week appeared in the pages of the *Canadian Forum,* a publication that was also started shortly after the end of the First World War. The *Canadian Forum* was founded in 1921 not only "to secure a freer and more informed discussion of public questions" but also "to trace and value those developments of art and letters which are distinctly Canadian."[3] Throughout the twenties it made a point of publishing articles about the writers who were emerging as the leaders of the movement we now know as modernism. It also opened its pages to several articles that specifically attacked the literary values that the Canadian Authors' Association stood for. Two of the most vigorous attacks on the prevailing literary standards are Douglas Bush's "Making Literature Hum" and A.J.M. Smith's "Wanted: Canadian Criticism." Both of these articles take up a theme that was sounded early in the *Canadian Forum*'s history by E.K. Broadus. In 1922 Broadus had warned: "Until we learn, *ruat coelum*, to substitute honesty for boosting, there will be no literary criticism in Canada."[4] Bush and Smith went further. They argued that the literary climate that existed in Canada was retarding the development of the country's literature. Until there was honest criticism of Canadian writing, they contended, there would be no Canadian literature that was worthy of serious attention.

Bush opened his article by decrying the "inflated rhetoric" and excessive "mutual adulation" that prevailed

---

[1] John W. Garvin, ref. of *A Native Argosy,* by Morley Callaghan, in *Canadian Bookman,* Feb. 1930, p. 38.

[2] John W. Garvin, "Interesting New Books," *Canadian Bookman,* Nov. 1930, p. 232.

[3] Editorial, *Canadian Forum,* Oct. 1920, p. 3.

[4] Edmund Kemper Broadus, "Criticism – or Puffery?" *Canadian Forum,* Oct. 1922, p. 20.

whenever Canadians discussed their national literature.[1] Most Canadian writing, he felt, simply did not deserve the fulsome praise it so often received. He complained that Canadian literary standards were distorted; work that achieved commercial success was praised beyond its deserts, while work of real merit went unnoticed: "Witness the slowness of Mr. D.C. Scott's conquest of an audience – while Robert Service, after a sensational welcome, settled down in the pleasant rôle of a Canadian classic" (72). Clearly, Bush is scornful of writing that he views as merely popular, and he reserves his approval for "serious" literature.

Bush's article provoked an indignant response from Watson Kirkconnell, who took offense at the slighting references to Canadian Book Week and the Canadian Authors' Association with which Bush began his article. Kirkconnell quite properly defended the Association by citing its unremitting efforts to improve Canadian copyright laws; he was less convincing, however, when he claimed: "most of the leaders of the C.A.A. have been men with as few illusions as himself regarding the shortcomings of Canadian literature."[2] Bush retorted: "Mr. Watson Kirkconnell writes in such a state of moral incandescence that he is neither consistent nor relevant."[3] Strictly speaking, Bush was right to claim that Kirkconnell's response was illogical. But Kirkconnell responded to the tone rather than to the letter of Bush's article. Kirkconnell was quite right in thinking that Bush had defamed a sacred cow.

Two years later, A.J.M. Smith launched an even more pointed attack on the Canadian Authors' Association. Smith claimed that Canadian critics, encouraged by the Canadian Authors' Association, had confounded commercial success with artistic value. "To the serious canadian writer," said Smith, "this is a vital question, for to him the confusion between commerce and art presents itself in the light of a

---

[1] Douglas Bush, "Making Literature Hum," *Canadian Forum*, Dec. 1926, p. 72. All further references to this work appear in the text.

[2] Watson Kirkconnell, Letter, *Canadian Forum*, Jan. 1927, p. 110.

[3] Douglas Bush, Letter, *Canadian Forum*, Feb. 1927, p. 141.

temptation to effect a compromise."[1] Canadian magazines offered no financial rewards for serious writing, but "poor imitations of the *Saturday Evening Post* are ready to pay him handsomely if he will cease to be an artist and become a merchant" (p. 600). Smith could not resist adding: "This is the temptation with which the devil has assailed the Canadian Authors' Association, and the whole communion has succumbed in a body" (p. 600). In such surroundings, Smith claims, the principal task of both critics and creative writers is to resist the prevailing social climate:

> First and foremost, as a sort of preliminary spade-work, the canadian writer must put up a fight for freedom in the choice and treatment of his subject. Nowhere is puritanism more disastrously prohibitive than among us, and it seems, indeed, that desperate methods and dangerous remedies must be resorted to, that our condition will not improve until we have been thoroughly shocked by the appearance in our midst of a work of art that is at once successful and obscene. Of realism we are afraid – apparently because there is an impression that it wishes to discredit the picture of our great Dominion as a country where all the women are chaste and the men too pure to touch them if they weren't. Irony is not understood. Cynicism is felt to be disrespectful, unmanly. (pp. 600-01)

In other words, Smith is arguing that Canada must finally leave behind the naive values of the frontier, and adopt the values of older and more civilized societies. At first sight, the stress Smith places on realism may seem surprising. It may seem that he has fallen away from the art-for-art's-sake position with which he is usually associated. This is not quite true. Eventually, Smith hopes, Canadian readers will learn to judge literature "after a consideration, not of its moral, but of its aesthetic harmony" (p. 601). In this article, however, Smith has accommodated his aestheticism to Canadian

---

[1] A.J.M. Smith, "Wanted: Canadian Criticism," *Canadian Forum*, April 1928, p. 600. All further references to this work appear in the text.

society as he finds it. Given the relatively undeveloped condition of Canadian fiction, it did not make sense to call for a full-scale modernism at this time. Thus, Smith did not call for symbolism or for psychological studies or for an exquisitely chiselled style, but for an open-minded attention to the circumstances of Canadian life. He advocates realism not as an end in itself but as a waystation on the road to a more sophisticated outlook.

The call for realism is also a feature in two book-length studies of Canadian writing that were published by academics during the twenties. In *Headwaters of Canadian Literature*, Archibald MacMechan complained that Canadian fiction was "tame": "Modern problems are as yet untouched, unapproached. Direct, honest realism is also sadly to seek, though subjects are crying aloud for treatment on every side .... So far Canadian fiction is conventional, decent, unambitious, *bourgeois*. It has nowhere risen to the heights or plumbed the depths of life in Canada."[1] In *Appraisals of Canadian Literature* (1926), Lionel Stevenson divided Canadian fiction into "two general classes, typified by the authors who have won the greatest success in practising them. There is the class of Ralph Connor and the class of L.M. Montgomery."[2] That is, Stevenson classes most Canadian fiction as either men's adventure stories or women's domestic fiction. Both kinds of fiction, he concedes, "are praiseworthy within their limitations" (p. 129). But in recent years, "it has been becoming apparent that the tradition is no longer satisfactory" (p. 131). In their place, a new kind of fiction has begun to appear: "Almost without exception, the noteworthy new novels show a determined effort towards a more serious treatment of life. In revulsion from egregious heroes and insipid heroines there is a distinct cult of unpleasant characters and an assumption of the harshness that is loosely termed realism" (p. 131). In *Highways of Canadian Literature*, John Daniel Logan and Donald G.

---

[1] Archibald MacMechan, *Headwaters of Canadian Literature*, New Canadian Library, No. 107 (Toronto: McClelland and Stewart, 1974), p. 215.

[2] Lionel Stevenson, *Appraisals of Canadian Literature* (Toronto: Macmillan, 1926), p. 128. All further references to this work appear in the text.

French also concede that realism is the hallmark of the most recent Canadian fiction. They comment grudgingly: "It was natural that a reaction should set in against the realistic romance with its insufficiency of motivation and its lack of fidelity to real life" (p. 312).

In the decade immediately after the First World War, then, our writers experienced a certain pressure to produce fiction that was in some way "serious" rather than purely escapist. If we survey the fiction of the twenties, however, we find that the distinction between old-fashioned romance and the newer realism is not always easy to make. In fact, many of our novelists seem uncertain whether they are working in a realistic or a romantic mode. They seem torn between the contradictory demands of popular fiction and serious fiction. Such a tension is clearly evident in the work of popular writers, such as Bertrand Sinclair, who sometimes tried to include contemporary social issues in their fiction. Sinclair's *Poor Man's Rock* (1920) told of a struggle by West Coast salmon fishermen to escape virtual serfdom to the large fish packing companies, and his *The Inverted Pyramid* (1924) was based on the actual failure of a Vancouver trust company. Postwar social upheavals, the restlessness of many returned soldiers, and the labour discontent that led to the Winnipeg General Strike were all reflected in Connor's *To Him That Hath* (1921) and in Douglas Durkin's *The Magpie* (1923). After the sentimental stories of childhood printed in *Explorers of the Dawn* (1922), Mazo de la Roche seemed to turn towards realism in *Possession* (1923) and *Delight* (1926), in both of which the sexual impulse provides the mainspring of the plot. But de la Roche's literary course was permanently shifted in the direction of popular romance by the success of *Jalna* (1927).

The conventions of popular fiction also provided the author's starting point in some works that had an obviously "serious" intention, such as Pierre Coalfleet's *Solo* (1924) and Beaumont Cornell's *Lantern Marsh* (1923). In both of these novels, the authors create sensitive young protagonists – potential artists – who struggle against the cultural limitations of their rural environments. But neither author seems to know what to do with his theme, and both novels conclude weakly. Fortunately, the work of modernizing Canadian fiction was undertaken with greater success by other writers, several of whom did their best work during the twenties. Yet their fiction too developed in a fruitful state of tension with our popular literature, for often their "serious" and "realistic" novels presented a critical view of attitudes and actions that were habitually portrayed with approval in the popular tradition.

In my previous chapter I argued that the prewar regional idyll laid the groundwork for the creation of a native literary tradition. Even in the era of their greatest popularity, regional idylls were lightly regarded by those who professed to take literature most seriously. Yet it is worth noticing that many of the pioneering works of Canadian realism deal with the same sort of rural settings that are found in the regional idyll. Although these early realistic novels are widely recognized as forming the backbone of the Canadian fictional tradition that had emerged at mid-century, their affinities with the earlier regional idyll have never been sufficiently examined. In fact, in books such as Martha Ostenso's *Wild Geese* (1925), Robert Stead's *Grain* (1926), Frederick Philip Grove's *Settlers of the Marsh* (1925) and *Our Daily Bread* (1928), Frank Parker Day's *Rockbound* (1928), and Raymond Knister's *White Narcissus* (1929) our authors deliberately began to challenge the optimistic vision that prevailed in many of the books that still dominated the fiction lists of Canadian publishers throughout the 1920s.

In fact, throughout the twenties numerous examples of the nostalgic regional idyll continued to be written by the authors who have aptly been called members of the "Sunshine School."[3] But books by Ostenso, Stead, Grove, Day, and Knister systematically contradicted the optimistic falsification of experience that was the stock-in-trade of the popular writers such as Ralph Connor, L.M. Montgomery, Hiram Cody, and Basil King. Instead, the work of Ostenso, Stead, Grove, Day, and Knister was informed by recent developments in British and American fiction, and they demonstrated a knowledge of contemporary ideas on social and psycho-

---

[1] Carlyle King, "Introduction," in Martha Ostenso, *Wild Geese*, New Canadian Library, No. 18 (Toronto: McClelland and Stewart, 1961), p. v.

logical questions. In a word, Ostenso, Stead, Grove, Day, and Knister tried to be "realistic" in their fiction.

Such a movement towards realism was desirable for more than reasons of literary fashion. It was necessary because Canadian writers of the early twentieth century still faced a dilemma that nineteeth-century American novelists had already resolved for their successors. Unlike American writers, Canadian writers had no agreed-upon picture of the principal concerns and the structure of their own society. Consequently, the arrival of modernism in Canadian fiction was combined with a development that had taken place much earlier in American fiction: the capturing in fictional form of the customs and attitudes of the writer's own society. Our early modernists, then, were primarily occupied in defining the fictional image of Canadian society. Like the settlers whose work of physical pioneering made the country habitable for European civilization, the new literary pioneers gave it an imaginative reality for its new inhabitants. Both kinds of pioneer needed to put aside cultural preconceptions and deal directly with the concrete details of their immediate world.

At this point, it may be useful to remind ourselves just how gingerly our authors took up the innovative techniques used by the leading European and American writers of modernist prose. For writers who wished to break away from the formulas of popular fiction, international modernism offered two main possibilities. On the one hand, writers could emulate the self-consciously elitist techniques of the European modernists; on the other hand, they could adopt some version of the naturalism favoured by many American writers. Most Canadian authors were reluctant to adopt either of these courses. The European modernists looked at the world from an elitist perspective, using the resources of European high culture to expose the shallowness and hypocrisy of bourgeois society. Most Canadian writers did not feel themselves to be above their society, although they might strongly disapprove of it in certain respects. Many American novelists combined a vernacular style with literary naturalism, and as a result seemed to specialize in writing documentary studies of lower-class life. Although Canadian writers no longer held an aristocratic conception of literature, most of them still thought that literature should retain a respect for genteel standards of decorum. They had no wish to emulate the vulgarity of American writers.

Typically, the European modernists favoured symbolism in poetry and the stream-of-consciousness or psychological novel in fiction. They rejected the nineteenth century's literal treatment of social questions, and approached social reality indirectly, by adopting a variety of ironic modes. That is, the modernists rejected the convention that cast the narrator of so many bourgeois novels as a reliable and omniscient observer, the spokesman for a collectively agreed-upon view of reality. In order to rebuild the house of fiction, they evolved techniques that were intended to mirror the inner workings of consciousness, the moment-by-moment flickerings of thought and feeling in the mind. By presenting their characters from the inside, the modernist authors hoped to satisfy readers who would not accept an omniscient author's authority. Readers familiar with the books of Henry James and Joseph Conrad had learned to question the surface meaning of events in a literary work. Such readers were prepared to conduct a painstaking and sceptical examination into the hidden motives of literary characters. The modernists wrote for readers who insisted on being shown the evidence, then being left to decide for themselves.

The psychological novel, as Leon Edel ably demonstrates, is an important branch of modernist fiction.[1] This kind of fiction is based on the belief that experience is fundamentally private, and cannot be adequately delineated by the mere rendering of external circumstances. The psychological novel is thus a literary extension of the nineteenth century's investigations into the hidden causes of biological and political events. Psychological fiction, however, was slow to develop in Canada. Unless we admit Ross's *As for Me and My House* (1941) as an example, no true instance of psychological fiction was produced by any member of the first generation of modernists. And not until the publication of the first three Manawaka novels by Margaret Laurence was stream-of-consciousness narration, the technique that is the

---

[1] Leon Edel, *The Psychological Novel 1900-1950* (London: Rupert Hart-Davis, 1955).

special trademark of the psychological novel, used to carry an entire book.

The modernist writers agreed in offering a severe critique of bourgeois values and bourgeois behaviour. Working in the aftermath of the First World War, the early modernists saw civilized values – and perhaps the value of civilization itself – called into question by the barbaric behaviour of their political leaders and the acquiescence of the common soldiers who carried out the leaders' wishes. A frequent modernist tactic was the procedure that Eliot, in a review of Joyce's *Ulysses*, christened the "mythical method," by which the author creates "a continuous parallel between contemporaneity and antiquity." This way of structuring a literary work, writes Eliot, provides "a way of controlling, of ordering, of giving shape and significance to the intense panorama of futility which is contemporary history.[1] The mythical method requires a learned author, who stands aside from his immediate society – James Joyce, say, or Ezra Pound, or Eliot himself. Not until Sheila Watson's *The Double Hook* (1959) does a Canadian author create a novel that is overtly based on mythological parallels.

Another important strand of modernist fiction, particularly in America, places less stress on the techniques by which moment-by-moment consciousness can be captured, and instead focuses on the attitude with which the protagonist confronts the world. The fiction of Ernest Hemingway provides several conspicuous examples of this development. The usual Hemingway protagonist preserves a stoical self-control in the face of a calamitous world. Virtue consists of maintaining one's equanimity in the face of death or disaster. The protagonist of "The Snows of Kilimanjaro," for example, is to be admired for facing death with greater self-possession than he has ever attained at any previous point in his life. Many of Hemingway's books portray the estrangement of the authentic individual from the hypocritical society around him. For example, Frederic Henry, the modern warrior-hero of *A Farewell to Arms*, must follow a

---

[1] T.S. Eliot, quoted in Jay Martin, ed., *A Collection of Critical Essays on "The Waste Land,"* Twentieth Century Interpretations (Englewood Cliffs, N. J.: Prentice-Hall, 1968), p. 7.

lonely, self-selected path. The emergence of modern mass society and mechanized warfare has destroyed the essentially feudal ideal of heroic service to one's community. For this twentieth-century knight-errant, the only honourable course is to run away from war, to embark on a quest for ways of affirming a personal rather than a collective faith.

Most Canadian writers do not separate themselves from their society as Hemingway does. Even when they are critical of prevailing community values, they still define themselves and their characters as assuming an adversary stance within the community. Their protagonists do not flee from society but – willingly or unwillingly – stay and do battle with repressive social forces. Typically the authors depict the effects of a climate of puritan psychological oppression on a sensitive individual. Often their novels tell the story of a character whose life is thwarted by the constricting and conventional standards of an unsophisticated and utilitarian rural community. Their novels often focus on generational conflicts within the family and on the plight of sensitive young people trapped within a self-consciously conventional culture. That is, their books seek to expose the faults and limitations of both the patriarchal families and the patriarchal society to which they belong. The Canadian writer's revolt – and the revolt of many of their fictional protagonists – is, in effect, the result of a family quarrel between restive youths and hidebound parental figures. The outcome is a suppressed or indirectly expressed antagonism that is less violent but more enervating than an open break would be. As a result, our fiction of the twenties and thirties, even when it shows the influence of the techniques and attitudes associated with modernism, remains close to the norms of the traditional bourgeois novel.

I have previously named several books that brought a critical scrutiny to bear on the darker side of rural life. During the twenties, some of our authors also began to conduct a critical examination of urban life. But Canadian authors, like Canadians in general, were comparatively slow to recognize the industrialization of their society. During the years from 1896 to 1921, according to Robert Craig Brown and Ramsay Cook, Canada "was a country being transformed."[1] The two historians have in mind the developments that reshaped Canada from a nation of farms and small towns into a predominantly urban society. The First World War completed Canada's swift initiation into the modern world, for the traumatic bloodletting in Europe seemed to shock the nation out of its prolonged Victorian sleep. Once awakened, many Canadians gazed in amazement at the busy commercial and industrial society that had grown up around them – as though seeing it for the first time. In the years that followed, social change was rapid. The automobile provided a heady new freedom of movement. The fear of Mrs. Grundy abated, as more Canadians left the restraining familiarity of small communities to live in the anonymity of large cities. The grip of orthodox piety relaxed, as muscular Christianity gave way to the social gospel or to a more thoroughly secular outlook. Industry boomed, and labour unions recruited new members; there was even a general strike in Winnipeg in 1919.

Only a few prewar works of fiction reveal any awareness that new forces were altering the apparently timeless rural world of the regional idyll. Most of these books are some form of the novel with an explicit social purpose. In them, literary values have been entirely subordinated to a moral or social message. For example, fictional versions of the social gospel can be found in many of the books of Ralph Connor, and in notable single novels by Agnes Maule Machar and Albert R. Carman, both of which deal with attempts to improve the lot of factory workers. In Machar's *Roland Graeme: Knight* (1892), there appears a revealing dedication to Lyman Abbott, whom Machar describes as "one of the first voices in America to enforce the relation of Christianity to the labor problem."[5] In the course of the novel the inadequacy of conventional "charity" as a solution to the problems of the working man is pointed out, and the long hours and starvation wages of the factory hands are somewhat alleviated. However, these results come more from goodwill on the

[1] Robert Craig Brown and Ramsay Cook, *Canada, 1896-1921: A Nation Transformed* (Toronto: McClelland and Stewart, 1974), p. 1.

[2] Agnes Maule Machar, *Roland Graeme: Knight: A Novel of Our Time* (New York: Fords, Howard, and Hulbert, 1892), p. 1.

factory owner's part than as a consequence of any concerted radical action. The action of Carman's *The Preparation of Ryerson Embury* (1900) reviews most of the alternatives to traditional religion that were in the air during the late nineteenth century. Ryerson tries in succession fundamentalism, liberal Christianity, free thought (atheism), the socialism of Henry George, and a kind of secular social gospel. He ends the book by departing for Montreal and planning to become a labour lawyer. Like Machar and Carman, Ralph Connor is also sunnily optimistic about the possibility of combining social idealism with Christian principles in order to produce an improved society. His ministers and heroes have a credo that is simplicity itself, like that of the missionary Brown in *The Foreigner* (1909): "Brown had a disconcertingly simple and direct method of dealing with the most complex problems. If a thing was right, it was right; if wrong, it was wrong, and that settled the matter with Brown."[6] The hero of *To Him that Hath* (1921), a later novel that Connor based loosely on the Winnipeg General Strike, argues that any and all social questions can be settled amicably if the solution is sought in the spirit of "the way of right doing, of brotherly kindness and of brotherly love which is the way of peace."[7]

With the appearance of books such as Jessie G. Sime's *Our Little Life* (1921) and Morley Callaghan's almost clinically detached early stories and novels, our urban fiction began to present a more dispassionate reflection of North American urban life. *Strange Fugitive* (1928), in particular, introduces a new kind of protagonist into Canadian fiction. Late in the novel Harry Trotter pays a visit to the town where he spent his childhood. Harry, then, is a fictional counterpart of the many Canadians who were leaving farms and small towns for the larger cities. But most earlier protagonists, such as Ranald Macdonald or Lorne Murchison, are remarkable for their intellect or for their moral fibre. In short, they are conventional fictional heroes. But unlike Ranald or Lorne,

---

[1] Ralph Connor, *The Foreigner: A Tale of Saskatchewan* (Toronto: Westminster, 1909), pp. 272-73.

[2] Ralph Connor, *To Him that Hath: A Novel of the West of Today* (New York: Doran, 1921), p. 277.

Harry Trotter is no story-book hero. Harry is not simply uneducated and unintelligent, he is a new kind of fictional character, the first anti-hero in our fiction. He is entirely without self-discipline, a bundle of sudden impulses and erratic emotions. Harry has no moral centre, no fixed ideas or values. Callaghan presents his existence as a moment-to-moment flux of sensations. One of the other characters describes Harry as a "natural" man – a sort of urban primitive.

I shall set aside any further consideration of urban fiction until a later chapter. By restricting the present discussion to rural fiction, I can more effectively illustrate how many of our early works of realistic or modernist fiction emerged out of the tradition of regional fiction that was so strong before the First World War. In most discussions of the development of Canadian fiction, the emphasis is placed on the discontinuity between postwar realistic fiction and pre-war popular romances.[1] In contrast, I want to emphasize the continuity of our literary development. In comparison to the revolution that modernism was working in international literary circles, the change in our fiction from sentimental romance to social realism was a relatively mild and conservative step – and a step taken with many a backward glance.

In a great many of our early modernist novels, an ironic or "modern" sensibility is trained on the world of the regional idyll. In Martha Ostenso's *Wild Geese*, for example, Lind Archer brings an educated urban sensibility to bear on the oppressive and unhealthy state of affairs in the Gare household, a state the family has taken as normal. In Stead's *Grain* the protagonist is explicitly described as the antithesis of a conventional hero. Stead writes: "Perhaps the term hero, with its suggestion of high enterprise, sits inappropriately upon the chief character of a somewhat commonplace tale; there was in Gander Stake little of that quality which is associated with the clash of righteous steel or the impact of

---

[1] See, for example, E.L. Bobak, "Seeking 'Direct, Honest Realism': The Canadian Novel of the 1920's," *Canadian Literature*, No. 89 (Summer 1981), pp. 85-101.

noble purposes."[1] In the novels of Ostenso and Stead, as in most of Frederick Philip Grove's fiction, we are shown the underside of that sunny rural world that is presented so benignly in most regional idylls.

When urban and rural characters meet one another in the fiction of the twenties, we can often interpret the meeting not simply as a sociological comment by the author but as an encounter between literary modernism and the older sensibility embodied in the regional idyll. To illustrate this clash of literary outlooks, I might have chosen to discuss any one of the early works of prairie realism by Ostenso, Stead, or Grove. But these novels are already quite familiar to most students of Canadian fiction. Raymond Knister's *White Narcissus*, on the other hand, is comparatively neglected. Moreover, an examination of *White Narcissus* discloses a writer visibly caught in the act of transforming his allegiance from the regional idyll to the modernist novel.[2]

Knister deliberately presents his novel as an anti-idyll. His protagonist, Richard Milne, has left the rural setting of his childhood, and has attained success as the urban world defines it. He now works in an advertising agency, and he has published three novels. Yet he is repeatedly drawn back to his childhood world. In part, he returns to woo the reluctant Ada Lethen, his long-time sweetheart. But in addition his own dissatisfaction with the city draws him back. Despite "all the years in which he had struggled for success there [in the city], it seemed that the only real and personal part of his life had been lived here, surrounded by trees, fields, river, which claimed him as though he had never left them."[3] But Richard Milne's homecomings are ambiguous. Each time he finds that "accompanying the return upon him bodily of the old life was the same sense of

---

[1] Robert J.C. Stead, *Grain*, New Canadian Library, No. 36 (Toronto: McClelland and Stewart, 1963), p. 15.

[2] Knister's familiarity with earlier Canadian fiction is clearly demonstrated by his editorship of one of the first anthologies of Canadian short fiction. See Raymond Knister, ed., *Canadian Short Stories* (Toronto: Macmillan, 1928).

[3] Raymond Knister, *White Narcissus*, New Canadian Library, No. 32 (Toronto: McClelland and Stewart, 1962), p. 32. All further references to this work appear in the text.

futility and uncertainty which he had known in those times –
the cause of his eventual determination to leave, and also of
his periodic returns" (p. 32). Knister later claims a general
significance for his protagonist's dilemma, when Richard
Milne muses that he suffers "the conflict of the conscious
ones of his whole generation, this confusion of outer freedom
and inner doubt" (p. 108).

Richard Milne's insecurity arises partly from his uneasiness with the idea of being an artist. He feels defensive about
his novels, and prefers to respond to questions about his
"work" by describing the advertising agency rather than
speaking of his literary efforts. "Nothing tried him more than
talking of his good work, his creative books, to curious or
indifferent people . . ." (p. 29). Richard's unease with his art
is in turn linked to his ambivalent feelings about his rural
origins. The rural community is "only two hours away from
the city" (p. 19), but emotionally it occupies another world.
The farm people can talk of the weather and of their crops;
they can exchange gossip and discuss local politics; but they
cannot speak of the innermost feelings that are important to
Richard, and are the core of his art. Surely Richard has done
well to escape from such a community.

Yet Richard's emancipation is incomplete. The power
that Richard's childhood world still exercises over him is
quickly made apparent in the novel. Images of confinement
are frequently applied to the countryside, which is described
as "a place of choked vistas" (p. 20) and "a prison cell up and
down which he walked" (p. 99). When he first returns, he
finds that the "fields, river banks, the astounding, over-
whelming sky he seemed to have forgotten, questioned him
as an alien" (p. 20). Yet after only a short visit, Richard "felt
that he had been a part of this for ever" (p. 75). All the
uncertainty of his youth returns, "until he found that to
himself he was at times that earlier uncouth boy, for whom
nothing was sure, not even his own hope or his smothered
longing to get away into the world" (p. 75). And the fate of
his neighbour Carson Hymerson, still at twenty-six the
servant of his cantankerous old father, is a warning of what
might have happened to Richard had he stayed.

Richard's long-standing attachment to Ada Lethen symbolizes the continuing hold that his childhood world exerts on

him. Ada is Richard's anima, his muse. We are told: "She had become the core of his life, of all his intimate work, the concern of his hours, so that he could not write an eloquent sentence, see a fair morning, or step aside from danger, without her face" (p. 76). Ada has stayed in the rural community, whereas Richard has left. But the same inhibitions and self-doubts permeate both of their personalities. Ada once showed a considerable gift for music, but she gave it up when she resolved to remain at home – the sufferings and uncertainty that go with artistic effort were too much for her to undertake. Yet her choice has not brought her release. Instead, in her white dresses and with her cool hands, Ada resembles one of the pale flowers that her mother raises. She is the living symbol of her parents' emotional barrenness, the withered progeny of "these slowly petrifying people" (p. 43).

Richard is determined to make a final attempt to persuade Ada to leave with him: "he knew that he could never be freed from the hold of this soil, however far from it he had travelled, though he were never to be called back by itself, but by a forfeit of love which in final desperation he had come to redeem or tear from its roots forever" (p. 21). Richard, then, wants liberation for both himself and Ada, and if Ada will not join him he has resolved to end their relationship for good. However, there is an additional possibility that is never openly mentioned in the novel, but is nonetheless implicit in Knister's imagery. Instead of freeing himself, Richard may succumb to the baneful influence of the countryside. If Richard cannot persuade Ada to come with him, he may risk losing touch with an important part of himself. The renunciation of Ada – his soul-mate, his alternative self – may be too drastic a step for Richard to take with safety.

Richard Milne, then, is poised between the countryside and the city, between the rural world of the regional idyll and the harsher urban world portrayed in most modernist fiction. His own art, we learn, is also suspended between these same two worlds. Like the authors of most regional idylls, Richard Milne has himself moved to the city but has chosen to locate his fiction in a rural setting. Although Richard's art deals with the rural milieu, he apparently displays a less sentimental outlook than do most authors of regional idylls. In fact, Richard's viewpoint grows less nostalgic and more "modern" in the course of the novel. His visit to his childhood home makes him reconsider his own fiction, and as he ponders we can see him resolve to adopt a different approach to his art:

> In his writing, Richard Milne had concerned himself with such people as these, typical farm characters. But while he had blinked none of their littlenesses, critics had claimed that his novels presented too roseate a picture of rural life. The reason was that he had seemed to find these temporal idiosyncrasies set off in due proportion against the elemental materials of life. But, he reflected now, that attitude was part of the nostalgia he experienced from his own past in such scenes; and it was a form of idealism which he saw as applicable no more to this milieu than to any province of life more or less open to primal forces. (p. 110)

Richard decides that he will no longer allow even this degree of nostalgia to appear in his work. He will become a more detached and ironic recorder of life as it is; he will apply to the rural scene the same standards that writers of his own day use in portraying urban settings: "He would not have idealized these [people] in a setting of commerce or of society, and he had been wrong to blur them in a scene which his boyhood had known. Hence, he foresaw, a further development in his own art. An increasing surface hardness seemed to be an inevitable accompaniment to the progress of the significant novelists of his and an earlier day" (p. 110). Richard, then, is poised between the countryside and the city, between the benign rural world of the regional idyll and the harsher world portrayed in most modernist fiction.

Knister's protagonist is an appropriate representative of Canadian fiction in the process of transforming itself from the sentimentality of the regional idyll to the harsher vision of modernism. Uncertainly, tentatively, perhaps belatedly, Richard Milne is modernizing his own art – just as Canadian fiction of the twenties was uncertainly adjusting itself to the example set by the younger British and American writers.

110

Knister's own novel is an excellent example of the uneasy accommodation with modernism that Canadian writers were reaching, for the book combines the regional idyll with elements of the psychological novel and symbolist fiction. Knister's modernism is evident both in his choice of psychological self-oppression as a central theme, and in his deliberate use of symbols, such as the sickly white narcissi that are associated with the emotional paralysis of the Lethen household. Knister's attachment to the regional idyll is most apparent in the happy conclusion he arranges for his story. Yet the nostalgia of that conclusion is, in a sense, qualified by Richard's apparent success in at last persuading the reluctant Ada Lethen to come away with him. Those who wish to develop inwardly to their full potential, Knister's story implies, must leave the rural life behind.

I have been arguing that, faced with hostility or incomprehension from many readers, literary modernism made slow headway in Canada during the twenties. It still had not taken firm root when the Depression imposed a sort of quick freeze on North American society. Nonetheless, by 1936, a Canadian poetic modernism did tentatively announce itself in the group anthology *New Provinces*.[1] In that book F.R. Scott's contribution included "The Canadian Authors Meet," which satirized the old-fashioned attitudes held by many members of the Canadian Authors Association, who measured writers "for their faith and philanthropics, / Their zeal for God and King, their earnest thought"(p. 55), rather than for artistic excellence. A.J.M. Smith, for his part, used the witty ironies of "News of the Phoenix" to castigate the indifference to culture shown by contemporary society. In "To a Young Poet" Smith urged young poets to create work that was "alien to romance," and he pictured the poet as a detached Joycean craftsman, who indifferently pared his fingernails after turning away from "a hard thing done / Perfectly, as though without care" (p. 74).

---

[1] *New Provinces: Poems of Several Authors* (Toronto: Macmillan, 1936). All further references to this work appear in the text.

Smith's "A Rejected Preface," originally written to introduce *New Provinces*, demonstrates his indebtedness to the ideas of the British modernists, especially his debt to Eliot's criticism.[1] The less contentious preface eventually provided by F.R. Scott also clearly indicated the adherence of the Canadian poets to the example set by British and American modernists. But, as F.W. Watt remarks, "the Depression era was like an intense magnetic field that deflected the courses of all the poets who went through it."[2] By the time *New Provinces* was published, the Depression had already altered the direction of Canadian writing away from a concern with new techniques and towards a more direct involvement with social issues. For this reason many of the poets in *New Provinces* found the work of the socially committed British poets of the thirties – writers such as Auden, Spender, and MacNeice – more useful than the ironic and fragmented poetry Eliot had published during the twenties.

Watt also remarks that the Depression brought about the "domination of fiction, for the first time in Canadian literary history, by contemporary themes" (p. 471). The Depression, then, reinforced what Watt calls "the movement towards contemporaneity and realism in fiction" (p. 471) that had begun during the twenties. It also discouraged our writers from emulating the more advanced techniques of the leading modernists. For example, the Depression shifted Morley Callaghan's fiction away from naturalism, and prompted him to write the moral fables he published during the 1930s, in which the traditional Christian virtues were offered as the proper response to Depression conditions. Hugh MacLennan, as well, tried to respond to the Depression in his fiction. His two unpublished novels from the 1930s deal with versions of the representative figure that MacLennan later, in *Two Solitudes* (1945), refers to as the "young man of 1933."[3] Sinclair Ross rode out the Depression as a bank clerk in

---

[1] A.J.M. Smith, "A Rejected Preface," *Canadian Literature*, No. 24 (Spring 1965), pp. 6-9.

[2] F.W. Watt, "Literature of Protest," in Klinck, ed., *Literary History of Canada*, p. 472. All further references to this work appear in the text.

[3] Hugh MacLennan, *Two Solitudes*, Laurentian Library, No. 1 (Toronto: Macmillan, n.d.), p. 333.

several Saskatchewan towns, where his work undoubtedly gave him an insider's knowledge of the physical and spiritual impoverishment he depicts in *As for Me and My House.*

The Depression, however, comes into Canadian literature more as an act of God than an act of man. It is to be remedied by greater faith, not by alteration in material conditions. In Morley Callaghan's novels of the thirties, the Depression is not an economic injustice to be blamed on specific social causes and remedied by specific social measures; rather it presents an opportunity for reforming the individual soul. *They Shall Inherit the Earth* (1935) ends with the birth of a child, the renewal of understanding between a father and his son, and a prayer for mercy; it appears that Michael Aikenhead cannot get a job as an engineer until he has expiated his guilt and recovered his ability to love. Even in the Depression, our authors looked for social reform to come about through a moral regeneration of the individual. Irene Baird's *Waste Heritage* (1939) is one of the few books that, by implication, supports a radical programme of social reform. Yet this book also evokes Biblical echoes by its transformation of Vancouver and Victoria into the cities of Aschelon and Gath.

The early career of George Stewart, in MacLennan's *The Watch That Ends the Night* (1959), is intended to illustrate the impact of the Depression on an entire generation. George remarks of himself and his contemporaries: "The Thirties lie behind us like the memory of guilt and shame."[1] Like so many others, George found that his society appeared to have little use for him, and he became convinced of "one of the most terrible things anyone can see – my own worthlessness" (p. 135). In this atmosphere of despair, people turned to extreme remedies. "This was a time," George tells us, 'in which you were always meeting people who caught politics just as a person catches religion" (p. 223). George himself was not immune to the contagion. He ruefully admits: "I learned the bitter language and thoughts of the period, as any sensitive man was bound to in a time when his elders and leaders betrayed him. I learned to profess a blanket

---

[1] Hugh MacLennan, *The Watch That Ends the Night* (Toronto: Macmillan, 1959), p. 123. All further references to this work appear in the text.

hatred for whole human groups, to talk wildly about politics and to encourage others to do the same" (p. 124). From this abyss of self-loathing and anger, George is rescued only by the intervention of Jerome and Catherine Martell, who become virtual surrogate parents to him.

Few Canadian novelists have written outright proletarian novels such as Irene Baird's *Waste Heritage* and Hugh Garner's *Cabbagetown* (1950). Yet the careers of an entire generation of writers were profoundly affected by the economic and social catastrophe that overwhelmed North American society in the decade before the Second World War. In consequence, many among the first group of Canadian modernist writers had isolated and difficult literary careers. Yet they did not make a virtue of isolation; they did not glory in a detached Joycean posture of silence, exile, and cunning. They remained within their society, but often in circumstances that made writing difficult. Ross worked for the Royal Bank; MacLennan taught at Lower Canada College; Mitchell worked for *Maclean's* before moving to High River to write full-time; Buckler retreated to farm life in the Annapolis valley.

These writers must have felt that they were not being sufficiently valued for the abilities on which they most prided themselves. For a glimpse of the way writers perceived themselves during this period we can examine a number of works that present artists as protagonists. In these works, our writers seem to share a common perception of the artist's social status: specifically, they agree in depicting the artist as a marginal member of Canadian society. For until quite recently, our writers have portrayed the lot of the writer in Canada as a lonely one. Len Sterner in Grove's *The Yoke of Life* is perhaps not a true artist, but he has an artist's sensitivity, and he is overwhelmed by the coarseness of the life he meets both in his home community and later in Winnipeg. Philip Bentley in Ross's *As For Me and My House* desires to be a painter but is thwarted by the pragmatism of his society and by his wife's highly possessive jealousy. David Canaan in Buckler's *The Mountain and the Valley* (1952) is set apart from his companions by the acute self-consciousness that makes him resolve to be a writer. The singer Monica Gall in Robertson Davies' *A Mixture of Frailties*

(1958) does develop her talents, but she must first be transported away from her provincial Canadian environment in order to find the proper climate in which to nurture her talents.

Sinclair Ross's story "Cornet at Night" provides an evocative image of a world that has no place for art. The story's protagonist, Tommy Dickson, is caught between a father who knows only the brute demands of farm labour and a mother whose version of culture – church, school, and music lessons – imposes standards that are as rigid as the demands of the land. In the music of the cornet, played by the young man he brings back from town, Tommy hears something that goes beyond his music teacher's metronome-governed conception of music: "the notes were piercing, golden as the cornet itself, and they gave life expanse that it had never known before."[1] The music embodies what is missing from the bleak, toil-filled lives of Tommy's mother and father. But such music is as out of place in the family's life as the cornet player is out of place in a wheat field. The story's conclusion implies that the music has changed Tommy in a fundamental way: "A harvest, however lean, is certain every year; but a cornet at night is golden only once" (p. 51).

When they depicted their lonely and isolated protagonists, our early modernist writers were asking an important question of their society. They were asking whether Canada had a meaningful place for its artists and writers. In other words, what is the place of the cultivated sensibility in Canadian society? For the space of a few decades, our novelists resolved this question by casting themselves as critics of society and as defenders of the humane values for which their society, a society grown increasingly industrial and commercial, found so little room. They remained inside the society they criticized, but in their fiction they grappled with the problems they diagnosed in the world around them.

---

[1] Sinclair Ross, "Cornet at Night," in *The Lamp at Noon and Other Stories*, New Canadian Library, No. 62 (Toronto: McClelland and Stewart, 1968), p. 49. The story was first published in *Queen's Quarterly*, 46 (1939-40), 431-52.

In my next chapter, I will examine some of the most distinctive features that their efforts have given to the Canadian tradition in fiction.

CHAPTER FIVE

Our Place on the Map

From that they found most lovely, most abhorred,
my parents made me ....
                                    – Alden Nowlan, "Beginning"

In *The Return of the Vanishing American* Leslie Fiedler
mentions only one novel by a Canadian author, Leonard
Cohen's *Beautiful Losers* (1966). Yet when Fiedler divides
the American novel into Northerns, Southerns, Easterns,
and Westerns,[1] he is speaking – whether he intends it or not
– in continental terms: his system of classification applies not
just to American writing but to all North American fiction.
Fiedler initially defines his four genres by their subject
matter. The Northern depicts the encounter with the land
itself; the Southern depicts the American's encounter with
the Negro; the Eastern portrays the American's return to
Europe; and the Western focuses on the American's encounter with the native peoples of this continent. In the
discussion that follows I will need to amplify these superficial definitions, just as Fiedler himself throughout his career
has extended and deepened his definition of the Western. In
addition, I will need to rectify a notable omission from
Fiedler's imaginative topography of American fiction. To the
four subgenres of the novel that Fiedler describes, we must

---

[1] Fiedler, *The Return of the Vanishing American*, pp. 16-20. All further
references to this work appear in the text.

117

add the novel of the city, a form that Fiedler might well have chosen to call the Urban. Later in this chapter, however, I shall adopt a more conventional terminology, and speak simply of urban fiction.

It must be borne in mind that these forms of fiction are the products of historical circumstances. They cannot be defined in purely aesthetic or purely formal terms. They must be understood as part of the response made by nineteenth century American society to the social forces at work within that society. That is, the creation of the Northern, Southern, Eastern, and Western as identifiable subgenres of the American novel is part and parcel of nineteenth-century America's effort towards cultural self-definition – part of the process by which Americans answered Crèvecoeur's famous question, found in the third of his *Letters from an American Farmer* (1782): "What then is the American, this new man?"[1] And the emergence of the Urban as a distinctive form of the American novel is intimately linked with the development of American society from its agrarian origins to its present condition. I should also add a warning that the Northern, the Southern, The Eastern, the Western, and the Urban do not divide American fiction into air-tight compartments. Rather, they are labels that identify tendencies – sets of related motifs and attitudes – that may exist separately or may be combined in any particular novel.

The Northern, the Eastern, and the Western can be understood as embodying divergent responses to a theme which is central to European culture and its new world offshoot. Specifically, they portray three different attitudes towards guilt. The European culture which spawned North American society was based on the individual conscience; it was a culture of guilt rather than a culture of shame.[2] Conformity to social standards was enforced by the individual's knowledge that he would feel guilty if he transgressed

[1] St. Jean de Crèvecoeur, *Letters from an American Farmer*, in *The Norton Anthology of American Literature*, ed. Ronald Gottesman et al. (New York: Norton, 1979), I, 442.

[2] Here, and in several subsequent passages, I make use of the analysis of American society given in David Riesman, with Nathan Glazer and Reuel Denney, *The Lonely Crowd: A Study of the Changing American Character* (New Haven: Yale Univ. Press, 1950).

those standards. In both its popular and elitist forms, the Western depicts characters who flee from guilt, characters who reject a maturity that would impose limits on the child's egocentric outlook. In contrast, the Eastern shows characters for whom the internalization of guilt that leads to social conformity is not a diminishing of the self, but a liberation of the individual's best potential. In the Eastern social conventions provide the necessary framework of rules within which the game of civilization may be played. If the Eastern shows social conventions as basically benign, the Northern expresses the view that social conventions are oppressive and stifling. The Northern is, above all else, the novel of the puritan conscience in action. The typical Northern studies the pernicious consequences of accepting a puritan or Calvinist picture of human nature.

The Southern must be understood in somewhat different terms. The Southern arises from a tradition-directed society, rather than from the inner-directed culture portrayed in the Northern, Eastern, and Western. Moreover, the Southern is an expression of a defeated culture, in which collectively established standards of honour and decency have ceased to hold authority. The Southern is the American counterpart of the European Gothic novel; in the Southern the dark places of the mind, unrestrained by social conventions, are externalized as mouldering plantations inhabited by a decadent aristocracy. Guilt festers abundantly in the Southern, but it is complicated by a gnawing sense of failure. The defeated society offers the individual no adequate scope for action, so that the guilty conscience can find no satisfactory outlet, no avenue of expiation. Instead, the attempt is made to deny guilt by projecting it onto the Negro, whose blackness is thought to symbolize his lower nature and so justify his historic enslavement. In fully mature versions of the Southern, of course, this process is recognized for the fallacious rationalization it is. Like the Western, the Southern readily crosses the boundary between elite or high art and popular art, so that the most familiar example of the form is probably Margaret Mitchell's *Gone with the Wind*, though its literary high point is found in the works of Faulkner.

American urban fiction frequently examines the consequences of pursuing the American Dream of unlimited material success. The pessimism displayed by the authors of many of the earliest American urban novels was influenced by the naturalism made fashionable in the late years of the nineteenth century by European writers such as Emile Zola. But American urban fiction can also be traced to native sources. After the Civil War, American fiction fell back into the hands of the sentimental writers Hawthorne had earlier denounced as the "d____d mob of scribbling women."[1] Although their literary paths eventually diverged markedly, W.D. Howells and his friend Henry James began their careers by reacting against the narrowly moralistic conception of fiction that the popular novelists had given widespread currency. James located much of his fiction in Europe, for only there did he find the cultivated taste, refined sensibility, and polished manners that in his eyes constituted a truly civilized society. By creating subtly crafted psychological studies, he staked a claim for those American novelists who would think of themselves, first and foremost, as artists writing for a limited audience of informed and sensitive readers. Howells, on the other hand, thought of the writer not as a pure aesthete but as a moralist and a social commentator. He used his fiction to explore the collision of traditional moral values with the new urban commercial society. Howells, then, stands at the head of a distinguished strain of American fiction – the urban novel or the novel of the big city – just as James stands at the head of the international novel or Eastern.

In his early novels Howells examined the shift from rural to urban society. In *A Modern Instance* he moved Bartley Hubbard from Equity to Boston; in *The Rise of Silas Lapham* he moved the Lapham family away from their farm to Boston. Both Bartley Hubbard and Silas Lapham encounter members of the patrician class that James depicts in novels such as *The Europeans*. The New England patricians, however, are not idealized by Howells, even though the best members of this class – Ben Halleck in *A Modern Instance* and Tom Corey in *The Rise of Silas Lapham* – do provide the

---

[1] Nathaniel Hawthorne, Letter to William D. Ticknor, 19 Jan. 1955, in *Letters of Hawthorne to William D. Ticknor, 1851-1864* (Newark, N. J.: Carteret Book Club, 1910), I, 75.

standard of comparison by which the other characters are judged. If we turn to the best of Howells' later novels, however, we can see him turning his attention to a further shift in American social conditions. In *A Hazard of New Fortunes* Howells moves Basil March from Boston to New York, and he involves March's affairs with those of the slangy promoter Fulkerson. Thus, he acknowledges that a new kind of person has gained the upper hand in American society. The new society is based on go-ahead Yankee ingenuity rather than on the inherited status and self-conscious cultivation of the Boston Brahmins. Novels by some of the writers Howells encouraged, such as Stephen Crane, Frank Norris, and Theodore Dreiser, blended Howells' attention to social conditions with the ideas of the European naturalists, and produced the typical American novel of urban life.

Urban fiction often studies the consequences of accepting the worship of Success that is the pervasive North American popular ideology. Instead of being primarily concerned with the influence of family background, the authors of urban fiction typically investigate the influence of the peer-group on the individual member of society. Frequently, therefore, urban fiction records the progress of that new kind of man whom the sociologist David Riesman terms "other-directed." The other-directed man appears in fiction in the numerous incarnations of that archetypally American figure, the self-made man or the apostle of Success. This figure – whatever his superficial disguise, whether he is a con-man or a business executive – is always fundamentally a salesman. He may not always sell a physical product, as Willy Loman does in Miller's *Death of a Salesman*, but he is perpetually on the market with one all-important product: himself. His fictional portrayal occurs in two main versions, one romantic and the other tragic. The romantic variant of the Urban is epitomized by the rags-to-riches story that was the stock-in-trade of the popular nineteenth-century author Horatio Alger. The tragic variant of the Urban portrays the moral decline – and often the material decline as well – of a protagonist who is engulfed by the indifferent mechanisms of urban society. Crane's *Maggie, A Girl of the Streets*, Norris' *McTeague* and Dreiser's *Sister Carrie* and *An American*

Tragedy can stand as representative examples.

The typology of North American fiction that I have just outlined can be used to isolate an important difference between the Canadian and American fictional traditions. American authors have erected the Western into a national myth. In doing this, they have chosen to emphasize a slightly different stage of historical development than have Canadian authors, who have until recently made the Northern the predominant form of serious Canadian fiction. We can say that American and Canadian authors have selected different "mythological moments" as the heart of the historical process by which European culture spread over the continent. American authors have chosen to elaborate upon – in effect, to seek to prolong – the moment immediately preceding settlement, when the frontiersman must decide whether he will stay put and turn into a settler or will retain his identity as a frontiersman by moving further west. In contrast, Canadian authors have chosen to dwell on the process of settlement, in which European or "civilized" values are imposed on the native landscape.

Ultimately this difference can be described in theological terms. American writing frequently asks: How can man escape the restrictions imposed by society? How can man regain his innocence? American writers frequently express the hope that sometime soon – perhaps tomorrow – man's natural goodness will become a demonstrated fact. But the American quest for freedom all too often leads to a realization that absolute freedom is unattainable and that natural goodness is a chimera: the New Adam still carries the Old Adam within himself. Therefore, the blackest American books confront the failure of the quest for innocence and freedom: frequently, the response is total despair. Canadian authors, on the other hand, usually start by doubting the notion of natural goodness. Canada's long history as a colony meant that there was no attempt to define the Canadian as a new man, free from the guilts and anxieties engendered by European society. Canadian authors feel that the restrictions imposed by religious and social conventions are necessary to control the Old Adam. But in the blackest Canadian books the repressive forces of family and society become forms of the trap that a repressive Calvinist society sets for the individual.

A good explanation of the psychological tensions at work in many novels that are central to the Canadian tradition is given in Ralph Connor's *The Man from Glengarry* (1901). When Mrs. Murray's Bible class discusses "the redoubtable ninth chapter" of Paul's Epistle to the Romans, the narrator tells us:

> It was significant that by Macdonald Dubh, his brother, and the other older and more experienced members of the class, the doctrine was regarded as absolutely inevitable and was accepted without question, while by Yankee and Ranald and all the younger members of the class, it was rejected with fierce resentment. The older men had been taught by the experience of long and bitter years, that above all their strength, however mighty, a power, resistless and often inscrutable, determined their lives. The younger men, their hearts beating with conscious power and freedom, resented this control, or accepting it, refused to assume the responsibility for the outcome of their lives. (p. 133)

In the bleakest Canadian fictions the puritan environment breaks the spirit of the younger generation. In more hopeful Canadian novels the younger generation strives towards a measure of emotional freedom.

The best-known of the forms Fiedler mentions is the Western. The Western is the novel of civilization evaded, in which Natty Bumppo and Chingachgook – and their numerous later avatars – wander in happy freedom through the forest, far from the constraints of a society whose principal embodiment is a God-fearing and emasculating Woman. Here we encounter an important difference between the American and Canadian traditions. The Western, in its traditional form, is a branch of the historical novel; and there exist in Canadian historical fiction none of those inseparable pairs of white and dusky males that recur throughout American fiction. The confrontation with the Indian, which Fiedler identifies as the heart of the Western, is not a common theme in Canadian fiction. Moreover, when the encounter between red man and white man does occur in Canadian books, it usually takes a different form than it does in the works of American authors. For example, in Howard O'Hagan's *Tay John* (1939) and in Rudy Wiebe's *The Temptations of Big Bear* (1973), the Indian does not stand for the deepest and truest self (as he does in so many American books), but for something beyond the self. The encounter with the Indian is inseparable from the encounter with the wilderness where the Indian dwells, and in Canadian fiction both Indian and wilderness are seen as embodying a timeless spiritual essence: the wilderness is a symbol of an eternal reality, and the Indian is an archetype of the fully integrated self in harmony with the cosmos.

If the Western is the novel of civilization evaded, then the Eastern is the novel of civilization regained, of sentiment affirmed, and of refinement acquired. The heart of the Eastern, says Fiedler, is the North American's return to Europe, which is "his Old Home, the place of origin of his old self, that original Adam, whom the New World presumably made a New Man" (p. 19). Only by seeing Europe does the American "know for sure that he *is* an American" (p. 19). Easterns are not as prominent in the American tradition as are Westerns, but the eminence of Henry James makes them an important feature of the American literary landscape.

A more commonly used term for the Eastern is "the international novel." An article by Oscar Cargill provides the best definition of this kind of fiction. "The international novel," Cargill says, "is not one in which a foreign setting merely gives a romantic interest. . . ."[1] Rather, the term should be applied only to fiction in which a character or characters from one nation attempt to cope with the customs and values of another national culture. As Cargill puts it:

An international novel is one in which a character, usually guided in his actions by the mores of one environment, is set down in another, where his learned reflexes are of no use to him, where he must employ all his individual resources to meet successive

---

[1] Oscar Cargill, "The First International Novel," *PMLA*, 73 (1958), 419. All further references to this work appear in the text.

situations, and where he must intelligently accommodate himself to the new mores, or, in one way or another, be destroyed. (p. 419)

Cargill's suggestion that the protagonist of an international novel will be destroyed if he (or she) fails to adjust to the new environment is certainly overstated. With this qualification, however, Cargill's account can be allowed to stand. The international novel, then, uses the experiences of its protagonist in order to compare two (or sometimes more) national cultures. Usually, in fiction written by English-speaking authors, one of these cultures belongs to a European nation and the other to the United States.

According to Cargill, Henry James's *The American* is the first true example of the international novel. That is, *The American* is the first novel that presents a clear contrast between European and American social myths. In James's novel, Christopher Newman, an American self-made man, goes to Europe in search of something he has not found in his North American life. At first, as he observes his new surroundings, the comparison seems to favour Europe. He recognizes that European civilization provides "a very rich and beautiful world, and that it had not all been made by sharp railroad men and stockbrokers."[1] He feels he has found the embodiment of his longings in Countess de Cintré, whose family appear to swallow their aristocratic prejudices and accept Newman as a suitor for their daughter's hand. But Newman is abruptly and unexpectedly rejected, just when his engagement has been publicly announced. "It is not your disposition that we object to, it is your antecedents," the Countess's mother, the forbidding Madame de Bellegarde, tells him. "We really cannot reconcile ourselves to a commercial person. We fancied in an evil hour that we could; it was a great misfortune" (p. 218). Although Claire de Cintré loves Newman, she obeys her mother's request to renounce him. Newman, the self-made man, finds this puzzling. Newman cannot understand that, as a member of an aristocratic

---

[1] Henry James, *The American*, Norton Critical Edition, ed. James W. Tuttleton (New York: Norton, 1978), p. 75. All further references to this work appear in the text.

European family, Claire de Cintré is simply not a free agent in the same way that Newman, the American, is. She feels that her very being is involved with her family and its traditions.

Canadian examples of the Eastern are not numerous, but they are nonetheless significant. The first noteworthy examples of the form occur in the fiction of Sara Jeannette Duncan, whose *An American Girl in London* (1891) and *Cousin Cinderella: A Canadian Girl in London* (1908) present the adventures of North American innocents abroad. Although Duncan's best-known novel, *The Imperialist* (1904), is not really an Eastern, it does include a brief visit by the central character to England, where he learns to define himself as a Canadian, a citizen of the New World. More recently, some of the leading features of the Eastern have appeared in the stories and novels of Mavis Gallant, and in some of the novels of Mordecai Richler. The most distinguished Canadian Easterns, however, have been written by Robertson Davies, whose entire literary career has been dominated by a concern for the precarious status of traditional or "high" culture in North American society.

Since the Southern, according to Fiedler, presents "the encounter with the Negro," it may seem that there should be no analogue to the Southern in Canadian writing. Yet intriguing comparisons have sometimes been made between the literature of the American South and the literature of Quebec.[2] The resemblances occur because both literatures come from defeated cultures, which often feel the past as an oppressive burden. The Gothic motifs common in both literatures – the ruined mansion, the frequently incestuous nature of the deepest emotional attachments – indicate a society that labours under a sense of failure, and as a result has turned inward to contemplate the pain of its unhealed historical wounds.

---

[1] See Margot Northey, *The Haunted Wilderness: The Gothic and Grotesque in Canadian Fiction* (Toronto: Univ. of Toronto Press, 1976), p. 50; see also John Lennox, "Dark Journeys: *Kamouraska* and *Deliverance*," *Essays on Canadian Writing*, No. 12 (Fall 1978), pp. 84-104.

The least familiar of Fiedler's four categories is the Northern, exemplified in his discussion by some of the novels of William Dean Howells and by Edith Wharton's *Ethan Frome*. The Northern is the novel of passion denied and sentiment repressed in the name of reason and social custom. Fiedler suggests that the Northern portrays a direct confrontation with the land. Certainly the Northern usually shows a human dwelling place, often a farmhouse or a small town, that is dwarfed by a hostile environment. However, the primary subject of the Northern is not the confrontation between man and environment; rather, the typical Northern studies the meeting between a sensitive individual and a puritanical society that inhibits the emotional and intellectual development of its members. Perhaps it is more accurate to say that environmental oppression and social oppression reinforce each other. The household at the centre of many Northerns is presided over by a patriarchal figure, joyless and forbidding, whose authority is reinforced by a punitive divinity and by a severe environment.

In his discussion of American literature, Fiedler is hard pressed to produce distinguished examples of the Northern; but part of the reason is that he has not cast his net widely enough. Within an imaginative geography of North America that includes Canada, the Northern is one of the major forms of literary expression. A great many of the most distinguished Canadian novels exemplify Fiedler's description of the Northern as "tight, gray, low-keyed, underplayed, avoiding melodrama where possible" (p. 16). A partial list would include most of the novels of Frederick Philip Grove, Martha Ostenso's *Wild Geese* (1925), Robert Stead's *Grain* (1926), Raymond Knister's *White Narcissus* (1929), Sinclair Ross's *As for Me and My House* (1941), Hugh MacLennan's *Each Man's Son* (1951), Ethel Wilson's *Hetty Dorval* (1947), Margaret Laurence's *The Stone Angel* (1964), *A Jest of God* (1966), and *A Bird in the House* (1970), Ernest Buckler's *The Mountain and the Valley* (1952), Patricia Blondal's *A Candle to Light the Sun* (1960), Rudy Wiebe's *Peace Shall Destroy Many* (1962), Harold Horwood's *Tomorrow Will Be Sunday* (1966), Percy Janes's *House of Hate* (1970), Alden Nowlan's *Various Persons Named Kevin O'Brien* (1973), and Matt Cohen's *The Disinherited* (1974).

Two well-known Canadian novels that can be used to define the typical contours of the Northern are Ross's *As for Me and My House* and MacLennan's *Each Man's Son*. In both books a work-obsessed husband retreats into a private study to drug himself with a self-imposed artistic or intellectual task – Philip Bentley draws pictures and Dr. Ainslie studies Greek. The central couples in both novels are childless, a condition that seems to be an index of their emotional barrenness. In both novels religion is depicted as an oppressive social force: Philip Bentley preaches a religion in which he does not even believe; Dr. Ainslie has rejected God but is nonetheless haunted by the demons of a lingering Calvinist heritage – guilt and self-doubt. Both novels end ambiguously. The central couples acquire children by adoption, but not before the mothers of both children are sacrificed to the harsh and unforgiving ethos that the two authors see as presiding over their fictional worlds. In both novels the happiness of an adopted child seems doubtful, for the adoptive parents are turning to the child in order to avoid confronting each other.

In both novels antagonism between the sexes motivates much of the action. *Each Man's Son* metes out a particularly harsh fate to many of its female characters. Dr. Ainslie acquires a son not by loving his wife but by sterilizing her and appropriating to himself the son of another woman, Mollie MacNeill, who reminds him of his own mother. Moreover, the parallel between Mollie and Dr. Ainslie's mother does not stop at physical resemblance: Dr. Ainslie's mother died as a result of sacrificing herself in an attempt to soften the effects of the uncompromising ambition that drove Dr. Ainslie's father; and Mollie dies at the hands of her returned boxer husband, who accomplishes what Dr. Ainslie has not dared to admit he wishes for. In *As for Me and My House*, on the other hand, the women triumph over the men, and attain a dominance that is depicted as joyless and unsatisfying. Mrs. Bird's control of her husband is described by Mrs. Bentley as a hard-won achievement. And Mrs. Bentley must constantly scheme for ways to keep Philip faithful to a marriage he entered without knowing it meant the death of his plan to become an artist. Philip's brief affair with Judith West is a short-lived movement away from bondage to his domineering wife, but he cannot maintain his freedom. At the novel's end he is even more firmly under the power of his parasitical wife, who can now secure his submission by holding out the threat of revealing young Philip's illegitimacy to the world.

Ross is not the first of our authors in whose work a sexual transgression and the resulting illegitimate child brings about a conflict with a narrowly puritanical society. Just before the turn of the century, for example, Joanna Wood in *The Untempered Wind* (1894) dissected a community that cruelly turns against a woman who bears a child out of wedlock. Of one of the townswomen, Wood writes: "Mrs. White was a very good woman, therefore she looked unutterable contempt at Myron Holder."[3] The unfeeling condemnation expressed by the town, especially the "merciless virtue" (p. 295) of the women, makes Myron's life a continual torment. However, even when Myron leaves the town to become a nurse, a rigidly moralizing preacher imposes upon her the duty of informing everyone she meets of her past misdeed, presumably so that she may be treated with the unkindness he thinks she deserves. Another unwed mother is ostracized by an intolerant community in Charles G.D. Roberts' *The Heart that Knows* (1906). In Robert Knowles' *St. Cuthbert's* (1905), the minister who narrates the story must learn to add a leaven of charity to his moral code when it is revealed that the man his daughter loves is the child of an illicit relationship. Bastard children must endure gibes and often physical torments in books ranging from Roberts' story to Stead's *The Smoking Flax* (1924) and Laurence's *The Stone Angel*.[4]

Romantic love is also particularly difficult for the characters of most Northerns to handle. Robert Stead's *Grain*, for example, contains two incipient romantic triangles whose development is inhibited by the emotional reticence of the protagonist, Gander Stake. The first triangle arises when Gander's attraction to the stranger from the city, Jerry

---

[1]Joanna Wood, *The Untempered Wind* (New York: J. Selwyn Tait, 1894), p. 7. All further references to this work appear in the text.

[2]The subject discussed in this paragraph is also considered in Moss, *Patterns of Isolation in English Canadian Fiction*, pp. 189-92.

Chansley, temporarily shakes his silent devotion to Jo Burge. Gander's fondness for Jerry represents a healthy awakening of his dormant emotions, but he lacks the self-confidence to respond to her advances. The second triangle emerges when Gander continues to be drawn to Jo Burge even after her marriage to Dick Claus. Gander's inhibitions and moral scruples prevent him from uniting with his soul-mate, Jo Burge, even after they have admitted their continuing mutual attraction. But at last Gander does realize what he has missed in life. Sadly, he accepts responsibility for his own unfulfilled life by signing his full name (rather than the childish nickname "Gander") to the note he leaves for Jo Burge when he decides to leave for the city.

A similar fear of romance is apparent in Raymond Knister's *White Narcissus*, in which Ada Lethen justifies her long resistance to Richard Milne by citing her duty to her parents, who quarrelled long ago because "each thought the other unfaithful" (p. 43). They have never spoken since, and their daughter denies herself an independent life in order to support her parents' existence. "They have been estranged so long that they are really dead to each other," she tells Richard Milne, "and yet if they were left alone together they would both ... die the bodily death as well" (p. 36). Nonetheless, Ada is the principal sufferer in this situation, having succumbed to "a sort of nihilism of the emotions" (p. 62) that makes her refuse Richard's love. In fact, it seems likely that Ada's appeal to duty is a cover for her fear of the very sexuality that also precipitated her parents' quarrel. The novel's resolution, which in a day undoes the results of a lifetime of repression, seems patently false. An ending that permanently divided the lovers would have been more convincing.

When he tries to set the American Northern within its historical context, Fiedler writes that Hawthorne's *The Scarlet Letter* "seems a *pre*-Northern, finally, describing the mythological origins of a world which wholly contains the later, true Northern" (p. 17). But it seems to me that the themes of *The Scarlet Letter*, along with the book's pre-eminent literary merit, make it not a forerunner of the Northern, but the epitome of the form. There are many important parallels between *The Scarlet Letter* and Fiedler's prime example of the Northern, Wharton's *Ethan Frome*. Both novels turn on a similar basic situation. The initial temptation is sexual: Ethan Frome and Arthur Dimmesdale are each attracted to a woman whom social convention forbids them to love. It does not matter that Ethan's attraction for Mattie Silver is not physically consummated. He feels his guilt just as intensely as he would if he had actually succeeded in running away with her. The guilt felt by both Ethan Frome and Arthur Dimmesdale enables another character to wage a kind of psychological guerrilla warfare, with the intention of increasing the victim's already considerable inner suffering. The wronged husband Chillingworth imposes a relentless moral torture upon Dimmesdale, and Mattie Silver exacts a bitter revenge by adding to the misery of Ethan's life. In both novels the inner guilt is symbolized by external physical marks: Ethan's bent body is a counterpart of the self-inflicted wounds which scar Dimmesdale's breast in Hawthorne's novel.

Similar patterns of psychological oppression occur in *As for Me and My House* and in *Each Man's Son*. In Ross's novel Mrs. Bentley assumes the Chillingworth role in a mordant comedy of puritan manners, and Philip Bentley enacts a pallid and tight-lipped Dimmesdale. In MacLennan's novel the tragedy of the puritan conscience is contained entirely within the central character. Dr. Ainslie is, to his own mind, both sinner and accuser, both Dimmesdale and Chillingworth. His wife wishes to free him from his guilt, but he won't accept her proffered liberation; he remains sexually and emotionally inhibited. At the end of MacLennan's novel we are told that Dr. Ainslie has learned how to live, but the assurance does not carry conviction. And it is a measure of the bleakness of Ross's novel that, when Judith West dies in childbirth, Mrs. Bentley confesses: "It's what I've secretly been hoping for all along."[1]

A psychological torment that resembles the manipulation of Dimmesdale by Chillingworth is also a leading motif in several other Canadian Northerns. In Grove's *Settlers of the Marsh* (1925) the witch-like Clara Vogel, formerly the

[1] Sinclair Ross, *As for Me and My House*, New Canadian Library, No. 4 (Toronto: McClelland and Stewart, 1957), pp. 161-62.

131

neighbourhood prostitute, torments her sensitive and guilt-ridden husband until he rebels by killing her. In Martha Ostenso's *Wild Geese* Caleb Gare uses his knowledge of his wife's past indiscretion to control and brutalize his entire family, whom he views as little better than farm animals. Other novels portray the destructive consequences of a dread of life that can arise when children are raised in an atmosphere of guilt. Grove's *The Yoke of Life* (1930) tells the story of a sensitive boy for whom the burdens of adult life – primarily the burden of his own sexuality – prove too much to bear. Len Sterner and his soul-mate prefer death by drowning during a Lake Winnipeg storm to continued existence in an imperfect world. A similar fate – though he does not take his lover with him – befalls Colin Ensley in Roderick Haig-Brown's *On the Highest Hill* (1949). Ernest Buckler's *The Mountain and the Valley* also ends with the death of an over-sensitive figure, for whom physical existence has proved too much to bear.

It is significant that one of the earliest Canadian Northerns, Raymond Knister's *White Narcissus*, explicitly places itself in the direct line of descent from Hawthorne. Knister's protagonist is himself a writer, and his fictional situation becomes a guide to Knister's understanding of his own literary antecedents. One of the three books that Richard Milne takes with him on his journey back to his childhood home is *The Scarlet Letter*. And Richard explicitly compares himself with Hawthorne's tortured male protagonist. "He was expiating Dimmesdale's secret sin yet, after two centuries. Love could not be free yet for men and women who had taken civilization as an armour which had changed to fetters upon them. What was his whole piacular story but that of Dimmesdale – prophetic name – a delusion no longer a delusion of sin, but of impotence and analysis which belied action and love?" And Richard goes on to claim a representative quality for his personal experience: "It was the conflict of the conscious ones of his whole generation, this confusion of outer freedom and inner doubt" (p. 108).

Like *The Scarlet Letter*, many Canadian Northerns are set in small communities in which religion is the dominant social force. In several turn-of-the-century books, the authors make quite subtle distinctions between different theological persuasions; and different styles of piety are matters for extensive analysis and heated comment by some of their characters. Turn-of-the-century writers often assign clergymen leading roles in their stories, or use them to enunciate the moral perspective of a novel. In later fiction, on the other hand, there are few examples of clerics as central characters, and they are seldom allowed to become spokesmen for the author's viewpoint. In fact, clerics such as Bishop Foley in Callaghan's *Such Is My Beloved* (1934) or Reverend Powelly in W.O. Mitchell's *Who Has Seen the Wind* (1947) are almost presented as members of the devil's party. Callaghan's Father Dowling is one of the very few clerical heroes from this period, but (he is too sincere in his beliefs for the institutional Church to tolerate.)A more typical clergyman is Philip Bentley in *As for Me and My House*, who no longer even believes in the religion he must preach to his congregation.

Most of our twentieth-century writers have seen small town religion as a hypocritical shell of conventional behaviour masking rigid and intolerant attitudes. The devout hypocrite Mrs. Abercrombie in W.O. Mitchell's *Who Has Seen the Wind* and the devout hypocrite Mrs. Finlay in Ross's *As for Me and My House* come to mind immediately. Certainly ministers remain among the leaders of fictional small town society, and their opinions are listened to with respect. But in twentieth-century novels the sphere over which religion claims control shrinks, and religion itself becomes more willing to tolerate a materialistic outlook. The rigidity of mind that was formerly associated with religion is now exercised in the name of respectability, resulting in extreme hostility towards all departures from the social norm.

The Northern, of course, does not encompass the whole of Canadian fiction. In most of the fiction by our first generation of modernists, however, the underlying pattern is clearly that of the Northern. The settings of these novels are rural, their plots are static, and their characters are isolated or confined, bound by family ties or by private inhibitions. The characters remain within their home towns, and much of the action takes place within the family home. Yet the protagonist's deepest longing, often unrecognized in any conscious way, is for escape – for a journey in search of personal identity. Buckler's David Canaan never leaves his home valley, but MacLennan, for example, sends many of his characters on such journeys. Usually the physical journey away from one's hometown is not a solution, for there is no escape from the self through mere physical motion. Therefore, many characters subsequently undertake a journey back to their origins. Such return journeys become metaphors for a confrontation with the self, an attempt to attain self-knowledge and self-respect.

The Manawaka novels of Margaret Laurence incorporate this motif, along with most of the other distinguishing features of the Northern. In Laurence's Manawaka novels the personalities of her characters are shaped by family and hometown to an extent that the characters only slowly recognize, and never entirely surmount. In consequence, her novels not only depict paradigms of entrapment, but also portray efforts to escape from the secular yet still guilt-ridden outlook that succeeds the overtly religious outlook presented in the fiction of earlier writers such as Ralph Connor. Her novels thus provide a good illustration of how a major Canadian can create an extensive fictional world from themes and patterns developed by her predecessors.

For example, Laurence has generously confessed her indebtedness to the example of Sinclair Ross's *As for Me and My House*. His novel, she has written, "had an enormous impact on me, for it seemed the only completely genuine one I had ever read about my own people, my own place, my own time."[1] Laurence did not set out simply to recreate the culture of guilt and hypocrisy that Ross describes, but rather she sought to explore the ways in which the individual might try to escape from such a culture. As a result, her characters often conduct an ongoing quarrel with the Calvinist God or with the work ethic that is Calvinism's secular legacy. In *The Stone Angel* Hagar takes into herself the strict self-control she learns from her father. Jason Currie is "a self-made man. He had started without a bean, he was fond of telling Matt

---

[1] Margaret Laurence, "Introduction," in Ross, *The Lamp at Noon and Other Stories*, p. 7.

and Dan, and had pulled himself up by his bootstraps."[1] Hagar marries Bram Shipley as an act of rebellion against her father, but discovers that she has brought to her marriage a prohibition on emotional self-expression that she has learned both from her father and from her town. "It was not so very long after we wed, when first I felt my blood and vitals rise to meet his. He never knew. I never let him know. I never spoke aloud, and I made certain that the trembling was all inner .... I prided myself upon keeping my pride intact, like some maidenhead" (p. 81).

For a long time Hagar blames Bram alone for the failure of their marriage, and for her decision to leave him. Eventually, however, Hagar does accept responsibility for her actions, especially when she admits the effect she has had on her son John. The result is not an uprush of guilt, but rather a release from the guilt she has never consciously acknowledged. "I could even beg God's pardon this moment, for thinking ill of Him some time or other" (p. 248), she confesses. Yet just before her death, Hagar reaffirms her refusal to submit to the wishes of anyone except herself. She will not even submit to God. Her unorthodox prayer runs: *"Bless me or not, Lord, just as You please, for I'll not beg"* (p. 307).

The first novel of Robertson Davies's Deptford trilogy also provides a good illustration of how a writer can deliberately work with – and fruitfully extend – the thematic preoccupations that are prominent in the Northerns that dominate the Canadian tradition. The action of *Fifth Business* (1970) starts in a psychological terrain that is thoroughly familiar to readers of Canadian fiction: Dunstan's home is dominated by his mother's self-righteous and self-denying personality. Dunstan's Presbyterian upbringing predisposes him to assume responsibility for the incident that sets in motion the events of *Fifth Business* – and eventually gives rise to the events described in *The Manticore* (1972) and *World of Wonders* (1975). The action of *Fifth Business* follows, as though by a sort of psychological syllogism, from the incident in which Dunstan ducks the snowball thrown by

---

[1] Margaret Laurence, *The Stone Angel*, New Canadian Library, No. 59 (Toronto: McClelland and Stewart, 1968), p. 7. All further references to this work appear in the text.

his "lifelong friend and enemy" Percy Boyd Staunton.[1] Dunstan's assumption of responsibility for the snowball implicates him in "a grossly sexual act – the birth of a child" (p. 19). "Forgive yourself for being a human creature, Ramezay" (p. 208), Father Blazon eventually urges Dunstan. And indeed, only after Dunstan forgives himself for his part in Paul Dempster's birth – and for his other human failings – can he accept his entire life, and cease his habitual self-recrimination.

In *Fifth Business* Davies shows an awareness of the Canadian tradition in fiction, and expresses his intention to modify that tradition. Early in the novel Dunstan announces his intention not to present the early phases of his story as a nostalgic idealization of childhood. "Can I write truly of my boyhood?" he asks. "Or will that disgusting self-love which so often attaches itself to a man's idea of his youth creep in and falsify the story?" (pp. 9-10). Not if Dunstan can help it – he has no wish to produce a regional idyll. Dunstan explicitly renounces both the sentimental outlook of the "regional" writer and the sensational approach of the debunker. Deptford, he tells us, is neither "inhabited by laughable, lovable simpletons" nor is it "rotten with vice, and especially such sexual vice as Krafft-Ebing might have been surprised to uncover in Vienna" (p. 10). Rather, Deptford is a smaller version of communities elsewhere, containing the usual balance of vices and virtues. "We were serious people," says Dunstan, "missing nothing in our community and feeling ourselves in no way inferior to larger places" (p. 13).

Fifth Business begins in a small town, but later moves to a more urban setting. It is therefore a blend of at least two of the kinds of fiction I have been discussing in this chapter: it modulates from a Northern into a sophisticated example of the Urban – it seems to include more than a dash of the Eastern as well. I make these remarks about Davies's novel as preparation for the more general observation that, at the same time as many Canadian authors were producing the Northerns for which the Canadian tradition is best known, a growing number of writers were beginning to publish books

---

[1] Robertson Davies, *Fifth Business* (Toronto: Macmillan, 1970), p. 1. All further references to this work appear in the text.

in which the city is the primary setting. Nonetheless, it is only quite recently that urban settings have become as frequent as rural settings in the work of our writers.

The most notable Canadian authors of urban fiction are Morley Callaghan and Mordecai Richler. Their books combine urban locales with an emphasis on the pitfalls that attend the pursuit of material success. However, neither writer endorses the materialistic outlook that so many of their characters espouse. In his novels Callaghan consistently shows how a materialistic society rejects characters who try to live by the light of an inward vision. Richler, too, always presents material success as a threat to moral values. In *The Apprenticeship of Duddy Kravitz* (1959), for example, the values of the Zeyda and of Uncle Benjy are preferable to the values of the Boy Wonder or Mr. Cohen. In fact, for a considerable number of years, Canadian writers have grappled with the problems attendant upon pursuing the North American kind of "success." Thus, although Canadian writers often examine themes which are closely parallel to the themes treated by American writers, they do not always reach the conclusions that Warren Tallman transfers from his reading of American literature. Except for Hugh Garner, whose *Cabbagetown* (1950) seems a naturalistic novel of the thirties that missed its historical moment, our novelists have held their characters morally accountable for their responses to urban conditions. An emphasis on moral responsibility, then, runs persistently through Canadian urban fiction.

Until quite recently, most general statements about Canadian fiction were necessarily statements about the Northerns that have predominated in the output of our writers. This is particularly true about the conclusions expressed in the remarkable series of critical studies that deepened our insight into the Canadian literary tradition during the 1960s and the early 1970s. The picture that emerged from the articles and books of the so-called thematic critics was in some respects a highly disconcerting one. Isolation, guilt, failure, and other negative themes were the most prominent elements that these observers found in the most familiar Canadian novels and stories. Although the thematic critics may have occasionally depicted the works of Canadian writers in overly bleak terms, in many respects the portrait they rendered of our literary tradition was an accurate one. Only if I concentrate my attention on recent novels by those writers who have begun to introduce a new emphasis into our fiction do I find it necessary to substantially modify many of the conclusions reached by the thematic critics.

I have in mind some comparatively recent treatments of the central themes of the Northern, in which our authors present characters who grow up to achieve some degree of escape from their repressive backgrounds. For example, Sheila Watson's *The Double Hook* begins with the overthrow of the agent of repression. Rachel Cameron in *A Jest of God* and Stacey Cameron in *The Fire Dwellers* (1969) not only physically leave home but mentally release themselves from their self-imposed bondage to the past. Even Hagar Shipley in *The Stone Angel* recognizes that pride was her wilderness, and so delivers herself from a self-created spiritual desert. The protagonists of Alice Munro's *Lives of Girls and Women* (1971) and *Who Do You Think You Are?* (1978) and the protagonists of Marian Engel's *Bear* (1976) and *The Glassy Sea* (1978) achieve an uneasy liberation from puritan backgrounds. There are also a substantial number of important Canadian books in which gloom plays little part. Such books may be understood as continuations of the regional idyll – in other words as pastoral versions of the Northern. Notable examples include Mitchell's *Who Has Seen the Wind* and *Jake and the Kid* (1961), and George Elliott's *The Kissing Man* (1962).

The later fiction of several writers who helped to create the Canadian tradition seems to announce the completion of a phase in that tradition's development. In a variety of ways, many of our most respected novelists have begun to grope their way beyond the apparent dead end reached in so many of the Northerns that until recently have dominated the Canadian tradition. MacLennan, Davies, Laurence, and Ross have in their later work striven to reach an accommodation with the society they once depicted in predominantly negative terms. In Ross's *Sawbones Memorial* (1974), for example, Doc Hunter doesn't reproach himself for his sexual adventures; and although the townspeople's petty jealousy and spite eddy around him at his farewell party, he never weakens in his assurance that his life has been justified. Indeed, throughout his life he has never yielded an inch to his community's standards of respectability. In *The Watch That Ends the Night* (1959), *Fifth Business*, and *The Diviners* (1974) the protagonists all come to view their Canadian origins with equanimity, even with pride. Instead of rejecting parental figures, George Stewart, Dunstan Ramsay, and Morag Gunn all affirm the possibility of continuity across the generations, and are able to take satisfaction from subscribing to traditional values.

It would not be amiss to mention Mordecai Richler's *St. Urbain's Horseman* (1971) and *Joshua Then and Now* (1980) in conjunction with this group of novels. Although Richler writes urban fiction rather than Northerns, his last two novels, like the novels I have mentioned by MacLennan, Davies, Laurence, and Ross, are books in which the protagonist must attempt both to understand and to accept what he has done and what he has become. In *A Fine and Private Place* (1975), Morley Callaghan has also written a novel that appears to be an apologia for his own career, though his book is markedly less successful than either of Richler's novels of this type. W.O. Mitchell, as well, in *Since Daisy Creek* (1984), has produced a novel in which the protagonist, like Mitchell himself an author and teacher of creative writing, is forced to review his career and reach a deeper understanding of himself.

All of these books, I suggest, signal the emergence of the Canadian novel from what we might call its "dark age" of gloom, pessimism, and guilt. With their appearance, it has become clear that Canadian authors can now achieve fully rounded literary careers. They need no longer remain stalled at the stage of youthful rebellion against a hostile and constricting social environment. In particular, MacLennan, Davies, Ross, Laurence, and Richler have done something that is especially significant. They have all made their protagonist's discovery of a personal pattern or meaning in life coincide to some extent with the protagonist's recognition that his or her private life is bound up with the life of the larger community. In other words, the stories of individual Canadians are no longer perceived in isolation, detached from the story of the nation's development. Personal development only takes place within a social setting, and so personal history is a microcosm of history in the conventional sense.

These novels were published at the end of a period that will almost certainly be recognized by future historians of Canadian letters as the first "classical" era of Canadian fiction, our first period of real literary maturity. The fiction of this period, it has shrewdly been suggested, is often marked by the realization that "you must go home" in order to find your true identity.[1] The pattern of self-exile and return is found in both *The Diviners* and *Fifth Business*. Hugh MacLennan's best novel, *The Watch That Ends the Night*, does not portray a conventional exile – George Stewart makes no youthful journey away from Canada. But George does undergo a species of internal exile when he teaches at Waterloo School, a bastion of lingering colonialism, before he is summoned to full participation in his society by Jerome Martell. And *Sawbones Memorial* celebrates the tenacity of a man who refused to feel out of place in his own town, despite the disapproval shown by many of the townspeople. Laurence, Ross, MacLennan, and Davies – these authors have surveyed their past and found their identity there. Richler and Mitchell, too, have contributed to this process in which the Canadian tradition in fiction is consolidating and modifying itself. The task of younger writers is to go on from the place their predecessors have reached. That is, the younger writers are among the "inheritors" to whom Morag passes her skill and her knowledge at the end of *The Diviners*. In the best novels of our "classic" writers, then, Canadian fiction has emphatically found its voice. And that voice, as I shall argue in the next three chapters, has taken on an unmistakably North American cadence and tonality, and increasingly over the years has expressed an outlook that is North American rather than European.

---

[1] Theodore Colson, "The Theme of Home in the Fiction of Canada, the United States, and the West Indies," *English Studies in Canada*, 4 (1978), 351-61.

CHAPTER SIX

The Superstitious Valuation
of Europe

In Alan's mind was the belief that neither he nor his country
had as yet proved themselves worthy of civilization.
— Hugh MacLennan, *Return of the Sphinx*

Throughout his career Henry James maintained that European society possessed a richness of established manners
that the American society of his day could not match. In an
early letter to his mother, for example, James offers a
scathingly critical account of the Americans he met in
Europe: "There is but one word to use in regard to them –
vulgar; vulgar, vulgar. Their ignorance – their stingy, grudg-
ing, defiant, attitude towards everything European – their
perpetual reference of all things to some American standard
or precedent which exists only in their own unscrupulous
wind-bags – ... these things glare at you hideously."[1]
Nonetheless, after a few years abroad, James softened his
condemnation of Americans. He came to recognize that
citizens of the new world, himself included, were often
inclined to feel an uncritical reverence towards all aspects of
the old world. As early as 1872, he wrote to Charles Eliot
Norton: "It's a complex fate, being an American, and one of
the responsibilities it entails is fighting against a supersti-

---

[1] Henry James, Letter to Mrs. Henry James Sr., 13 Oct. 1869, *Letters*,
ed. Leon Edel (Cambridge, Mass.: Belknap, 1974), I, 152.

tious valuation of Europe."[1]

Coming from James, the last assertion may sound a bit unexpected. Of all American writers, surely James places the highest value on everything European. This is true, however, only in a special sense, for James's assessment of European society as literary material is not necessarily the same as his moral judgments of that society. In his fiction that treats the "international theme," James subjects European institutions and customs to a searching and at times critical examination. Indeed, in his international novels James habitually gives the moral upper hand to his American characters. Christopher Newman, for example, is shabbily treated by the de Bellegarde family. Yet when given the opportunity, Newman does not stoop to a petty, personal revenge. Although he has learned a discreditable fact about the de Bellegardes, he decides not to make his knowledge public.

Sara Jeannette Duncan is the Canadian writer in whose work we can find the closest parallel to James's treatment of the international theme. In fact, of all the writers who published fiction before the First World War, only Duncan consistently makes the contrast between European and North American societies a prominent feature of her work. No subsequent writer has attempted the detailed comparison of national cultures that Duncan offers in her best work, although perhaps some of Robertson Davies' work comes close to matching the Jamesian type of fiction that Duncan writes. Among contemporary writers, however, Davies is unique in the exaggerated deference he pays to almost all aspects of European culture. Although several major twentieth-century Canadian writers have started their careers with a bow towards Europe, in the end they have used their fiction to express their discovery that their deepest commitment is to their own continent, their own country, and their own community.

Duncan's first book, *A Social Departure: How Orthodocia and I Went Round the World by Ourselves* (1890), describes an unconventional journey around the world that Duncan undertook in company with a fellow journalist, Lily Lewis. In

---

[1] Henry James, Letter to Charles Eliot Norton, 4 Feb. 1872, *Letters*, I, 274.

a sense, since it describes visits to Japan and India, *A Social Departure* deals with the international theme on a global scale. But Duncan's view of non-Western societies is distinctly superficial. She remains locked within her Western prejudices, and gives what is really a tourist's patronizing account of quaint or picturesque local sights. *A Social Departure*, however, does announce one persistent feature of Duncan's writing: it deals with a contrast between two or more cultures.

On the Indian leg of her journey, Duncan met Everard Cotes, a museum official in Calcutta, whom she married in 1890. As a result, one of her favourite fictional subjects became the difficulties that confront members of the Anglo-Indian ruling class in British India. Her Anglo-Indian fiction, however, is not my concern here. I will deal only with those novels that in some way explore a contrast between British and North American societies. For the most part, these novels present simple versions of the international courtship story that James used so resourcefully in most of his international fiction. But in Duncan's hands, with only one exception, the international theme yields only a series of mildly amusing anecdotes that illustrate the more superficial aspects of upper-class social life on either side of the Atlantic.

The first of Duncan's international novels is *An American Girl in London* (1891), in which the heroine is an American heiress, Mamie Wick of Chicago. For the most part, the novel is a loosely connected series of incidents that highlight amusing peculiarities of British social life. The novel's climax turns specifically on the contrast between British reticence and American openness. Mamie learns that the self-effacing and helpful Mr. Mafferton has in fact been courting her, but his attentions have been so formal and proper that Mamie has not become aware of his feelings. For the most part Duncan's observations are no more penetrating than the following passage, in which Mamie Wick contrasts the sedateness of the pedestrians on a British street with the bustle that she attributes to Americans: "Hardly anybody was laughing, and very few people were making unseemly haste about their business. There was no eagerness and no enthusiasm. Neither was there any hustling. In a crowd like that in Chicago everybody would have hustled, and nobody would have minded it."[1] In a subsequent novel, *A Voyage of Consolation* (1898), Duncan takes Mamie Wick to the continent, and in another novel, *Those Delightful Americans* (1902), she reverses the direction of travel, and observes American life through the eyes of a visiting Englishwoman.

Only in *The Imperialist* (1904) and *Cousin Cinderella: A Canadian Girl in London* (1908), does Duncan expand her international contrasts to include Canada. *Cousin Cinderella* is merely another version of the Jamesian transatlantic love story. In *The Imperialist*, however, Duncan extends the range of her fiction far beyond the social trivialities that dominate her other international fiction. In this novel she deals with an entire society, not just with the leisure classes that her earlier international fiction had depicted. There are two romances in *The Imperialist*, but the love theme takes second place to Duncan's other concerns. Specifically, Duncan wants to show British readers what Canada's political outlook really is. She wants "to present the situation as it appears to the average Canadian of the average small town, inarticulate except at election times, but whose view in the end counts for more than that of those pictorial people whose speeches at Toronto banquets go so far to over-colour the British imagination about Canadian sentiment."[2] In fact, Duncan accomplishes much more than this. Her novel shows that Elgin's own manners and values are every bit as well established as those of British society.

Elgin, Ontario is meant to be a representative Canadian community. As Duncan's narrator remarks: "Elgin market square, indeed, was the biography of Fox County and, in little, the history of the whole Province" (p. 73). Duncan makes it clear that Elgin's interests are determinedly parochial. "The politics of Elgin's daily absorption," she remarks, "were those of the town, the Province, the Dominion" (p. 59) – and probably in that order of interest. Elgin has little time for the higher or non-utilitarian aspects of

---

[1] Sara Jeannette Duncan, *An American Girl in London* (New York: Appleton, 1891), p. 27.

[2] Quoted by Francis Zichy, "Sara Jeannette Duncan," in Jeffrey M. Heath, ed., *Profiles in Canadian Literature*, I (Toronto: Dundurn, 1980), 39.

civilized culture: "The arts conspired to be absent; letters resided at the nearest university city; science was imported as required, in practical improvements. There was nothing, indeed, to interfere with Elgin's attention to the immediate, the vital, the municipal" (p. 60). In this environment, idealists such as Lorne and Advena Murchison are not appreciated at their true worth, for they are so obviously different from the majority of the town's inhabitants, "and a difference is the one thing a small community, accustomed comfortably to scan its own intelligible averages, will not tolerate" (p. 44). Yet Duncan does not condemn Elgin. The town's faults are merely the natural drawbacks of its newness, inseparable from the drive that has made Elgin a rising commercial centre. Throughout the novel, in scene after scene, Duncan illustrates how characters who consciously espouse the old conservative values and who profess to admire all things British actually live their lives by the new liberal American standards. In its public professions Elgin is enthusiastically pro-British, and its society preserves social distinctions of a nicety that "may not be easily appreciated by people accustomed to the rough and ready standards of a world at the other end of the Grand Trunk" (p. 14) – that is, in the United States. Yet when Canada meets England, in the form of Alfred Hesketh, Esquire, Canada shows itself to have distinctly democratic social attitudes. For example, Hesketh feels a momentary hesitation when he discovers that he is expected to treat Lorne Murchison's father, a tradesman, as an equal. In addition, Duncan makes it clear that Canada, as represented by the electors of rural South Fox, finds Hesketh's campaign speech too full of offensive words like "colony." Hesketh, says Duncan's narrator, makes "too many allusions to the nobility for a community so far removed from its soothing influence" (p. 195). One quick-witted member of the audience pointedly asks him: "Had ye no friends among the commoners?" (p. 195). Hesketh's audience are not Americans, but neither are they Englishmen. They are really "democrats who had never thrown off the monarch – what harm did he do there overseas?" (p. 191). The qualification is significant. If the monarchy did interfere, it would soon be gone.

Probably the figure in the book who is most representative of the Canadian outlook is Octavius Milburn, the
President of the Elgin Chamber of Commerce. Mr. Milburn
"had inherited the complacent and Conservative political
views of a tenderly nourished industry" (p. 52). We are told:
"His ideal was life in a practical, go-ahead, self-governing
colony, far enough from England actually to be disabused of
her inherited anachronisms and make your own tariff, near
enough politically to keep your securities up by virtue of her
protection" (p. 51). Although Mr. Milburn has often said
"that he preferred a fair living under his own flag to a
fortune under the Stars and Stripes" (p. 51), his loyalty to
Britain does not extend as far as renouncing the known
commercial advantage of the National Policy for the unknown and problematical benefits of expanded imperial
trade. No amount of rhetoric by the Lorne Murchisons of the
country can alter his dollars and cents calculations: "Mr.
Milburn wouldn't say that this preference trade idea, if
practicable, might not work out for the benefit of the Empire
as a whole. That was a thing he didn't pretend to know. But
it wouldn't work out for his benefit – that was a thing he did
know" (p. 212).

Lorne Murchison overcomes the bad impression made by
Alfred Hesketh's speech "by the simple expedient of talking
business" (p. 195). Later in his election campaign, however,
Lorne is not so astute. He believes, as he tells Dora Milburn,
that England has "developed the finest human product there
is, the cleanest, the most disinterested, and we want to keep
up the relationship – it's important" (p. 98). He becomes
infatuated with his own imperialist rhetoric, and eventually,
as his opponents gleefully notice, he puts "sentiment in
politics" (p. 207), making him a ready target for satire. When
he is dropped as his party's candidate in the new election,
Lorne is told that he "didn't get rid of that save-the-Em-
pire-or-die scheme" soon enough: " 'The popular idea seems
to be,' said Mr Farquharson judicially, 'that you would not
hesitate to put Canada to some material loss, or at least to
postpone her development in various important directions,
for the sake of the imperial connection' " (p. 262). Farquharson is saying that Lorne, in his youthful idealism, carries
things too far. Putting principle before material advantage

would, in the view of both political parties, be an unforgivable sin.

Even Lorne Murchison, however, finds that his loyalty to England is stronger at a distance. In fact, as a result of his visit to England, Lorne acquires a more self-conscious awareness of his Canadian identity. Lorne, "with his soul full of free airs and forest depths," is depressed by the pitifully confined open spaces of a London park, which are the nearest approach to the countryside that London can offer its residents for a Sunday outing. Lorne and the other members of his party find that the self-absorption of the English people and the country's "cumbrous social machinery, oppressed them with its dull anachronism in a marching world." North Americans, says Duncan, have acquired "that new quality in the blood which made them different" from Englishmen (pp. 125-26). In fact, Duncan's entire novel is an astute portrait of a society that is developing a now social fabric, a society in the process of dropping its allegiance to British customs and adopting the customs of the new world.

After the First World War there was a striking change in the nature of trans Atlantic literary relations. North American writers no longer went to Europe primarily in order to become reacquainted with their cultural heritage. In part, they went abroad for the practical reason that the cost of living was low in postwar Europe. In addition, they found that in Europe they did not have to apologize or feel defensive about being artists. But, although they had escaped from the philistine culture of America, the members of the lost generation remained unabashedly North American in their work. That is, although many of them wrote fiction set in Europe, they no longer made detailed cultural comparisons in the Jamesian manner. As Stephen Spender remarks: "In American novels of the 'twenties which have European settings, the main characters are Americans, and the Europeans have only walking-on and sleeping-with parts."[1] Canadian authors, however, show a greater deference to the traditional prestige of European culture. Especially in the

---

[1] Stephen Spender, *Love-Hate Relations: A Study of Anglo-American Sensibilities* (London: Hamish Hamilton, 1974), p. xvii.

works of Hugh MacLennan, Mordecai Richler, and Robertson Davies, a continuing effort to come to terms with the cultural authority of Europe is visible.

In the immediate postwar years, however, the most important Canadian writers who made the pilgrimage to Paris were Morley Callaghan and John Glassco. Leon Edel, himself another of these literary pilgrims, has said of this group: "We were all very pleased because we had fled the lingering Victorianism in Canada and found ourselves youthful members of the literary avant-garde."[1] But Edel points out that Callaghan's outlook differed from the outlook of Glassco and his friend Graeme Taylor. Edel says of Callaghan: "I found him very young, very robust, *very* Toronto, and thus foreign to the insouciant hedonism of the young Montrealers" (p. x). In other words, Callaghan never became a true part of the artistic Bohemia that the North American expatriates created in Paris. As a result, the primness of Callaghan's account of his time in Europe, *That Summer in Paris* (1963), contrasts sharply with the raunchiness of Glassco's *Memoirs of Montparnasse* (1970). It would be unthinkable for Callaghan to confess, as Glassco happily announces, that his "first experience of a French prostitute was a revelation. I had, quite simply, never enjoyed myself so much in my life" (p. 86). Hugh MacLennan and Robertson Davies later made sojourns to Europe, after which they returned to the places where they were to set the bulk of their fiction.

After the Second World War, a new group of young authors made the journey to Europe. Mordecai Richler, Norman Levine, and Mavis Gallant are the most prominent of these later expatriates. Gallant is the prime example of an expatriate writer who has preferred Europe to her homeland. Despite Gallant's recent return to Canada, her subject-matter remains predominantly international. Linnet Muir, Gallant's most autobiographical protagonist, announces at one point: "I did not feel a scrap British or English, but I was not

---

[1] Leon Edel, "Introduction," in John Glassco, *Memoirs of Montparnasse* (Toronto: Oxford Univ. Press, 1970), p. viii. All further references to this work appear in the text.

an American either."[1] Yet neither is Linnet Muir conspicuously Canadian. Indeed, whether Gallant's stories are set in Europe, the United States, or Canada, her characters all seem rootless; their background gives them no stable values or secure sense of identity. Gallant does not write about coming home, but about having no home. In the work of Mordecai Richler aand Norman Levine, on the other hand, Canada has retained a special importance. Joseph Grand, the autobiographical protagonist of *From a Seaside Town* (1970), discovers that, although he has gone to England to live, he cannot leave his past life behind. In fact, a great deal of Levine's work has examined his enduring ties to his family and to his childhood in Ottawa's Lower Town. Similarly, Richler has written: "No matter how long I continue to live abroad, I do feel forever rooted in Montreal's St. Urbain Street. That was my time, my place, and I have elected myself to get it right."[6]

The two World Wars forced many North Americans to reconsider their view of Europe as the repository of the best features of Western civilization. As Mordecai Richler has remarked: "We've lived through two great horrors, in our time, the murder of the Jews and Hiroshima, and the rest disappears. This is what we lived through in our time and one must, you know, figure out where he stands in relation to it just as at one time you had to figure out where you stood in relation to the Communist Party."[7] Richler has remarked that "the holocaust . . . is at the very core of most serious Jewish writing since the war."[8] Certainly, this statement is true of his own work. A similar preoccupation with Europe's violent recent history is evident in Henry Kreisel's two novels, *The Rich Man* (1948) and *The Betrayal* (1964), as well as in a series of novels by writers who took part in the

---

[1] Mavis Gallant, "In Youth is Pleasure," in *Home Truths: Selected Canadian Stories* (Toronto: Macmillan, 1981), p. 220.

[2] Mordecai Richler, "Why I Write," in *Shovelling Trouble* (Toronto: McClelland and Stewart, 1972), p. 19.

[3] Donald Cameron, *Conversations with Canadian Novelists: Part Two* (Toronto: Macmillan, 1973), p. 125.

[4] Mordecai Richler, "The Holocaust and After," in *Shovelling Trouble*, p. 95.

Second World War: Earle Birney's *Turvey* (1949), Colin McDougall's *Execution* (1958), and Douglas LePan's *The Deserter* (1964). More recently, Timothy Findley has examined humanity's destructive impulse in *The Wars* (1977). In *Famous Last Words* (1981) he has explored the contradictions that exist in a culture that can produce both high art and excessive violence. Yet for some writers Europe remained the home of Western culture, the place where art and artists are treated with a respect they do not receive in pragmatic North America. More persistently than any other of our writers, Hugh MacLennan and Mordecai Richler have wrestled with this apparent contradiction, as they struggled to reconcile the violence of modern European history with Europe's traditional role as the source of Western culture.

The chaos that overtook European society in the aftermath of the First World War is prominently featured in the two unpublished novels that MacLennan wrote during the thirties. Both of these novels resemble the book that Paul Tallard unsuccessfully attempts to write in *Two Solitudes* (1945). Paul's novel is called *Young Man of 1933*, and it is about "a young man caught between the old war that was history and the new one whose coming was so certain it make the present look like the past even before it had been lived through."[7] Eventually, Paul realizes that the underlying conception of his novel is not in keeping with his desire to celebrate human individuality, for by writing about socially significant issues he has created characters who are dominated by circumstances – and whose fates are shaped by conditions in the old world. As Neil Macrae does in *Barometer Rising* (1941), Paul turns away from the old world and its failures to the new world and its buoyant aspirations.

In *Barometer Rising* the First World War awakens Halifax from its long nineteenth-century sleep. Prewar Halifax is still an outpost of the waning British Empire. Uncle Albert and Aunt Maria are characters left over from the Victorian era. The Wains are an old-fashioned extended family, which seeks to retain control over its younger generation. In *Two Solitudes* MacLennan creates similar

---

[1] MacLennan, *Two Solitudes*, p. 333. All further references to this work appear in the text.

portraits of the restrictive traditional society that exists in both rural Quebec and the Montreal business community. But in both novels MacLennan shows a far-reaching social change taking place during and after the First World War. In both Halifax and Montreal, the younger generation are adapting themselves to the new reality of a world dominated by technology. Penny Wain and Neil Macrae are both gifted ship designers. Paul Tallard combines a knowledge of classical literature with a scientific education. Early in *Two Solitudes*, Canada is described as the place where two "old races and religions meet ... and live their separate legends, side by side" (p. 2) However, the book holds out the hope that the hatreds inherited from the European past may be bridged by a new generation of Canadians, more open to the possibilities of the future. Late in the novel Paul sees a group of workers in an all-night restaurant as a symbol of the coming reconciliation: "They were relaxed and easy with each other, French and English together, radio technicians, theatre operators, telegraphers, men who had walked up from the railroad stations. None of them seemed worried or strained. They were together because of the nature of their jobs, and because the rest of the city was asleep" (p. 375). At the end of the novel Paul thinks that the country has taken "the first irrevocable steps towards becoming herself"; the people are realizing that they are "alone with history, with science, with the future" (p. 412).

Recently, in *Voices in Time* (1980), MacLennan seems to have returned to the preoccupations of his early, unpublished fiction. The atomic catastrophe that MacLennan imagines in *Voices in Time* might seem to express a deep pessimism about the future of North American civilization, which has become infected with the sickness of European society. But MacLennan's novel also shows a younger generation at work building a new society out of the ruins of the old one. MacLennan, then, appears to think that a purified European civilization may yet be created in the new world.

Like MacLennan, Mordecai Richler began his literary career by writing about Europe. In four of Richler's novels – *The Acrobats* (1954), *A Choice of Enemies* (1957), *St. Urbain's Horseman* (1971), and *Joshua Then and Now* (1980) – the protagonist's journey to Europe plays an important part in

the action. Another novel, *Son of a Smaller Hero* (1955), ends
with the departure of its protagonist on such a journey. In
these novels, many of Richler's characters are haunted by
sinister figures associated in some way with Nazi Germany.
In order to make peace with themselves, Richler's characters
must reach an accommodation with these figures, who are
really embodiments of the dark side of their own nature. For
example, André Bennett in *The Acrobats* is haunted by
Colonel Kraus. Before André dies he has a moment of insight
in which he associates Kraus with the most shameful episode
from his own past. In this way, André finally acknowledges
his own dark side. In *A Choice of Enemies* Norman Price
eventually says of the German refugee Ernst Haupt, who
unintentionally killed Norman's brother Nicky: "wherever he
is let him go in peace. Let him be."[1] The case of Jake Hersh is
more complicated. Throughout most of the novel Jake imagines that his brother Joey is an avenging Nazi-hunter, the
relentless pursuer of the notorious Dr. Mengele. Near the
end of the novel, when Jake receives news of Joey's death, he
must himself take on the role of the Horseman. This does not
mean that Jake will turn into a bloodthirsty Jewish avenger;
it simply means that he will at last assume full responsibility
for making his own moral judgments – a responsibility he
has hitherto avoided by fantasizing about his missing brother.

If the Second World War and the holocaust are Richler's
version of the Fall, then his Eden is a prewar world in which
political choices seemed transparently simple and inevitable.
For several of Richler's protagonists, notably for André
Bennett, Norman Price, Jake Hersh, and Joshua Shapiro,
this simpler and more comprehensible world is located in the
era of the Spanish Civil War. In *A Choice of Enemies*, for
example, we learn that Norman Price's father, a Montreal
surgeon, was killed in the Spanish conflict. Yet Norman
looks back to this era without bitterness, indeed with
nostalgia for a time when the world seemed to make more
sense: "in those days, Norman remembered fondly, the choice

---

[1] Mordecai Richler, *A Choice of Enemies*, New Canadian Library, No.
136 (Toronto: McClelland and Stewart, 1977), p. 215. All further
references to this work appear in the text.

of enemies had been clear. Today you were no longer altogether sure" (p. 62). And Richler tells us: "When John Osborne's Jimmy Porter, in *Look Back in Anger*, mourned that there were no more good, clean causes left, Joshua glowed in his Royal Court seat, nodding yes, yes, but once there was Spain."[1] Joshua has also expressed his nostalgia for this period by writing *The Volunteers*, a book about the North Americans who fought on the republican side in Spain.

As the epigraph for his second novel, *Son of a Smaller Hero*, Richler uses Dostoyevsky's remark that if God does not exist, then everything is lawful. Most of the protagonists in his fiction face a modern version of this dilemma, for Richler has never stopped exploring the plight of man who is at sea in a world where traditional moral standards have become unfashionable. As Chaim says of André Bennett in *The Acrobats*, "he knows and understands all the things that he is against, but he still doesn't know what he is *for*."[2]

Richler's major protagonists all have difficulty in finding a set of values that will bring a satisfying moral order into their lives. In Richler's world, adherence to any of the existing systems of values usually implies support of a specific political cause or membership in a particular ethnic community. As Richler points out in *A Choice of Enemies*, such groups are defined as much by what they oppose as by what they stand for. In this novel Richler suggests that the choice of enemies has become more a matter of convenience that a matter of morality: by choosing the same enemy as others have chosen, you solidify your membership in your own social group. Therefore, as Sally MacPherson notices, there is really little difference between Norman Price's left-wing friends and their right-wing opponents: "It seemed to Sally that Norman and his friends were not, as they supposed, non-conformists, but conformists to another rule" (p. 42).

Since they cannot rely on traditional inherited standards, each of Richler's protagonists must seek out his own values. This is what Norman Price eventually realizes he must do: "If there was a time to man the barricades, Norman thought,

---

[1] Mordecai Richler, *Joshua Then and Now* (Toronto: Seal, 1981), p. 197.

[2] Mordecai Richler, *The Acrobats* (New York: Putnam's, 1954), p. 36.

then there is also a time to weed one's private garden. The currency of revolution is invalid as long as both tyrannies bank big bombs .... All alliances had been discredited. The enemy was the hit-and-run driver of both sides. . . . His cause was just. He knew what was good for you and he was above small virtues" (p. 215). Norman's comments anticipate Jake Hersh's deprecating self-assessment in *St. Urbain's Horseman*: "What Jake stood for would not fire the countryside: decency, tolerance, honor. With E.M. Forster, he wearily offered two cheers for democracy. After George Orwell, he was for a closer look at anybody's panacea. Jake was a liberal."[11] Cultivating your own private garden, as Jake recognizes, may not yield a life that is very impressive to other people. Nonetheless, Jake does his best to live with decency in a difficult time. He tries not to betray his personal standards.

In *St. Urbain's Horseman* Jake Hersh's view of Europe is complicated by feelings that arise from his Canadian origins. Richler attributes to Jake an attitude that he remembers from his own childhood: "We were governed by Ottawa, we were also British subjects, but our true capital was certainly New York. Success was (and still is) acceptance by the United States."[12] Consequently, as Richler tells us: "Jake, Luke, and others of their generation were reared to believe in the cultural thinness of their own blood. Anemia was their heritage" (p. 182). Once they reach London, Luke and Jake feel doubly inferior. Not only are they colonials, but also they lack the moral cachet that comes from a history of colonial oppression. They feel out of place "amid so many exiles from nineteenth century tyranny, heirs to injustices that could actually be set right politically, thereby lending themselves to constructive angers" (p. 182).

In *St. Urbain's Horseman* Jake is ostensibly on trial for sexual peccadillos committed when he unexpectedly walked in on the activities of Harry Stein and the compliant *au pair* girl Ingrid Loebner. But for Jake, the trial involves larger

---

[1]Mordecai Richler, *St. Urbain's Horseman* (Toronto: Bantam, 1972), p. 287. All further references to this work appear in the text.

[2]Mordecai Richler, *The Street* (Toronto: McClelland and Stewart, 1969), p. 59.

154

issues: "What he couldn't satisfactorily explain to Nancy was that he was more exhilarated than depressed by the trial because at last the issues had been joined. Joined, after a fashion" (p. 81). For Jake, the Canadian, the trial provides a way of measuring his moral worth against the standards used in the most famous seat of British justice, the Old Bailey. Jake feels he has evaded all the important moral issues of his time:

> Wrong place, wrong time. Young too late, old too soon was, as Jake had come to understand it, the plaintive story of his American generation. Conceived in the depression, but never to taste its bitterness firsthand, they had actually contrived to sail through the Spanish Civil War, World War II, the holocaust, Hiroshima, the Israeli War of Independence, McCarthyism, Korea, and, latterly, Vietnam and the drug culture, with impunity. (p. 80)

But after the trial, when Jake has protected the repellent Harry Stein – who nonetheless represents the darker side of Jake's own personality – he can tell himself: "The trial's over, Yankel. You did not behave badly" (p. 430). In addition, after the trial Luke Scott invites Jake to direct his latest script. And Jake, after some vacillation, agrees. These two Canadians have finally learned to trust each other's talents. However tentatively, they finally see themselves as the equals of any European artist.

The publication of *St. Urbain's Horseman*, then, was Richler's assertion that his own work measured up to international standards. After making this declaration, he no longer felt compelled to remain in England. In 1972, Richler and his family moved to Canada, and his next novel, *Joshua Then and Now*, centres on Montreal rather than on London. Like Jake Hersh, Joshua is obsessed with recent events in European history, though his attention focuses on the Spanish Civil War rather than the holocaust. But Europe plays a relatively small part in this novel. When Joshua revisits Spain, foolishly seeking to atone for what he sees as his youthful cowardice, he finds that his gesture is completely unnecessary. The once-threatening Dr. Mueller now

155

seems a comic figure; the Freibergs were never in danger of losing their hotel. Joshua realizes, almost too late, that his real testing-place is Montreal, where his wife is undergoing a nervous breakdown. Like Jake Hersh, Joshua has married a *shiksa*, a girl from Westmount. And during Joshua's difficulties, both his father, a former boxer and small-time hoodlum, and his father-in-law, a former Member of Parliament and now a Senator, rally to Joshua's defense. This Jewish-Wasp family solidarity seems to indicate that Richler himself has now become reconciled to the two ghettos – the Jewish and the Canadian – from which he once tried to free himself.

The last writer whose response to Europe I want to examine at length is Robertson Davies. As a young man, Davies has reported, he sometimes "fretted against the ill-fitting clothes that – in a cultural sense – we all [in Canada] seemed to be wearing .... In modern terms, I wondered, why isn't Canada getting a piece of the action? And like thousands of young Canadians, when the time came I tried to solve the problem by leaving Canada and going to where the action seemed to be."[1] Davies studied at Oxford, and then he spent a brief period working in the London theatre. When he returned to Canada in 1940, Davies still hoped to write plays for the British stage, and for a long time he considered himself primarily a dramatist rather than a novelist. Although my concern in this study is with the development of Canadian fiction, I want to consider Davies' plays as well as his novels, because the novels deal with themes that found their first expression in the plays.

During the 1940s, when British theatrical companies showed little interest in performing his plays, Davies began to tailor his writing to the amateur companies that were available in Canada. He wrote a number of one-act plays, pieces with small casts and simple settings. Such works were eminently suitable for entry in the Dominion Drama Festival, the pinnacle of Canadian theatrical life at that time. Not surprisingly, the first play Davies wrote for Canadian performance was a vigorous indictment of his country's impoverished cultural life. *Hope Deferred* (1945) opens as

---

[1] Robertson Davies, "The Canada of Myth and Reality," in *One Half of Robertson Davies* (Toronto: Macmillan, 1977), p. 283.

Frontenac, the Governor of New France, is welcoming the return to Quebec of Chimène, a native girl whom he had sent to France to be educated. In France Chimène has undergone a surprising transformation, for there she has been exposed to the French classics and trained as an actress. Frontenac now plans to use her talents to bring high culture to the rude society of New France, proposing to start with a performance of Molière's *Tartuffe*. This plan, however, is opposed by the colony's religious authorities, and in the ensuing test of influence Frontenac is defeated. Chimène decides to return to France, where her newly acquired talents will be properly appreciated.

The outlook expressed in this play is cultural snobbery at its most blatant. European culture is presented as wholly admirable, in fact as a necessary attribute of any civilized society. For example, Frontenac pours scorn on Chimène's state before she was exposed to French culture: "your ambition was to grow fat so that some young Huron would love you and let you carry his pack for him."[8] When he is asked to cancel his plans to perform *Tartuffe*, Frontenac angrily exclaims: "Are you asking me to reduce the intellectual tone of this whole country to what is fit for Indians and shopkeepers?" (p. 70). Although *Hope Deferred* is set in the colonial era, the play expresses Davies' view of the cultural backwardness of his own time. Canada, Davies feels, is dominated by a rigorous and unimaginative puritanism, which can only be redeemed by an infusion of European sophistication. As he yields to the church's wishes, Frontenac laments: "There is no tyranny like that of organized virtue" (p. 76). Chimène tells Bishop Laval that he is wrong to want only virtue for New France, "because goodness without the arts demands a simplicity bordering on the idiotic. A simple man without the arts is a clod, or a saint, or a bigot: saints are very rare: clods and bigots are many. Are you trying to put my country into their hands?" (p. 74).

In *Overlaid* (1946), another early one-act play, Davies portrays the cultural poverty of a society that been ruled by

---

[1] Robertson Davies, *Hope Deferred* in *Eros at Breakfast and Other Plays* (Toronto: Clarke, Irwin, 1949), p. 58. All further references to this work appear in the text.

precepts that are narrowly pragmatic and moralistic. This limited outlook is embodied in Pop's daughter Ethel, an "emotionally understimulated" woman whose secret ambition is to purchase a massive granite tombstone for the family plot. Ethel is challenged by her eccentric father, whose rebellion takes the form of listening to the Metropolitan Opera broadcast each Saturday afternoon, while wearing a comical burlesque of formal dress. An unexpected windfall from a forgotten insurance policy precipitates a power struggle between Pop and Ethel. Pop wants to use the money to make a journey to New York, where he will indulge the side of his nature that his local culture has starved:

> I'll tell you what I'd do, since you're so nosey: I'd get some stylish clothes, and I'd go into one o' these restrunts, and I'd order vittles you never heard of – better'n the burnt truck Ethel calls food – and I'd get a bottle o' wine – cost a dollar, maybe two – and drink it all, and then I'd mosey along to the Metropolitan Opera House and I'd buy me a seat right down beside the trap-drummer and there I'd sit an' listen, and holler and hoot and raise hell whenever I liked the music, an' throw bookies to the gals, an' wink at the chorus, and when it was over I'd go to one o' these here night-clubs an' eat some more, an' drink whisky, and watch the gals that take off their clothes – every last dud, kinda slow an' devilish till they're bare-naked – an' maybe I'd give one of 'em fifty bucks for her brazeer – [1]

In the end, however, Ethel wins out over Pop, who announces that he has been "overlaid" by Ethel's morality. As Pop resigns his dream, he admits: "There's a special kind o' power that comes from the belief that you're right. Whether you really are right or not doesn't matter: it's the belief that counts" (p. 108).

Additional studies of Canada's cultural impoverishment

---

[1] Robertson Davies, *At My Heart's Core and Overlaid* (Toronto: Clarke, Irwin, 1966), p. 98. All further references to this work appear in the text.

are contained in several of Davies' later full-length plays. In
At My Heart's Core (1950), for example, Davies explores the
historical origins of our cultural limitations. Phelim, the
irresponsible Irish storyteller, sadly compares Canada with
the old world:

> In the old land, now, I could get a fine living; sure,
> the people were that wretched they'd be glad of a tale
> or a song to beguile them from hunger and the
> thoughts of death and injustice. but here the poorest
> ruffian of them all has his bit o' land, and his pig,
> maybe, and the ones with good arms and good heads
> on them is thrivin' so fast they never feel the need of
> a story at all. They're not the same people I knew,
> God help them. They're a strange lot entirely, with
> the blush o' health on their cheeks and the maggot o'
> respectability in their brains. (p. 27)

Fortune, My Foe (1948) presents a more contemporary study
of Canada's cultural poverty. This time European culture is
embodied in the puppets created by the Hungarian immigrant Franz Szabo, and Canada's dominant culture is represented by the civic officials who want to make his art a
means of imparting didactic messages to children.

In the novels of the Salterton trilogy, Davies again
explores the cultural deficiencies of Canadian society. In
Tempest-Tost (1951) the most deprived figure is Hector
McIlwraith, a schoolmaster whose faith in reason has stunt-
ed his emotional development. Many of the novel's characters
are condemned by their failure to measure up to the roles
they play in an amateur production of Shakespeare's *The
Tempest*. The only truly self-possessed characters have
attained their knowledge and maturity elsewhere:
Humphrey Cobbler in England and Valentine Rich in New
York. In *Leaven of Malice* (1954) Humphrey Cobbler is again
prominent. His eccentric escapades not only provide farcical
comedy; they also demonstrate that Cobbler is a free man in
a way that most of the novel's other characters are not. Solly
Bridgetower and Pearl Vambrace are dominated by oppressive parents; Puss Pottinger is governed by absurd social
conventions; Bevill Higgin is ruled by a malicious spirit of

revenge; and even Gloster Ridley, until late in the novel, places an overly high valuation on the honorary degree he hopes to receive from Waverley University.

All three of the Salterton novels can be viewed as illustrations of a distinction that Sir Benedict Domdaniel makes in *A Mixture of Frailties* (1958). "There are, the world over," Sir Benedict tells Monica Gall, "only two important political parties – the people who are for life, and the people who are against it .... I'm an Eros man myself, and most people who are any good for anything, in the arts or wherever, belong to the Eros party. But there are Thanatossers everywhere – the Permanent Opposition."[1] Hector McIlwraith is the leading Thanatosser in *Tempest-Tost*, as his attempted suicide indicates. The domineering parents of Pearl and Solly are the worst examples in *Leaven of Malice*. In *A Mixture of Frailties*, the Thirteeners, a fundamentalist group to which Monica's parents belong, substitute a narrow set of prohibitions for genuine spirituality. Sir Benedict later suggests that Monica "has obviously been in contact with a lot of these crypto-Thanatossers – probably educated by them, insofar as you have been educated at all" (p. 108). But in these novels Davies does hold out some hope for Canadian society. Hector McIlwraith is not entirely without feelings – he attempts suicide, after all, only because he cannot deal with his newly awakened emotions. Pearl Vambrace and Solly Bridgetower finally decide to marry, in spite of their parents' opposition. And Monica Gall is liberated from her barren environment.

Much more openly that either of its Salterton predecessors, *A Mixture of Frailties* centres on the importance of artistic culture. When Sir Benedict Domdaniel first hears Monica Gall sing, he tells the Bridgetower trustees: "the great thing that seems to be wrong with her, considered as a possible artist, is [not] that she has lived for twenty years in circumstances which are . . . discouraging to art – . . . but in which art in any of its forms is not even guessed at" (p. 55). So Monica must go to Europe to be educated as an artist. But

---

[1] Robertson Davies, *A Mixture of Frailties*, Laurentian Library, No. 7 (Toronto: Macmillan, 1968), p. 108. All further references to this work appear in the text.

160

Monica's training involves much more than merely acquiring a good singing technique. In addition to her musical studies, Sir Benedict prescribes a crash course in the entire European cultural heritage. Monica must also learn what it means to be a true artist. Sir Benedict tells her that there are two kinds of singer: the self-centred prima donna and the "bardic singer" who effaces herself in favour of the music itself. "With the bardic singer, the music comes first, and self quite a long way second" (p. 107). Eventually, she finds that music satisfies her "yearning toward all the vast, inexplicable, irrational treasury from which her life drew whatever meaning and worth it possessed" (p. 311). In other words, through her training in European classical music Monica has acquired the spiritual insight that Davies sees as the highest goal of art.

Davies' place in Canadian literature rests above all on *Fifth Business* (1970). It is certainly likely that Davies' use of familiar Canadian themes in this novel helps to explain its popularity with Canadian readers. It is also possible, I suggest, that these familiar, yet highly charged, materials helped Davies to produce his best writing. I am not trying to argue the crudely nationalist position here. I do not mean that *Fifth Business* is a good novel simply because it deal with themes that are common in other Canadian novels. I think, however, that Davies may have been spurred to achieve his best work by the fact that he was drawing, for once, upon the full resources of his own country's literary and cultural traditions. Certainly, the resulting novel has a special resonance for Canadian readers.

Magnus Eisengrim expresses one of the major themes of *Fifth Business* when he explains his *Soirée of Illusions* to Dunstan: "nowadays the theatre has almost abandoned charm; actors want to be sweaty and real, playwrights want to scratch their scabs in public. Very well; it is in the mood of the times. But there is always another mood, one precisely contrary to what seems to be the fashion. Nowadays this concealed longing is for romance and marvels" (p. 244). Only in *Fifth Business*, I think, has Davies successfully made his own country a place of romance and mystery. Dunstan Ramsay is the first of Davies' characters to complete a heroic inner struggle in a Canadian setting. Although Dunstan does go to Europe and Latin America to acquire knowledge of the saints, he finds his own personal saint, Mary Dempster, in his childhood village. When Liesl asks Dunstan how he proposes to get young Paul Dempster out of Canada and "into a country where big spiritual adventures are possible" (p. 256), the dismissal of Canada should be attributed to Liesl's European cultural snobbery rather than to Davies's own prejudices. For by this stage in the novel Dunstan has already learned that "big spiritual adventures" are possible in Canada. In the remaining two books of the Deptford trilogy, however, Davies returns to the idea that Europe is the place where spiritual quests are best carried out.

The Manticore (1972) begins where *Fifth Business* ends, with the scene in the Royal Alexandra Theatre during which a voice shouts out, "Who killed Boy Staunton?" As the Brazen Head speaks its reply, Dunstan has his heart attack, and – we now learn – Boy Staunton's son, David Staunton, having shocked himself by blurting out the question, hastily retreats from the theatre. Upset by his conduct, David conducts "the usual examination" of his own state of mind.[1] The result, some readers may think, is extreme. David immediately flies to Zurich and presents himself as a prospective patient at the Jung Institute. Just consider this sequence of events. As soon as David Staunton meets a situation that is beyond his control, he flees to Europe, the cradle of Western civilization. Only in Europe, it seems, can the wounds that Canada has inflicted on his psyche be healed.

Fifth Business contains, in Boy Staunton, an example of the spiritual atrophy that Davies feels is caused by North American materialism. To his son David, Boy Staunton has always seemed to radiate self-assurance, and throughout his life David has been flaying himself because he feels he hasn't measured up to his father's standards. But during his Jungian analysis with Joanna von Haller, David comes to understand both himself and his father better. He realizes that Boy unconsciously recognized the void within himself when he launched a genealogical inquiry into the Staunton

---

[1] Robertson Davies, *The Manticore* (Toronto: Macmillan, 1972), p. 1. All further references to this work appear in the text.

family's origins. This search was intended to provide ancestors who would compensate for Boy's sense of personal incompleteness. As Adrian Pledger-Brown explains to David:

> "so many of you New World people, up to the eyebrows in all the delights of republicanism, hanker after a link with what is ancient and rubbed by time to a fine sheen. It's more than snobbery; more than romanticism; it's a desire for an ancestry that somehow postulates a posterity and for an existence in the past that is a covert guarantee of immortality in the future. You talk about individualism; what you truly want is to be links in a long unbroken chain." (pp. 233-34)

Boy, however, could never see himself as part of something that transcends his individual being. Boy's strained efforts to acquire the trappings that he feels should go with wealth contrast with the effortless culture displayed by Judy Wolff's family, who are European Jews: "There was a sophistication in that house that was a continual refreshment to me. Not painted on, you know, but rising from within" (p. 145).

In *World of Wonders* (1975) Europe is again the location of the mystery that the hero must seek out to make himself whole. In North America Paul Dempster learns the mechanics of sleight-of-hand manipulation from the vulgar Willard. But in order to be initiated into the spiritual meaning of his vocation, he must go to Europe and be reborn as the disciple of the romantic actor Sir John Tresize. The audience that Davies assembles to hear Magnus Eisengrim's confessions contains three Europeans and only one Canadian. In addition to Liesl, the Europeans are the Bergman-like film director Jurgen Lind and the BBC executive Roland Ingestree. The Canadian is, of course, Dunstan Ramsay. But the Dunstan of *World of Wonders* is a pale shadow of the opinionated student of myth who speaks to us in *Fifth Business*. Now that Dunstan is a permanent guest at Sorgenfrei, Liesl's Swiss chateau, he has degenerated into a conventional historian, hot on the trail of the very sort of factual accuracy that he previously denounced. "Give me a document, every time,"[1] this new Dunstan says. Surely this is a false note, out of keeping with everything we learned of Dunstan in *Fifth Business*.

In *World of Wonders* Eisengrim describes a tour of Canada undertaken by Sir John Tresize's company. Sir John's personal acting style, as well as his company's repertoire, was considered passé in London and New York. But in Canada Sir John still drew substantial and appreciative audiences. Eisengrim says that Sir John was popular, not because Canadians were unsophisticated, but because his romantic theatre "was speaking to a core of loneliness and deprivation in these Canadians of which they were only faintly aware. I think it was loneliness, not just for England, because so many of these people on the prairies were not of English origin, but for some faraway and long-lost Europe. The Canadians knew themselves to be strangers in their own land, without being at home anywhere else" (pp. 292-93). Here, in a nutshell, is Davies's recurrent assessment of Canadian culture. It is a partial culture – a culture too exclusively concerned with pragmatic and material things. Canadians do not feel at home in their own land because it does not nourish all aspects of the human spirit. The Canadians who yearned for "some faraway and long-lost Europe" were not homesick in any literal sense. Rather, they yearned to be part of a culture that would feed all aspects of their nature. In Davies's view, I am arguing, such cultural wholeness is usually found in a European setting.

In *The Manticore*, for example, David Staunton is engaged in the same quest that Davies assigns to all of his major protagonists: the search for one's inner self. Davies might argue that self-exploration is a universal theme; the geographical location of the spiritual voyager is an secondary feature of his adventures. Certainly, David's journey to Zurich becomes a metaphor for his journey into the recesses of his own personality. But David's quest is specifically described by Joanna von Haller as a search for an alternative

---

[1] Robertson Davies, *World of Wonders* (Toronto: Macmillan, 1975), p. 63. All further references to this work appear in the text.

to North American values, when she warns David to put aside his North American notion that individual happiness is the ultimate goal of life:

"You New World people are, what is the word, hipped on the idea of happiness, as if it were a constant and measurable thing, and settled and excused every- thing. If it is anything at all it is a by-product of other conditions of life, and some people whose lives do not appear to be at all enviable, or indeed admirable, are happy. Forget about happiness." (p. 236)

Davies has always argued that romance and marvels are necessary to psychic health. But Davies's images for romance and marvels are almost invariably European. Europeans do this kind of thing better than North Americans – that is the clear tenor of Davies's thought.

An obeisance to European culture is evident even in those works that Davies locates entirely in a Canadian setting. The action of *The Rebel Angels* (1981), for example, is set in a Canadian university that emulates the cloistered atmosphere or Oxford or Cambridge. The novel features gypsies and eccentric scholars; the plot revolves around a manuscript by Rabelais; there are allusions to many figures drawn from European intellectual history. In short, although Canada provides the novel's immediate physical setting, its mental geography remains European. In the play *Question Time* (1975) Davies also transposes his habitual themes to a Canadian setting. The Prime Minister's psychomachia is another example of a symbolic technique for the onstage dissection of personality that Davies has used before – playfully in *Eros at Breakfast* (1947) and more seriously in *General Confession* (1956). Although the Prime Minister's spiritual guide is an Eskimo shaman, the wisdom he offers is the same wisdom that is purveyed by European sages such as Liesl and Father Blazon. All of Davies' spiritual seekers act on the advice that Richard Roberts offers in *A Jig for the Gypsy* (1954): "We're too much concerned nowadays with helping other people: we don't do enough to help ourselves. If a man wants to be of the greatest possible value to his fellow-creatures let him begin the long, solitary task of perfecting himself."[1]

I think Davies is right to see Canadians as longing to become part of a larger cultural environment. I think he is wrong to look so exclusively towards Europe for that environment. It does seem likely, however, that Davies is the last major Canadian writer who equates European culture with the very possibility of art. Most of our younger writers do not look to Europe for their cultural roots, but find mythic resonances within the Canadian past and the Canadian present, as Margaret Laurence and Rudy Wiebe have done. Laurence's *The Diviners* (1974), in particular, offers a clear picture of the way the typical Canadian attitude towards Europe has changed. Morag is a representative figure, a writer who personifies an entire generation. Like many Canadian writers, Laurence herself included, Morag left her home, but found that, in both her life and her art, she had to come to terms with her origins. Like Paul Tallard in MacLennan's *Two Solitudes*, Morag longed to acquire an essentially foreign cultural heritage, and tried hard to claim it as her own. Eventually, however, she had to return from an exile that was as much mental as physical. She learns that "the town inhabits her, as once she inhabited it."[2]

An important theme of *The Diviners*, then, is the necessity to recognize that Canadian society and the Canadian landscape provide the proper basis for a Canadian art. Morag is an aspiring writer who feels ashamed of her adoptive parents – Christie is the town garbage collector and Prin is an almost grotesquely fat woman. Morag moves away from Manawaka to seek a culturally richer environment, and it takes her a considerable time to recognize that her true home is Christie's country. She must realize that her own past is not a garbage heap, but provides the very soil out of which her inmost self has grown. In other words, Christie's culture is just as valid as – though it is different from – the imported European culture that Morag encounters at university and that she embraces in the person of Brooke Skelton. Morag eventually realizes that in both her life and her art she must

---

[1] Robertson Davies, *A Jig for the Gypsy* (Toronto: Clarke, Irwin, 1954), p. 85.

[2] Margaret Laurence, *The Diviners* (Toronto: Bantam, 1975), p. 227.

rely on her experience of her native place. She learns to accept as part of herself not only the meaner aspects of life in Manawaka but also Christie's language, Christie's drunken tales, and even Jules's subversive version of Canadian history. And she uses many of these things as the basis for her own novels.

A strong sense of Canada's cultural maturity is also expressed by the principal narrator of Hugh Hood's multi-volume cycle of novels, *The New Age / Le nouveau siècle*. It is clear that Matt Goderich does not see Canadian culture as a radical departure from the European precedent, but as a continuation of the human race's age-old collective project, civilization. In *A New Athens* (1977) Matt tells us that he has learned not to laugh at the idea of naming a small Ontario town after the centre of classical Greek culture. When the rural community of Farmersville was incorporated as a village, it formally renamed itself Athens "because of the unquestioned excellence of the two schools in the village."[1] Matt comments:

> When I first heard of this, I considered it a ridiculous presumption on the part of those good Athenians – the grand name, as somebody remarks, for the mean thing. I was wrong. Oh yes, I was wrong. What they had done wasn't to insinuate that their village was as great, as central to culture as the city of Athena, but only that their schools were in the tradition of the Academy, that human culture is continuous, that a Canadian school two generations removed from the wilderness is the same kind of school as the Academy, that human nature persists, remains self-identical through many generations of superficial changes. (p. 59)

Matt is here suggesting that high culture is at the centre of Canadian life, not on the periphery – a brave and challenging assertion, however dubious it may be as an account of our actual society. Hood still looks to high culture as the

---

[1] Hugh Hood, *A New Athens* (Ottawa: Oberon, 1977), p. 23. All further references to this work appear in the text.

167

repository of all that is best in civilization. But, as other novels in *The New Age* make clear, he does not scorn North American popular culture. Plainly, he feels that all levels of Western culture have been successfully transplanted to North America. This is a sentiment that many of our contemporary writers would endorse. Whatever Davies may think, most contemporary Canadian writers and artists no longer find it necessary to look uneasily over their shoulders at Europe.

CHAPTER SEVEN

Against the Success Man

to furnish, out of the traffic and smog and the shambles of
dead precursors,
a civil habitation that is
human, and our own.

— Dennis Lee, *Civil Elegies*

When Canadian authors portray urban settings, they usually
have one eye cocked towards the American example. In fact,
from Sara Jeannette Duncan and Stephen Leacock to Robertson Davies, leading Canadian writers have examined the
fundamental values on which the American way of life is
based. Most obviously, they repeatedly criticize the obsession
with "success" in all its forms that characterizes both
American life and many American novels. A great many of
our authors would agree with Morley Callaghan, who once
told Robert Weaver: "in my own way I'm against the success
man."[1] The figure Callaghan calls the "success man" occurs
frequently in Callaghan's own novels, appears occasionally in
the fiction of Hugh MacLennan, and is common in Mordecai
Richler's work. In *Fifth Business* Boy Staunton may pattern
his social self on a British model, but the business career
Dunstan watches with fascinated distaste is thoroughly
North American in spirit.

Today, many Canadian authors view the city as the

---

[1] Robert Weaver, "A Talk with Morley Callaghan," *Tamarack Review*,
No. 7 (Spring 1958), p. 23.

natural habitat of their fiction. But the extensive use of urban settings is a comparatively recent development in our fiction. Before I look at the books in which our authors explicitly scrutinize the values that lie behind the obsession with material success, I want to examine the way urban fiction entered the Canadian tradition. Inevitably, as writers responded in their work to the shift from a rural to an urban way of life, they reflected some important changes in Canadian society. Repeatedly, their books document the decay of the traditional family, the continuing decline of traditional religion, and the accompanying rise of materialistic values.

One of the most striking portrayals of the break-up of the family-centred rural way of life is contained in Frederick Philip Grove's *Our Daily Bread* (1928). In Grove's novel John Elliot has a dream "of seeing his children settled about him as the children of the patriarchs of Israel were settled about their fathers."[1] Yet as his children grow up, they all leave him, and many of them make marriages that he views with disfavour. All of John Elliot's children eventually lead lives of which he cannot approve, and most involve themselves in conditions of great economic hardship. In part, the novel criticizes the psychological effects of Elliot's authoritarian rule: many of the children's problems stem from weaknesses of character that are traceable to their upbringing. But the gulf between John Elliot and his children also illustrates the way social conditions have changed. John Elliot and his children belong to different generations, with entirely different values. A revealing incident takes place when Elliot goes to visit his daughter who lives in Winnipeg. He is asked if he is making progress. He replies indignantly, "Farmers don't make progress. They make a living" (p. 168). Elliot's children have set their courses and measured their success by different standards from those of their father. When the children are gathered for the last time at their father's funeral, they sense that "with him the last link had been broken which so far had held the many divergent forces at

[1] Frederick Philip Grove, *Our Daily Bread*, New Canadian Library, No. 114 (Toronto: McClelland and Stewart, 1975), p. 7. All further references to this work appear in the text.

work within the family together as in a sheaf. Henceforth, their eyes would be focused on their own, individual futures" (p. 390).

In *Our Daily Bread* Grove is responding to a significant aspect of Canada's shift from a rural to an urban society. His novel is an example of the harsher realism that was slowly gaining ground in Canadian fiction between the Wars. In most earlier fiction, the family receives a sympathetic and often idealized treatment. Children are on good terms with their parents, and often they remain at home long past adolescence. Marriage, which may come quite late in life, is the orthodox reason for finally quitting the parental roof. Parental opinion may weigh quite heavily with children, who do not lightly go against their parents' wishes in choosing a career or a mate. In more recent urban fiction, on the other hand, the family is not automatically the dominant institution shaping the individual. In fact, many characters in urban novels acquire their values from society at large, not from their families. The authors of urban novels sometimes feel no need to inform readers of their characters' family backgrounds. In urban fiction, children and adolescents often find the family a source of conflict, rather than of reassurance or support. Frequently, the children pursue goals that are different from the goals that satisfied their parents. Often the family comes to be seen not as the source of standards and security, but as the cause of psychological problems, as it is in Mordecai Richler's *The Apprenticeship of Duddy Kravitz* (1959) or in Margaret Atwood's *Surfacing* (1972) and *Lady Oracle* (1976).

The move to the city is usually accompanied by a weakening in the influence of traditional religion. The Presbyterian Church is a vital force in the rural community portrayed in Ralph Connor's *The Man from Glengarry* (1901) and is still important in the small town depicted in Sara Jeannette Duncan's *The Imperialist* (1904). Duncan, however, suggests that material and spiritual values are becoming confused when she remarks: "In Elgin religious fervour was not beautiful, or dramatic, or self-immolating; it was reasonable. You were perhaps your own first creditor; after that your debt was to your Maker" (p. 60). In Leacock's *Arcadian Adventures with the Idle Rich* (1914), we see evidence of the further decline – even the debasement – of religion in an urban setting. The Presbyterian St. Osoph's Church has among its leading members the Overend brothers. "Not that they were, by origin, presbyterians," Leacock remarks. "But they were self-made men, which put them once and for all out of sympathy with such a place as St. Asaph's. 'We made ourselves,' the two brothers used to repeat in defiance of the catechism of the Anglican Church."[1]

Leacock's book shows that the pursuit of wealth seems to have become the root motivation of North American society. The principle of profit and loss is conspicuous not only in business affairs, but also in social life, in the university, in politics, and in religion. The business mentality finds its most blatant expression in the merger of the two rival churches, which is based on sound financial principles and on no theological principles at all. Of course, the charge that society is pervaded by the desire for monetary gain is by no means new. Roland Graeme and Ryerson Embury, for example, had accused factory owners of putting profits ahead of the welfare of their workers. But Leacock is unique in the blanket application he makes of this criticism. The human feeling that softens all human contacts in Mariposa does not exist in Plutoria. In *Sunshine Sketches*, no one is hurt; in *Arcadian Adventures*, as we are reminded in the last sentence of the book, the rich exist only on the backs of the poor.

In *Arcadian Adventures* the story of Tomlinson, the wizard of finance, is Leacock's sardonic commentary on the typical American rags-to-riches success story – the Alger-like myth that Americans like to attach to everyone who gains a great deal of wealth. Leacock tells us, "there were all sorts of stories afloat in the weekly illustrated press" (p. 29) about the origins of Tomlinson's fortune:

> They agreed mostly on the general basis that Tomlin-
> son had made his vast fortune by his own in-
> domitable pluck and dogged industry. Some said that
> he had been at one time a mere farm hand who, by

---

[1] Stephen Leacock, *Arcadian Adventures with the Idle Rich*, New Canadian Library, No. 10 (Toronto: McClelland and Stewart, 1959), p. 111. All further references to this work appear in the text.

sheer doggedness, had fought his way from the hay-mow to the control of the produce market of seventeen states. Others had it that he had been a lumberjack who, by sheer doggedness, had got possession of the whole lumber forest of the Lake district. Others said that he had been a miner in a Lake Superior copper mine who had, by the doggedness of his character, got a practical monopoly of the copper supply. These Saturday articles, at any rate, made the Saturday reader rigid with sympathetic doggedness himself, which was all that the editor (who was doggedly trying to make the paper pay) wanted to effect. (p. 29)

In reality, of course, Tomlinson "was attempting to carry out a *coup* greater than any as yet attributed to him by the Press. He was trying to lose his money" (p. 29), so that he could return to his family's farm beside Tomlinson's Creek in Cahoga County, just below Lake Erie. For Tomlinson's story, like the last chapter of *Sunshine Sketches of a Little Town*, reminds us that the wish for Mariposa still exists within the hearts of many residents of Plutoria.

In *Arcadian Adventures* Leacock points out the pervasiveness in North American of what the economist Robert Heilbroner calls the "monetization" of society. According to Heilbroner, the members of our modern pluralistic society share only one fundamental value: their willingness to judge almost any object or activity in terms of its monetary worth. "Shorn of fixed status, deprived of a guaranteed level of life," says Heilbroner, "the individual must win his own salvation *in the market place*, and it is this necessity, and not avarice, which makes him and his society money-valuing, money-oriented and money-*minded*."[1] Money-mindedness is not confined to North America, but it achieves its apotheosis there. As Robert Fulton, an English immigrant, says in Jessie G. Sime's *Our Little Life* (1921), "in older countries there are things still (not many) that can be had without money; but in the new countries there is nothing which can be had without

---

[1] Robert L. Heilbroner, *The Quest for Wealth: A Study of Acquisitive Man* (New York: Simon and Schuster, 1956), p. 212.

173

money – things unbuyable and unsaleable don't exist there."[1]

Money-mindedness does not become a major theme in our fiction until after the First World War, but its influence is visible in several prewar pictures of Canadian society. For example, money-mindedness casts its shadow even in Mariposa. As Leacock's narrator remarks: "it was a favourite method in Mariposa if you wanted to get at the real worth of a man, to imagine him clean sold up, put up for auction, as it were."[2] And one of the subtle sources of humour in *The Man from Glengarry* is the incongruity of Yankee Jim's monetary metaphors, when he tries to discuss theology with solemn Scottish-Canadian Presbyterians. The citizens of Duncan's Elgin rejoice exceedingly on the Queen's birthday, but they are also proud of belonging to a highly "go-ahead" society: that is, a society devoted to the pursuit of individual happiness by acquiring money.

The money-mindedness of North American society is usually justified by the argument that the pursuit of wealth is only a means to the pursuit of happiness. The monetized society is viewed by its advocates as a great democratic levelling instrument. But in a completely monetized society, the only medium for transactions between individuals is money. Other considerations become secondary or irrelevant in measuring an individual's status. Thus, the monetization of society means that the individual becomes a social atom, identical to every other individual in the only respect that matters – the ability to receive and to spend money. In a fully monetized society, men would need no more personality than a bank pass-book. But if men are reduced to being simply buyers and sellers, mere getters and spenders of money, what happens to the other aspects of their personalities? This question has been asked in a significant number of books by Canadian writers. Consequently, there exists a significant group of Canadian novels that critically examine the American myth that material success is the principal desideratum in life and is freely available to anyone who seeks it with industry and determination.

---

[1] Jessie G. Sime, *Our Little Life: A Novel of Today* (New York: Frederick A. Stokes, 1921), p. 8.

[2] Leacock, *Sunshine Sketches of a Little Town*, p. 34.

Grove's *A Search for America* (1927), for example, contains his most detailed criticism of the materialism that has become the dominant creed of North American society. In Grove's novel the most important discovery made by Phil Branden is the existence of not one, but two Americas. There is the America that first strikes a stranger like Phil Branden: the America of the great barbecue, vulgar and commercial, devoted to the ruthless pursuit of success. In contrast, there is also the America of Abraham Lincoln, a land devoted to individual self-fulfillment and to aiding others to achieve their own self-realization. Phil Branden finds the commercial America mainly in the cities, where slick confidence men lurk in hotel lobbies and clever businessmen scheme to extract money from the unwary. He finds the America of Abraham Lincoln chiefly outside the cities – "in little villages, little hamlets, little farmsteads and smithies – wherever men sacrificed their own selfish ends for the general good. . . ."[1] Moreover, in a footnote late in the novel Grove adds: "I have since come to the conclusion that the ideal as I saw and still see it has been abandoned by the U.S.A. That is one reason why I became and remained a Canadian" (p. 382). Canada, then, is the continuing custodian of the true American dream of justice for all.

John Marlyn's *Under the Ribs of Death* (1957) also tells of a protagonist whose success in achieving the materialistic North American dream does not bring emotional satisfaction. In the central episode of this novel, young Sandor Hunyadi reads a book that is clearly one of the many popular romances written by Horatio Alger. Alger's stories enact the American success myth, the rags-to-riches saga of the self-made man. Thus, Sandor, the immigrant Hungarian-Canadian, is influenced by the archetypal American vision of success and happiness. But Marlyn does not resolve his story by allowing Sandor either to succeed in the manner of a Horatio Alger hero or to fail in the manner of the protagonist of a naturalistic novel. The Depression intervenes, like an act of God punishing a blasphemously materi-

---

[1]Frederick Philip Grove, *A Search for America*, New Canadian Library, No. 76 (Toronto: McClelland and Stewart, 1971), p. 306. All further references to this work appear in the text.

alistic society. Sandor ultimately realizes that his father's humanistic values are preferable to the materialism of the death-like Mr. Nagy.

At the same time as Grove was beginning his career as a North American writer, certain other writers were trying to find a tone that would be more appropriate to portray the speeded-up, anxiety-filled urban scene. Jessie G. Sime's *Our Little Life* perhaps owes a great deal to the sedate prose of Arnold Bennett or to the H.G. Wells of *Kipps* and *Mr. Polly*. Morley Callaghan's *Strange Fugitive* (1928), however, is thoroughly North American in both its subject-matter and its literary antecedents. Callaghan's commitment to creating an art that is North American rather than European is clearly illustrated in a story he has told about the days when he was a student at the University of Toronto, and was just starting his career as a writer:

> By this time I had become aware that the language in which I wanted to write, a North American language which I lived by, had rhythms and nuances and twists and turns quite alien to English speech. When I showed some of my first stories to academic men highly trained in English literature, I could see them turning up their noses. "A failure of language," one said to me; and feeling encouraged I said, "No, a failure on your part to understand the language." I had decided that language of feeling and perception, and even direct observation had to be the language of the people I wrote about, who did not belong in an English social structure at all.[1]

The professor equates literary language with a cultivated and genteel style; for him, literature proclaims its superiority to everyday life through its contrived style. On the other hand, in Callaghan's lexicon "literature" is a perjorative term; he insists, "I wanted to get it down so directly that it

---

[1] Morley Callaghan, "An Ocean Away," in *Times Literary Supplement*, 4 June 1964, p. 493; rpt. in *Morley Callaghan*, ed. Brandon Conron, Critical Views on Canadian Writers, No. 10 (Toronto: McGraw-Hill Ryerson, 1975), p. 17.

wouldn't feel or look like literature."[1] We can say that the professor has an aristocratic conception of the style that is proper in real "literature." Callaghan, on the other hand, sets himself the populist goal of transcribing the life around him in everyday language. From the start of his career, he commits himself to using North American language, as well as treating North American subjects.

In *Strange Fugitive* Harry Trotter inhabits a world from which all values save those of the predatory business ethic seem to have been removed. Callaghan presents Harry Trotter's progress from workman to one of the unemployed to bootlegger to corpse with the objectivity of a scientist observing a rat attempting to find its way through a maze. Indeed, the novel is very like a laboratory experiment. It reads as though Callaghan said to himself: I'll create a man who is entirely the creature of his times, with no carryovers from the past such as religion or respect for the conventional taboos; he won't be too smart but he won't be too dumb either, just an average guy. Then I'll turn him loose in a modern city, without the headstart of wealth or the handicap of poverty, and watch what happens to him. The results, from a moral point of view, are appalling. Left to his own devices, Harry Trotter simply goes to ruin. His demise does not condemn his society, for throughout the novel the reader can see Harry's fate approaching – Harry himself is simply unable to read the signs. Nor does Harry have any of the redeeming qualities that would turn his squalid death into a tragic example of the waste of a worthwhile human life.

To illustrate the new tone that Callaghan brought into Canadian writing, I want to quote a longish passage that describes how Harry Trotter ends a working day at Pape's lumber-yard:

> In the three-by-four compartment he had erected for himself in the corner of the warehouse he started to clean up. He got the pail from a corner and went back to the tap for water. He took off his khaki shirt, his undershirt, and, bare-bodied, dipped the soap in

---

[1] Morley Callaghan, *That Summer in Paris*, Laurentian Library, No. 40 (Toronto: Macmillan, 1976), pp. 21-22.

water, making lather for his face and rubbing well down his shoulders and hairy chest. Scooping water in his palms he splashed his face, blowing out through his mouth and his nose, and getting soap out of his eye with the thumb-joint. He stood up well-rubbed with the towel, peeled off his overalls, and kicked off his heavy boots. He remembered that to-night one of the ball teams practised in the park near his place, and, standing in his underwear, putting on a clean shirt, wished he had time to make a place on one of the teams. The soft collar he circled with a sky-blue tie, snappy, conservative, the knot tied fastidiously. He looked squarely and seriously at his image in the jagged piece of looking-glass hanging on the wall, and wondered if Vera would want to do anything after supper that would prevent him from going over the park. Slowly he brushed his thick hair, took a straw sailor from a nail and adjusted it at a sporty angle on his head. He handled carefully his shining, tan low shoes. He emerged from the warehouse, altogether aloof from the yard, no bum, not just a hunky boss, no cheap skate from a lumber yard. He walked confidently along the platform, the flash of thick blond hair under the hat brim well cut, his tanned, high-cheekboned face free from stubble, his stylish tweed suit with a high waist-line, well cut and form-fitting.[1]

Notice the wealth of physical detail: the pail, the water, the lather, the hairy chest, the sky-blue tie, the straw hat. Notice too the unobtrusive blending of external and internal viewpoints. Only the two sentences in which Harry thinks about watching the baseball practice are conventional omniscient narration. Yet the rest of the passage is actually written in the *style indirect libre* that Callaghan has learned from Joyce, who in turn had learned it from Flaubert. The physical details of Harry's actions and appearance are not observed by an invisible narrator's eye; rather, they record

---

[1] Morley Callaghan, *Strange Fugitive*, Laurentian Library, No. 15 (Toronto: Macmillan, 1973), p. 7.

Harry's awareness of what he is doing, and reveal how he thinks of himself.

Most of Callaghan's later fiction searches for a way out of the societal dead-end that is depicted in *Strange Fugitive*. For example, Father Dowling in *Such Is My Beloved* (1934) and Kip Caley in *More Joy in Heaven* (1937) are enmeshed in society in a way that Harry Trotter is not. In many ways Kip Caley is just Harry Trotter writ larger. But Kip discovers within himself a secure basis for his "big special feeling";[1] therefore, the entire society depicted in the novel can be judged in relation to Kip's values. If Kip is destroyed by the society he has tried to improve, then that society is criticized. (Similarly, the madness of Father Dowling is as much an indictment of society as it is a comment on Dowling's own immaturity and naïveté.)

(The stories of father Dowling and Kip Caley hold out the possibility that the individual may still be able to save his own soul although society as a whole may be irredeemable.) Callaghan's most comprehensive examination of North American society, however, is found in *They Shall Inherit the Earth* (1935). In this novel Callaghan holds out a larger hope – the hope that the innate virtue of the little people shall in the last analysis become the basis for a renewed society. As the novel opens, we meet Andrew Aikenhead, who has lived his life according to the business ethic. Yet we find him seeking to renew contact with his son and feeling "as though he had at last taken a necessary step that would bring joy again into his life."[2] The system by which Andrew has lived is expressed by his partner, Jay Hillquist, with whom as a young man Andrew "had made such ardent plans to make money" (p. 135). When Andrew's personal problems distract him from the affairs of their advertising firm, Jay is angry that sentiment should interfere with his sense of business efficiency: "As he muttered 'To think I'd ever see the day when I'd let a personal relationship interfere with business,'

---

[1] Morley Callaghan, *More Joy in Heaven*, New Canadian Library, No. 17 (Toronto: McClelland and Stewart, 1960), p. 13.

[2] Morley Callaghan, *They Shall Inherit the Earth*, New Canadian Library, No. 33 (Toronto: McClelland and Stewart, 1962), p. 11. All further references to this work appear in the text.

his heart was troubled and he was full of secret shame. Yet he would not let himself respond to the urge from the deeper part of his nature, for he felt it would be a betrayal of everything he stood for in his daily life" (p. 135).

Andrew's son, Michael Aikenhead, doesn't quite know what he is seeking, but he knows that he cannot find it by following his father's business ethic. During a hunting trip in the Ontario countryside, Michael is prompted to burst out violently against the predatory nature of the capitalist system:

"A wolf is an individualist," Mike said. "They kill out of the sheer lust of killing, and they kill without sense .... If you want it to be clear that a man is ruthless and an enemy of society you call him a wolf, don't you? ... Any enemy of the race you call a wolf because he knows no moral law, and that's why you can't organize society, because it's full of wolves, and they don't know justice, and don't want it. The financial brigands and labour exploiters and the war profiteers and the Wall Street sharks and nearly anybody who tries to put his head up in a world of private profit, what are they? Wolves I tell you." (pp. 189-90)

What Michael has been searching for, he realizes at last, is a way of feeling "single and whole" within himself. He must have a single set of values to live by, and all aspects of his life must be compatible with those values. That is, he cannot be happy while his life is compartmented, as Jay Hillquist's is. He cannot be compassionate in private life and predatory in his business affairs.

Michael's resolution is finally achieved not by means of any intellectual system such the Communism of his friend Bill Johnson or the Catholicism of the former Jew Nathaniel Benjamin, but through his love for Anna Prychoda. Anna embodies in herself the wholeness that Michael seeks. In her, there is no separation between external behaviour and the "deeper part" of her nature:

She went on from day to day, living and loving and exposing the fulness and wholeness of herself to the life around her. If to be poor in spirit meant to be without false pride, to be humble enough to forget oneself, then she was poor in spirit, for she gave herself to everything that touched her, she let herself be, she lost herself in the fulness of the world, and in losing herself she found the world, and she possessed her own soul. (p. 242)

The emotional release brought about by Michael's relationship with Anna Prychoda allows him to forgive himself for the part he played in the drowning of his half-brother, David Choate, and to accept his father's offer of a renewed family tie. Callaghan can permit a happy resolution to this story because he sees human nature as having an underlying unity. Men are united by their common core of morality, which is the same in each individual and does not depend for its existence and authority on an external God or a formalized system of beliefs.

It is interesting to compare this novel with the American novel that in all probability gave Callaghan the germ of his plot, Theodore Dreiser's *An American Tragedy* (1925). Let me quickly summarize the plot of Dreiser's novel. Clyde Griffiths, after an impoverished childhood, begins to move into a new level of society when he gains work at a factory owned by some of his well-off relatives. He starts an affair with a working girl, Roberta Alden, but at the same time he aspires to marry his wealthy cousin. When Roberta becomes pregnant, Clyde takes her on a boating excursion, and brings about her death by drowning. Clyde is arrested, tried, and hanged. Notice the parallels with Callaghan's novel: in both books, the protagonists make lower-class girls pregnant; and both protagonists are responsible for a death by drowning.[1] But the outcome of Callaghan's novel is very different from the outcome of Dreiser's story. Michael Aikenhead realizes

---

[1] Even if Dreiser's novel did not prompt Callaghan's book, my main point is not substantially weakened. Comparison of the two novels still reveals a striking difference in the characteristic outlooks of American and Canadian urban fiction.

that nothing is more precious than life; he repents his part in David Choate's death. In Callaghan's eyes, Michael's inner reform is sufficient. Callaghan allows Michael to marry Anna Prychoda, to rejoice at the birth of his son, and to be reconciled with his father. Callaghan, then, has moved a long way from the deterministic outlook that lies behind Dreiser's early example of American naturalism.

Father Dowling, Kip Caley, and even Michael Aikenhead have all, in different ways, stepped aside from the struggle for material success that is at the heart of capitalist society. In these novels, a belief in conventional values – above all, a belief in wealth and power – is embodied in secondary characters such as Mr. Robison) in *Such Is My Beloved*, Senator Maclean in *More Joy in Heaven*, and Jay Hillquist in *They Shall Inherit the Earth*. In some of his later fiction, however, Callaghan has turned to a more direct examination of the career of the "success man." The principal examples are the stories of Jim McAlpine in *The Loved and the Lost* (1951), Harry Lane in *The Many Colored Coat* (1960), and Ira Groome in *Close to the Sun Again* (1977). These figures are all haunted by a need for something that they cannot obtain by pursuing a conventional version of success.

In *The Loved and the Lost* Jim McAlpine must choose between two women who represent very different ways of looking at the world. Catherine Carver is the daughter of Senator Carver, the Montreal newspaper publisher who wants to hire Jim to write a regular column on international affairs. Becoming engaged to Catherine would help to launch Jim's newspaper career and would guarantee his acceptance by the Westmount society to which the Carvers belong. That is, marriage with Catherine would offer Jim "not only all the familiar delightful emotions that could come from a woman in love but the success he had sought since his boyhood."[1] Jim, however, is also fascinated by Peggy Sanderson, a nonconformist who extends her friendship to a very mixed assortment of misfits and social outcasts, including several Negro jazz musicians. Jim knows that Peggy would be regarded with suspicion by people like the Carvers, and he

---

[1] Morley Callaghan, *The Loved and the Lost*, Laurentian Library, No. 9 (Toronto: Macmillan, 1970), p. 103.

finds himself concealing his growing friendship with Peggy. When Peggy finally is willing to accept Jim as her lover, he discovers that he still has reservations about her unconventional behaviour. He leaves her alone in her apartment, and later that night she is murdered. Jim feels responsible for her death, because he knows that when he distrusted Peggy he failed to live up to her generous and open standard of conduct.

When we first meet Harry Lane in *The Many Colored Coat*, he seems to be merely a typical public relations man. He is a well-known glad-hander, someone whose principal stock-in-trade is conviviality. He has, as the bank manager Scotty Bowman says, a "talent for making people feel all his success belongs to them too."[1] Scotty Bowman's friend Mike Kon is more sceptical. He says of Harry Lane: "All he needs in his phony job is to be a little smoother, a little faster on his feet and a little more intelligent than most guys" (p. 12). When Scotty Bowman is tried for embezzlement, Mike Kon's testimony places Harry Lane in a bad light. Harry is outraged at the accusation that he deliberately manoeuvred Scotty into deceiving the bank, and he embarks on a quixotic campaign to vindicate himself. In fact, Harry wants nothing less than a renewed courtroom encounter with Mike Kon.

Both Harry and Mike are unwilling to let their disagreement rest; they are apparently governed by a desire for absolute justice. In the process, however, Harry loses his job and Mike Kon's tailoring business falls off badly. If Harry were behaving pragmatically, he would take the cynical advice offered by the advertising executive Ted Ogilvie. "If I were you," Ted tells Harry, "I'd handle it just like I'd handle a television account. As I see it, we con people. It's our job. But they know we con them and they don't care as long as we're nice guys. . . . Who cares about my ethics, and my nice points of honor, and my goddamned integrity if they know I'm in the great American image? The nice guy making a buck" (p. 179). In fact, when Harry looks for a new job, he is rebuffed in words that seem a deliberate echo of Arthur Miller's *Death of a Salesman*: " 'a businessman has to be well

---

[1] Morley Callaghan, *The Many Colored Coat* (Toronto: Macmillan, 1960), p. 12. All further references to this work appear in the text.

liked, Mike,' Singerman said quietly. 'Are you well liked now, Mike?' " (p. 192). Surprisingly, however, when Harry's wish for a new trial is eventually granted, he does not appear in court to testify on his own behalf. And when Mike Kon takes the stand, he withdraws his condemnation of Harry Lane. "I had no right to make that accusation and try to stick by it," he announces. And he adds: "Maybe I had no right to judge Harry Lane" (p. 308). That is, he obeys the Biblical injunction to judge not, lest you be judged.

A major problem with these two novels is their utter implausibility. This is not just a matter of their unlikely plots, for the stories of Father Dowling and Kip Caley are equally far-fetched. The problem arises because Callaghan is now trying to write a different kind of novel than he wrote previously. His major works from the thirties are moral parables, whereas *The Loved and the Lost* and *The Many Colored Coat* are attempts at the novel of character. By virtue of their direct and simple idealism, Father Dowling and Kip Caley become powerful figures, challenging the reader's complacent acceptance of the status quo. Jim McAlpine and Harry Lane, on the other hand, seem like confused and petulant children rather than clear-eyed moralists. A similar implausibility also weakens the story of Ira Groome in *Close to the Sun Again*. As he lies dying, Ira Groome relives a long-suppressed episode that had started him "down a road on which he had turned his back on the perplexity and the mystery of people that made up the real adventure in life."[1] That is, only when it is too late does Ira Groome realize that there are things that are more important than the financial rewards and the social prestige that accompany success in the business world.

Hugh MacLennan is best-known for the literary nationalism that is expressed in his first two novels, *Barometer Rising* (1941) and *Two Solitudes* (1945). But in his third novel, *The Precipice* (1948), MacLennan turns his attention to a study of the American Dream. The characters and plot of this novel are drawn with a simplicity that is almost allegorical. Lucy Cameron, the inexperienced girl from

---

[1] Morley Callaghan, *Close to the Sun Again* (Toronto: Macmillan, 1977), p. 168.

Granville, Ontario, is unexpectedly courted by the visiting American engineer, Stephen Lassiter. Lucy, whose childhood was dominated by the strict Calvinist beliefs whose impact Maclennan explores so memorably in *Each Man's Son* (1951), embodies both Canadian inhibitions and Canadian virtues. Stephen Lassiter, the American engineer, represents the old American frontier ideal of mastering the environment by physical effort and mechanical ingenuity. Carl Bratian, Lassiter's employer, represents the newer American ethos of salesmanship and advertising. Stephen goes wrong when he goes to work for Bratian's advertising agency, and takes Lucy with him to New York, "the city, where, no matter how many people pretended otherwise, the really successful men chose to live."[1] Stephen slides into extramarital sexual adventures, and chronic drunkenness. At the novel's end, however, he seems to be redeemed by Lucy's continuing love. According to MacLennan, then, Canadian virtue supplies the antidote to the worst features of American life.

MacLennan has often expressed reservations about the dominant tendencies of modern American fiction (a point to which I shall return in the next chapter). As early as 1949, he was arguing that, despite the merits of their fiction, writers such as Dos Passos, Hemingway, and Mailer had brought American fiction to a spiritual dead end. His best novel, *The Watch That Ends the Night* (1959), can be seen as his own attempt to counteract the dominant tendency of North American fiction, and to make his own work reveal what he has called "the dynamics of goodness itself."[2] During the years when he was writing this novel, MacLennan has said: "my intuitions were forcing me to utter something socially blasphemous in those years. They were asserting that God had not been outmoded by the Christian Church, Bertrand Russell, the social scientists, and modern education."[3] George Stewart is not a representative Canadian like

---

[1] Hugh MacLennan, *The Precipice* (Toronto: Collins, 1948), p. 86.

[2] Hugh MacLennan, "Changing Values in Fiction," *Canadian Author and Bookman*, 25 (Autumn 1949), 17.

[3] Hugh MacLennan, "Reflections on Two Decades," in his *The Other Side of Hugh MacLennan: Selected Essays Old and New*, ed. Elspeth Cameron (Toronto: Macmillan, 1978), p. 252.

Lucy Cameron, but a twentieth-century Everyman, looking for salvation in a world where individual actions no longer seem to matter. George's story is set in a new Montreal whose citizens "were learning to live like New Yorkers" (p. 5). But George, faced with the impending death of his much-loved wife Catherine, is forced to ask himself questions about the ultimate significance of life in this world. His answer is essentially a religious one:

> Nobody – this I knew – can ever know in advance how he will feel when he encounters the finality. Often I dreaded it; often I rebelled against this fate of ours. But toward that summer's end I had almost ceased to think about the future, and she never thought of it at all. Remembering the years when she had wrung life and joy out of pain and perpetual exhaustion, I knew, deep inside, that this struggle was not valueless. (p. 373)

In the sonorous, cadenced passages that conclude the novel, George makes his final affirmation: "In the early October of that year, in the cathedral hush of a Quebec Indian summer with the lake drawing into its mirror the fire of the maples, it came to me that to be able to love the mystery surrounding us is the final and only sanction of human existence" (p. 372).

Like Callaghan in *They Shall Inherit the Earth*, Mordecai Richler in *The Apprenticeship of Duddy Kravitz* may be replying to a specific work of American fiction. At the bar-mitzvah where Duddy is making his first film, Irwin Shubert sarcastically exclaims, "look who's here. Sammy Glick."[1] Later in the novel, when Duddy is briefly reconciled with Yvette, she tells him: "Duddy, if you start running again I'll leave you" (p. 282). Then when Virgil has an epileptic fit, after discovering that Duddy has forged a cheque on his bank account, we are told: "Duddy ran, he ran, he ran" (p. 306). It is very probable, I suggest, that Richler had in mind Budd Schulberg's *What Makes Sammy Run?* as he composed his own novel. Of course, Duddy's career in the

---

[1] Richler, *The Apprenticeship of Duddy Kravitz*, p. 147. All further references to this work appear in the text.

movies is very small potatoes compared with Sammy Glick's rise to the control of a major Hollywood studio. But Duddy is motivated by the same dream that urges Sammy on: he wants to succeed, to make it big in North American terms.

There is, however, an important difference in the way these two authors view their protagonists. Late in Schulberg's novel, Al Manheim, Schulberg's narrator, goes to visit Sammy's parents, who still live on Rivington Street in the New York City slum from which Sammy has escaped. Throughout much of the novel, Al Manheim has been fascinated by Sammy's ruthless pursuit of success. Now, after he hears the story of Sammy's childhood, he sees Sammy in a different light:

> I thought of Sammy Glick rocking in his cradle of hate, malnutrition, prejudice, suspicions, amorality, the anarchy of the poor; I though of him as a mangy little puppy in a dog-eat-dog world. I was modulating my hate for Sammy Glick from the personal to the societal. I no longer even hated Rivington Street but the idea of Rivington Street, all Rivington Streets of all nationalities allowed to pile up in cities like gigantic dung heaps smelling up the world, ambitions growing out of filth and crawling away like worms. I saw Sammy Glick on a battlefield where every soldier was his own cause, his own army and his own flag, and I realized that I had singled him out not because he had been born into the world any more selfish, ruthless and cruel than anybody else, even though he had become all three, but because in the midst of a war that was selfish, ruthless and cruel Sammy was proving himself the fittest, the fiercest and the fastest.[1]

In Schulberg's novel, Sammy's conduct is explained as the result of his childhood environment. In the peroration with which the book concludes (modelled loosely on the

---

[1] Budd Schulberg, *What Makes Sammy Run?* (New York: Random House, 1941), p. 249. All further references to this work appear in the text.

conclusion of *The Great Gatsby*, just as the whole of Schulberg's novel is an attempt to update Fitzgerald's masterpiece), Al Manheim remarks of Sammy:

> It was too late to hate him or change him. Sammy's will had stiffened. It had been free for an instant at birth, poised bird-free in the doctor's hand that moment in the beginning before it began to be formed in the life-molds, the terrible hungers of body and brain, the imposed wants, the traditional oppressions and persecutions, until at last Sammy's will had curled in on itself, like an ingrown hair festering, spreading infection. (p. 303)

Richler does more than avoid this sort of rhetoric. He is also morally tougher on his protagonist. He supplies enough details about Duddy's early childhood to make it clear that Duddy, after the death of his mother, received less than his share of approval and affection. But Richler does not let Duddy's childhood excuse his later moral failings: Richler's novel is not based on a deterministic outlook.

In *The Apprenticeship of Duddy Kravitz* Richler takes what we might call the North Americanization of our fiction a stage beyond the point reached by Callaghan. Richler's novel is saturated with allusions to North American popular culture. Duddy's ambitions, for example, are expressed in terms that owe everything to Duddy's exposure, through newspapers, magazines, and radio, to the American myth of success:

> He knew what he wanted, and that was to own his own land and to be rich, a somebody, but he was not sure of the smartest way to go about it. He was confident. But there had been other comers before him. South America, for instance, could no longer be discovered. It had been found. Toni Home Permanent had been invented. Another guy had already thought up Kleenex. But there was something out there, like let's say the atom bomb formula before it had been discovered, and Duddy dreamed that he would find it and make his fortune. He had his heroes. There was

188

the stranger who had walked into the Coca Cola Company before it had made its name and said, "I'll write down two words on a piece of paper, and if you use my idea I want a partnership in the company." The two words were "Bottle it." Don't forget, either, the man who saved that salmon company from bankruptcy with the slogan, *this salmon is guaranteed not to turn pink in the can.* There was the founder of the *Reader's Digest* – he'd made his pile too. The man who thought up the super-market must have been another shnook of a small grocer once. (p. 75)

Specifically, Duddy aspires to emulate Jerry Dingleman, the Boy Wonder, whose rise to wealth and influence, as told by Duddy's father, has become for him a mythic version of the American rags-to-riches saga. But the novel's final scene, in which Duddy has replaced the Boy Wonder as the hero of Max's tales, announces Duddy's failure rather than his triumph.

I have already asserted that Warren Tallman misreads *The Apprenticeship of Duddy Kravitz*. Specifically, Tallman neglects Richler's clear signals that Duddy should ultimately be judged a moral failure. Duddy exploits his only genuine friends, Virgil and Yvette. In so doing, he betrays Simcha's trust in his better nature and loses the respect of the member of his family whose opinion he values the most. Duddy's inner battle immobilizes him in bed with what Yvette later describes as a nervous breakdown. But Duddy's venal side wins out in the end. Uncle Benjy's letter to Duddy puts the matter quite plainly:

There's more to you than mere money-lust, Duddy, but I'm afraid for you. You're two people, that's why. The scheming little bastard I saw so easily and the fine, intelligent boy underneath that your grandfather, bless him, saw. But you're coming of age soon and you'll have to choose. A boy can be two, three, four potential people, but a man is only one. He murders the others. (p. 279)

189

Richler's point is that Duddy had the potential to behave differently, but by the novel's end he has destroyed his better self. Just as he has supplanted the Boy Wonder as the hero of Max's rags-to-riches saga, so he has become no better than the Boy Wonder. Tallman's unconditional approval of Duddy, then, displays exactly the same moral failing that Richler attributes to Duddy.

The cost of success has continued to be one of the most persistent themes in Richler's fiction. For example, when Duddy Kravitz reappears as a minor character in *St. Urbain's Horseman* (1971), he is a successful Toronto businessman, a millionaire. But the dubious nature of his success is indicated by the story of his first coup: he unknowingly markets a brand of reducing pill that contains a tapeworm, and when he discovers the pill's active ingredient he adroitly manoeuvres his unsuspecting partner into buying the entire operation. Later, when Jake Hersh meets Duddy in London, he finds that Duddy's money has not made him secure within himself. Where Duddy formerly wheedled and schemed to take advantage of his friends, now he dispenses his own money freely in order to purchase the affection he feels he does not deserve for his own sake alone. His self-loathing is demonstrated when he pathetically asks Jake: "Who in the hell could love Duddy Kravitz?" (p. 196).

Although Jake Hersh, the protagonist of *St. Urbain's Horseman*, and Joshua Shapiro, the central figure of *Joshua Then and Now* (1980), are not businessmen, they have both avidly pursued success – Jake as a film director, and Joshua as a sportswriter and television commentator. Jake and Joshua have each attained a degree of stature in their chosen professions, yet in middle age each man is beset by doubts about his own competence and about the importance of his profession. Both men feel that their private lives provide a more abiding satisfaction than their professional careers. Jake and Joshua, then, are unusual protagonists in an age when the self-centred and preferably suicidal artist *maudit* is the prevalent fashion in creative figures. Richler has said about *Cocksure* that in this novel he "was making a case for that much-abused man, the square."[1] The same thing can also be said about his purpose in *St. Urbain's Horseman* and *Joshua Then and Now*.

Between the publication of *The Apprenticeship of Duddy Kravitz* and the appearance of *St. Urbain's Horseman*, Richler also published two extravagantly satiric short novels, *The Incomparable Atuk* (1963) and *Cocksure* (1968). In the first of these novels, Richler's main target is Canadian cultural nationalism. He is particularly scathing at the expense of self-important celebrities who boast, as one of his characters does, that they are world-famous all over Canada. Richler's point is that Canadians are now thoroughly imbued with American values. In the words of the novel's epigraph: "if full sovereignty were invoked and the southern border were sealed tight against American mass culture ... Canada would have to produce her own."[2] In Buck Twentyman, Canada has even produced her own American-style business tycoon, though Richler's low assessment of this figure is implied in his name. In contrast to the sketchily portrayed Twentyman, the Star Maker, the Hollywood mogul portrayed in *Cocksure*, is a compellingly horrific incarnation of American capitalism. With the assistance of compliant doctors and his expendable spare parts men, the narcissistic and totally amoral Star Maker turns himself into a chillingly literal illustration of the words he speaks to Mortimer Griffin: "Remember this, Griffin. The revolution eats its own. Capitalism recreates itself."[3]

I want to conclude this survey of fictional Canadian reactions to the United States by taking another look at Robertson Davies's *Fifth Business*. It may seem strange that I include Davies's novel in a chapter on urban fiction. The novel is best-known for the portrayal of small-town life in its early pages, and for Dunstan's later exotic encounters with religion and magic. Like Magnus Eisengrim, Davies has always gone against the mood of his time: he has always

---

[1] Cameron, *Conversations with Canadian Novelists: Part Two*, p. 116.

[2] Richard H. Rovere, quoted in the epigraph to Mordecai Richler, *The Incomparable Atuk*, New Canadian Library, No. 79 (Toronto: McClelland and Stewart, 1971).

[3] Mordecai Richler, *Cocksure* (New York: Bantam, 1969), p. 135.

favoured romance and marvels over the sweaty realism that is common in the first wave of North American urban fiction. Yet *Fifth Business* does deal with one of the central themes of urban fiction, for in Boy Staunton's story Davies offers his severest critique of the North American obsession with material success. Boy Staunton's life illustrates one of the things Davies finds most objectionable in North American society: its conviction that people should put all their energies into attaining material success. By doing this North Americans neglect the self-cultivation that Davies feels is much more important.

Davies has an active interest in the American cult of success, and this interest helps to shape his account of Boy Staunton's life and death. Lest some readers think that I am attributing an excessive knowledge of the literature of success to Davies, I will digress briefly to examine a chapter from his collection of informal essays about books and reading, *A Voice from the Attic* (1960). In one chapter of that book, Davies surveys the inspirational self-help book – the success manual – from Samuel Smiles to Norman Vincent Peale. As he often does, Davies treats the nineteenth-century figure with considerable respect; but he is less complimentary about most of the twentieth-century figures he mentions, especially those apostles of success whose message has a religious flavour. Such gurus are anathema to Davies, for they express "an intensely materialistic concept of religion which is common in our day."[1] Davies scathingly dismisses the idea that is "the message of a majority of these books: success is from God, and God can be cajoled or compelled to give it to you. One need not be of a profoundly religious nature to find this shocking" (p. 59).

In *A Voice from the Attic* Davies quotes a passage taken from *The Art of Real Happiness* by Norman Vincent Peale and Smiley Blanton. Elsewhere in their book Peale and Blanton assure their readers: "God never meant us to carry around our necks the millstones of old misdeeds. We can be free of a sense of guilt about them. We can move, clear-eyed,

---

[1] Robertson Davies, *A Voice from the Attic*, New Canadian Library, No. 83 (Toronto: McClelland and Stewart, 1972), p. 73. All further references to this work appear in the text.

with a buoyant heart and mind, toward a successful future."[1] This is what Boy Staunton has tried to do. When Dunstan reminds him of the incident in which he threw the snowball that hit Mrs. Dempster and caused Paul Dempster's premature birth, Boy scoffs at the notion that an adult should feel guilt over the results of a childhood prank. In fact, Boy denies any recollection of the event. He does not quite deny that the incident took place, but he proudly tells Dunstan: "The difference between us is that you've brooded over it and I've forgotten it" (p. 310). Boy's subsequent suicide, however, shows that a part of his mind has not forgotten the incident. When Dunstan reminds Boy of the snowball incident, he also urges Boy "to recover something of the totality of your life. Don't you want to possess it as a whole – the bad with the good?" (p. 311). Boy refuses to do this. Instead, like the Prince of Wales he admires so much, Boy abdicates. He drives away from his responsibility to himself, and ends up at the bottom of Toronto Harbour.

Fifth Business contains several references to figures who contributed to the American cult of success. For example, at one point, Dunstan refers to Dr. Emile Coué, whose method of autosuggestion was supposed to help Boy's wife Leola "to acquire moral energy, after which social grace, wit, and an air of easy breeding would surely follow" (p. 179). Emile Coué is a French psychologist, who visited the United States during the early twenties to publicize his teachings. His method, as Dunstan points out, set many Americans to murmuring: "Every day in every way, I am getting better and better."[2] Dunstan says of Coué: "His system was really a form of secularized, self-seeking prayer, without the human dignity that even the most modest prayer evokes" (p. 180).

Boy is also impressed by a minister he meets during his honeymoon voyage to Europe. Dunstan sarcastically describes the Reverend George Maldon Leadbeater as "a great prophet from a fashionable New York church" (p. 137).

---

[1] Norman Vincent Peale and Smiley Blanton, *The Art of Real Happiness* (New York: Prentice-Hall, 1950), p. 73. Davies quotes from this book in *A Voice from the Attic*, p. 55.

[2] See Emile Coué, *My Method: Including American Impressions* (Garden City, N.Y.: Doubleday, Page, 1923).

Leadbeater is Davies's own invention. However, he seems to be based on two actual figures, one of them dating from the twenties and the other from the fifties. The clergyman whom Leadbeater resembles, in his materialism and in his position as pastor of a fashionable New York congregation, is Norman Vincent Peale. But Leadbeater's interpretation of Jesus closely resembles the view embodied in a best-selling book published in 1925 by Bruce Barton, who was an advertising executive rather than a minister (although he was a minister's son).

Barton achieved wide celebrity during the twenties and thirties with his version of the life of Jesus, titled *The Man Nobody Knows*.[1] The thrust of Barton's book is sufficiently indicated by his chapter titles: "The Executive"; "The Outdoor Man"; "The Sociable Man"; "His Method"; "His Advertisements"; "The Founder of Modern Business"; "The Master." In other words, Barton portrays Jesus as a man whom any modern Chamber of Commerce or Rotary Club would be proud to have as a member. Boy Staunton ascribes a similar conception of Jesus to Leadbeater. The passage in which he describes Leadbeater's ideas is worth quoting at length:

"He makes Christianity make sense for the first time, so far as I'm concerned. I mean, Christ was really a very distinguished person, a Prince of the House of David, a poet and an intellectual. Of course He was a carpenter; all those Jews in Bible days could do something with their hands. But what kind of a carpenter was He? Not making cowsheds, I'll bet. Undoubtedly a designer and a manufacturer, in terms of those days. Otherwise, how did He make his connections? You know, when He was travelling around, staying with all kinds of rich and influential people as an honoured guest – obviously He wasn't just bumming his way through Palestine; He was staying with people who knew Him as a man of substance who also had a great philosophy. You know, the way those Orientals make their pile before

---

[1] Bruce Barton, *The Man Nobody Knows* (Indianapolis: Bobbs-Merrill, 1925).

they go in for philosophy. And look how He appreciated beauty! When that woman poured the ointment on His feet, He knew good ointment from bad, you can bet. And the Marriage at Cana – a party, and He helped the host out of a tight place when the drinks gave out, because He had probably been in the same fix Himself in His days in business and knew what social embarrassment was. And an economist! Driving the money-changers out of the Temple – why? Because they were soaking the pilgrims extortionate rates, that's why, and endangering a very necessary tourist attraction and rocking the economic boat. It was a kind of market discipline, if you want to look at it that way, and He was the only one with the brains to see it and the guts to do something about it."(pp. 137-38)

In content, this passage is virtually a précis of Barton's book. In tone, as well, it catches the breezy note of vulgar materialism that is Barton's hallmark.

Boy is Davies' representative specimen of the North American millionaire. As Dunstan watches Boy and his "moneyed, influential friends" (p. 194), he comes to the conclusion that these people do not understand themselves. They believe they have succeeded by "hard work and great personal sacrifice" (p. 194). Dunstan, however, contends that they simply possess "a rather rare talent ... the talent for manipulating money" (p. 194). Dunstan thinks that financiers should regard themselves as artists of a special sort. He exclaims: "How happy they might have been if they had recognized and gloried in their talent, confronting the world as gifted egotists, comparable to painters, musicians, or sculptors!" (p. 194). Eisengrim does this, and so does the Bergman-like film director in *World of Wonders*. But Boy and his rich friends balk at self-knowledge; they prefer to hide their true nature even from themselves.

Dunstan Ramsay, on the other hand, is Davies' embodiment of the Canadian alternative to the American pursuit of material success. He is, in fact, Davies' version of the Canadian hero. In a speech given, appropriately enough, to an American audience, Davies describes his conception of this unlikely character by borrowing a phrase from Douglas LePan's poem "Coureurs de bois." The Canadian, Davies says, is "Wild Hamlet with the features of Horatio." Still referring to LePan's poem, he says: "The Canadian voyage, I truly believe, is this perilous voyage into the dark interior of which the poet speaks. It is a voyage in which many are lost forever, and some wander in circles, but it is the heroic voyage of our time." Davies concludes his speech with a passage in which he surely has the hero of his own best novel in mind: "There is the Canadian. The appearance is that of the secondary character, the hero's friend, the confidant; but the opportunity and heart – if he has the courage to trust it – is that of one who may be a hero, and a new kind of hero, a hero of conscience and spirit, in the great drama of modern man."[1]

Like Davies, the novelists Leo Simpson and Richard Wright have recently dealt with the American presence in Canadian life by creating a relatively passive "Canadian" character who watches in fascination or horror as a vigorous and amoral "American" character performs a series of devious manipulations. This pattern is conspicuous in Simpson's *Arkwright* (1971) and in Wright's *Farthing's Fortunes* (1976). In all likelihood, neither of these authors would endorse Davies' notion that the inner adventures of the Canadian hero can redeem the modern world. But, like other contemporary Canadian writers such as Margaret Atwood and Dave Godfrey, both Simpson and Wright appear to share Davies' uneasiness about the direction in which American values are taking Canadian society.

Most twentieth-century Canadian authors have repudiated the primacy of European culture and have cast their lot with North America. But this choice brings its own dangers, which must be countered in their turn. Did Canadians throw off their subservience to Europe only to be swallowed by the powerful apparatus of American popular culture? I have argued that a significant number of Canadian authors have examined this question in their fiction. Taking the United States as the paradigm of modern urban society, these

---

[1]The quotations in this paragraph are from Davies, "The Canada of Myth and Reality," in *One Half of Robertson Davies*, pp. 285-86.

writers express a hope that Canadian life can be governed by standards that differ from the prevailing values of American life.

CHAPTER EIGHT

The Colloquial Style
and the Tory Mode

"If, Sir," said Mr. Hopewell, with much earnestness, "if instead of ornamenting your conversation with cant terms, and miserable slang, picked up from the lowest refuse of our population, both east and west, you had cultivated your mind, and enriched it with quotations from classical writers, you would have been more like an Attaché, and less like a peddling clockmaker than you are."
        – Thomas Chandler Haliburton, *The Attaché*

In the twentieth century the majority of important American novelists have adopted a style that is direct, simple, energetic, and often slangy or colloquial in tone. In *The Colloquial Style in America* Richard Bridgman describes how the style of modern American fiction has been shaped by such "popular" influences as dialect humour and newspaper style.[1] Even the experiments with language conducted by leading American writers such as Ernest Hemingway, Gertrude Stein, and William Carlos Williams are based on the resources of vernacular speech rather than the elaborate refinements of educated discourse. In the United States, then, the representatives of elite and popular cultures have cooperated in forming a "democratic" style, a style appropriate to the supposedly classless society of the new world. As the linguist

---

[1] Richard Bridgman, *The Colloquial Style in America* (New York: Oxford Univ. Press, 1966). All further references to this work appear in the text.

Edward Sapir has written: "The modern mind insists on having the process of standardization (in 'prestige forms' of speech) take the form of a democratic rather than an aristocratic process."[1]

According to Bridgman, the three main factors shaping the colloquial style of American fiction are "romantic individualism, nationalistic pride, and practical necessity" (p. 41). None of these forces has been a dominant influence in shaping Canadian literature. The Canadian West was opened to settlement much later than the American West, and its development was to a considerable extent managed by the government. As a result, the mythic paradigm for Canadian westward expansion is the collective national enterprise celebrated in E.J. Pratt's *Towards the Last Spike* and Pierre Berton's *The National Dream*, not a version of the frontier individualism portrayed in, say, Cooper's Leatherstocking novels. Throughout most of Canadian history, the country's ambiguous political situation has not encouraged nationalistic boasting. Certainly Canadians have never been noted for the "ring-tailed roaring" found in so much of the American folk humour that forms one of the main tributary streams of the colloquial style. And American pragmatism has never received official sanction from most Canadian arbiters of intellectual probity and artistic taste. Indeed, from time to time certain Canadians have thought of themselves as custodians of a higher standard of political morality and cultural purity than that prevalent in the United States: Canadians not infrequently portray themselves as a Tory leavening in the democratic lump of North American society.

In this chapter, I want to argue that the prevailing conservatism of the Canadian temperament has also found an outlet at the level of prose style. Throughout this study, I have been examining the process by which our writers turned their fiction into a reflection of Canadian society. But even in the work of writers who have made Canadian experience the primary material of their fiction there are often lingering traces of the writer's initial reverence for

---

[1] Edward Sapir, quoted in M.H. Scargill, *Modern Canadian English Usage: Linguistic Change and Reconstruction* (Toronto: McClelland and Stewart, 1974), p. 12.

Europe. This residual deference to European culture is most apparent in the language our writers choose to employ rather than in their overt subject-matter.

In most American and Canadian fiction from the first half of the nineteenth century, vernacular speech was confined to the periphery, to the speech of lower-class characters and juveniles. In the United States, however, during the later half of the century vernacular speech gradually took over the whole of the narrative, as it does most notably in *Huckleberry Finn*. A parallel development did not take place in nineteenth-century Canadian fiction, where vernacular speech was still confined within strict limits. In *The Imperialist* (1904), for example, Sara Jeannette Duncan pointed out that the speech of Elgin "was clearly an American product" (p. 49). Her own style, however, is indebted to the studied ironies of Howells and James. Her narrator's formal sentences and complex witticisms clearly mark her as more sophisticated and worldly than most of the novel's characters. The contrast is most strongly marked if we compare the narrator's usual style with the style of the few speeches that the less educated residents of Fox County are allowed to make. As an example, here is Elmore Crow's deflating response to Lorne Murchison's imperial vision of a vaster Britain: " 'You keep your hair on, Lorne,' he advised. 'We ain't going to get such big changes yet. An' if we do the blooming syndicates'll spoil 'em for us' " (p. 149). This sort of breezy informality, however, is kept to a bare minimum in Duncan's novel. Even in the twentieth century, the colloquial style has until quite recently remained a comparative rarity in our fiction. The few aggressively colloquial writers – Morley Callaghan, Hugh Garner, or, more recently, Mordecai Richler – have been stylistic odd-men-out in Canadian letters. Instead of wholeheartedly following the American example, Canada has developed a linguistic split personality that Stephen Leacock wittily describes by saying that Canadians "use English for literature, Scotch for sermons and American for conversation."[1]

On strictly linguistic grounds, the stylistic conservatism of Canadian fiction is somewhat unexpected. A considerable

---

[1] Stephen Leacock, *How to Write* (New York: Dodd, Mead, 1943), p. 119.

body of linguistic research confirms the strong resemblance we would expect to find between the English spoken in Canada and that spoken in the United Stated. In *Speaking Canadian English*, Mark M. Orkin points out:

> ... the greater part of English-speaking Canada east of the Great Lakes was not in the first instance settled by Englishmen at all, but by Americans. The United Empire Loyalists were our Founding Fathers, and the language which they brought with them was that of the inhabitants of eighteenth-century New York and Pennsylvania, many of whose distinctive words may to this day be found embedded in our daily speech.[1]

Moreover, as Orkin adds: "The pronounced 'American' cast of much of the English spoken in Western Canada is attributable to the fact that the English-speaking West was settled almost entirely from Eastern Canada and the United States" (p. 58).

However, Canadian literary style has not simply followed the country's prevalent speech patterns. Although Canadian popular culture is dominated by American influences, Canada's educated culture has often deliberately turned away from the United States and instead looked towards Britain. Through the deliberate policies of its educational institutions and through the example of the CBC, Canada has long resisted standardizing the "prestige forms" of speech in the direction of the language of the masses. Orkin is able to assert: "That part of Canadian education however, which concerns itself with syntax, grammar and spelling has for a hundred years and more been based almost exclusively on British models" (p. 42). Canadian educational authorities, it would seem, have tried to resist the democratization of everyday standards of speech, which they viewed as resulting from a sort of linguistic version of Gresham's law: shoddy usage drives out good usage.

---

[1] Mark M. Orkin, *Speaking Canadian English: An Informal Account of the English Language in Canada* (Toronto: General, 1970), p. 48. All further references to this work appear in the text.

Especially in our universities, this attitude survived for a long time. During the early 1960s, Robert L. McDougall could still lament: "I mistrust our universities. I mistrust, from the point of view of literary criticism, the mob they house of gentlemen who write with ease, who are cosmopolitan and urbane to the last drop of sherry that flows in their veins."[1] That is, whatever their country of origin may be, the professors about whom McDougall is complaining are thoroughly steeped in the British intellectual tradition. Today, of course, the situation in our universities is quite different. Most of the prevailing intellectual fashions – along with many of the professors themselves – are now imported from the United States. In other words, our universities have gradually caught up with the developments that have been taking place in the rest of Canadian society.

The first generation of Canadian modernists grew up in a country that was more and more coming to be dominated by urban centres and their values. Increasing urbanization also meant greater acceptance of American values, for the urban centres to which Canadians were attracted in increasing numbers resembled American rather than European cities. We might well expect this generation of writers to be noticeably influenced by the colloquial style that was coming to dominate American writing. Actually, it is surprising how seldom the American influence took hold. In the first place, by the time it became the dominant mode in American fiction, the colloquial style – Mark Twain's example notwithstanding – was basically an urban rather than a rural style. It reflected the ragged, speeded-up materialistic life of the city. Its slang was no longer the expression of an advancing western frontier but the product of an urban ethos. This urban influence may help to explain why Grove, Buckler, Ross, and Mitchell, who locate most of their stories in rural settings, do not adopt the colloquial style as their primary vehicle of expression.

---

[1] Robert L. McDougall, "The Dodo and the Cruising Auk: Class in Canadian Literature," *Canadian Literature*, No. 18 (Autumn 1963), pp. 6-20, rpt. in Mandel, ed., *Contexts of Canadian Criticism*, pp. 230-31.

Instead of a version of the colloquial style, Grove, Buckler, Ross, and Mitchell use a controlled and cultured language, which conspicuously marks them as educated men. These writers all create many characters who speak in an uneducated manner, but none of them habitually commits his own voice entirely to vernacular rhythms and vocabulary. Grove is perhaps a special case. Older than the others and educated in the Europe of another era, he naturally acquired the notion that literature should be set apart from ordinary life or should comment on ordinary life from a superior moral and cultural plane. Even in Grove's urban novel, *A Search for America* (1927), the language is ponderous and formal, with no use of slang. Like Grove himself, Phil Branden possesses "a rather extensive reading and arguing vocabulary which however showed – and, by the way, to this day shows – its parentage by a peculiar stiff-necked lack of condescension to everyday slang" (p. 3). Buckler's prose is noted – and is even notorious – for its highly wrought syntax and imagery. Ross's *As for Me and My House* (1941) is filled with prose counterparts of the Waste Land imagery prevalent in much early modernist poetry. Even Earle Birney's *Turvey* (1949), a novel that contains a virtual anthology of Canadian ethnic accents and regional speech patterns, assumes that readers and author measure the vernacular speech of the characters against a shared standard of "correct" grammar. In the stories of *Jake and the Kid* (1961) Mitchell does give over the narration to a colloquial speaker. But *Jake and the Kid* falls within the special province of humour, where vernacular idiom has long been one of the recognized devices. In his manifestly "serious" novels Mitchell embeds the informal speech of his characters within a matrix of his own more conventionally literary prose.

The strength of Mitchell's commitment, at the outset of his career, to a conspicuously educated or "literary" style can be gauged by examining the opening paragraphs of the first edition of his best-known novel, *Who Has Seen the Wind* (1947):

Here was the least common denominator of nature, the skeleton requirements simply, of land and sky – Saskatchewan prairie. It lay wide around the town, stretching tan to the far line of the sky, clumped with low buck brush and wild rose bushes, shimmering under the late June sun and waiting for the unfailing visitation of wind, gentle at first, barely stroking the long grasses and giving them life; later, a long, hot gusting that would lift the black top soil and pile it in barrow pits along the roads or in deep banks against the fences.

But for now, it was as though a magnificent breath were being held; still puffs of cloud were high in the sky, retaining their shapes for hours on end, one of them near the horizon, presenting a profile view of blown cheeks and extended lips like the wind personification upon an old map.

Over the prairie cattle stood still as the clouds, listless beside the dried-up slough beds which held no water for them. Where the snow white of alkali edged the course of the river, a thin trickle of water made its way toward the town low upon the horizon. Silver willow, heavy with dust, grew along the river banks, perfuming the air around with its honey smell.[1]

The passage differs somewhat from the version that has been read and studied in so many Canadian classrooms. In the second edition of the novel, Mitchell dropped the second paragraph with its ostentatious allusion to the wind-rose drawings found on so many Renaissance charts. Even the revised version, however, is conspicuously "poetic," obviously a piece of fine writing by an author who is making clear the sensitivity of his response to the natural landscape.

Among the early Canadian modernist prose writers, Callaghan, MacLennan, and Davies are the leading chroniclers of life in middle-sized or large urban centres. The colloquial style might therefore seem to be their natural medium of expression. Only in Callaghan's fiction, however, does the colloquial style pervade the narration as well as the dialogue. MacLennan and Davies, on the other hand, use styles marked by a high incidence of slightly old-fashioned

---

[1] W.O. Mitchell, *Who Has Seen the Wind* (Toronto: Macmillan, 1947), p. 1.

syntactic habits. Their habitual tone is formal and dignified, occasionally verging on stuffiness. Robertson Davies, in particular, has been described as writing in "the Tory mode."[1] This term deserves a wider application, however, for it aptly describes the style that Davies, MacLennan, and several other Canadian authors have selected as the appropriate vehicle for articulating their conservative philosophies.

As used by Davies and MacLennan, the Tory mode is not simply an isolated stylistic quirk, but is a stylistic reflection of a larger commitment to conservative values. In their fiction and in their essays, MacLennan and Davies offer critiques of the materialism prevailing in modern society – by which they mean an urban society patterned after the American model. Similarly, their styles are deliberately cultivated alternatives to the colloquial manner that is prevalent in American fiction. The persistence of the Tory mode, not only in MacLennan and Davies, but in more recent writers such as George Grant, Scott Symons, and Hugh Hood, is part of a continuing effort by some Canadians to keep alive in North America a way of life that differs from the way of life pursued in the country to the south.

The pronounced resistance to the vernacular that is evident in the styles of MacLennan and Davies is entirely consistent with other features of their careers. Both men were strongly influenced by sojourns in England for post-graduate education. Both men have repeatedly announced their preference for British rather than for American literary models. Davies, in particular, has shown himself to be more sympathetic to British writing than American writing. In MacLennan and Davies, then, adherence to the Tory mode is part of a consistent literary ideology, part of a coherent set of ideas concerning the nature of fiction and the function of style in literature. In fact, the comments on style that have been offered by MacLennan and Davies constitute the most complete apology yet written for the Tory mode in Canadian fiction.

In most discussions of modern American fiction, the style of Ernest Hemingway is inevitably a central point of refer-

---

[1] Robert Cluett, "Robertson Davies: The Tory Mode," *Journal of Canadian Studies*, 12 (Feb. 1977), 41-46.

ence. It is illuminating to examine MacLennan's and Davies's attitudes towards the famous Hemingway manner. My concern is not the extent to which MacLennan and Davies have been influenced by Hemingway's style, but rather the reasons they have offered for rejecting Hemingway's example as a suitable model for their own fiction. For the critical writings of both MacLennan and Davies make it clear that their stylistic choice is part of a systematic rejection of values that are prominent in American fiction.

MacLennan's view of the Hemingway style is expressed in an essay titled "Homage to Hemingway."[1] MacLennan's central argument is that Hemingway's gifts were those of a stylist rather than a story-teller: "As a prose writer he is superb; as a novelist he must be regarded as little better than second-rate" (pp. 85-86). MacLennan draws an analogy between Hemingway's stylistic revolution and the overhauling of English prose style that took place during the Restoration. Hemingway "understood that between him and his reality lay a mountain-range of hackneyed words and phrases which had crushed the evocative powers of the English language. He sought by trial and error for a means of setting down with truth and vividness what his five senses told him, knowing that what they told him was much subtler than anything his predecessors had been able to communicate. And he found it" (p. 92). However, Hemingway applied his purified style to a purpose of which MacLennan cannot entirely approve: "What Hemingway has done has been to restore order and clarity to our use of the English language. But unlike the followers of Dryden, who insisted on clarity as a means to accurate thinking, he has used this classic criterion of style to represent accurate feeling. The style of the eighteenth century produced intellectualism; the style of Hemingway has made sensualism an end in itself" (p. 93). MacLennan's objection to the Hemingway style is, in the last analysis, a moral one. The Hemingway style is exquisitely crafted, but socially irresponsible.

In MacLennan's view, the proper use of language is to

---

[1] Hugh MacLennan, "Homage to Hemingway," in *Thirty and Three* (Toronto: Macmillan, 1954), pp. 85-96. All further references to this work appear in the text.

communicate conclusions reached through rational and responsible thought. As an illustration of the responsible use of language, he cites the eighteenth century's creation of "a kind of universal prose style which almost any educated man could acquire" (p. 90). He explains:

> It was the clarity and order of this universal style that made possible the political documents of Locke and Jefferson, the literary ease with which Berkeley and Hume discussed metaphysics, the urbanity brought to journalism by Steele and Addison ....
>
> This rational approach did more than produce clear writing; it also changed the history of the world, because for a time it eliminated misunderstandings between educated men. It is no accident that the development of stable government in England coincided with the period in which clarity of prose expression reached its apogee, just as it is also no accident that Germans in our own century, whose prose is often as formless and confused as Milton's, were unable to protect their minds against the incantations of Adolph Hitler. (pp. 90-91)

In MacLennan's eyes, then, prose style and politics are inseparable.

Robertson Davies' attitude towards style is similar in many respects to MacLennan's outlook. In *A Voice from the Attic* (1960) Davies has written at length on books and reading, and it is here that his conception of style can be most readily examined. In fact, *A Voice from the Attic* is specifically intended to offer American readers an alternative or "Canadian" perspective on the world of books. In this book, Davies offers a spirited apologia for the educated, genteel style that he favours. This style is very much a modern version of the same eighteenth-century style that MacLennan admires. It is a classical "middle" style, the style of a gifted personal essayist – and both Davies and MacLennan excel in this genre. In other words, both Davies and MacLennan are committed through their styles to an old-fashioned picture of the author as an educated gentleman. Both writers want to lead their readers to the intellectual high ground of rational argument and timeless values.

Nowhere in *A Voice from the Attic* does Davies comment directly on Hemingway's style; but he does refer scathingly to other recent American writers. Paraphrasing the conclusions reached in Edmund Fuller's *Man in Modern Fiction*, Davies disparages "a body of American novelists of whom James Jones and Norman Mailer are but two, who have exalted what he [Fuller] calls 'the Yahoo-hero' – a coarse-fibered vulgarian, grotesque in his thinking, and immature in his attitude toward life, who lives for the kicks he can get out of it" (p. 344). Davies decries the picture of the human condition that these writers present; they hold "a notion (concept is too definite a word) of man as a derelict and irresponsible creature existing in a world where no moral values apply" (p. 343). He comments with asperity on the sexual activities of their characters: "It is significant that many of these books are war books, or books about groups of men under stress, in which we find that there is exaggerated sexual activity with women who are described in terms of the uttermost contempt, whereas the true sentiment, the real love, is reserved for the 'buddy,' and is plainly homosexual" (p. 106). These comments make it plain that the writers about whom Davies is talking belong in the American tradition of what Fiedler describes as "homoerotic" fiction, a tradition that runs from Twain through Hemingway to Mailer.

With few exceptions, modern American fiction is not to Davies's taste. However, the worst sin that American writers have committed is not their treatment of sex but their anti-intellectualism. "Their chief defect," says Davies, "seems to be that they are desperately badly educated; potentially powerful intelligences have been given nothing to feed on, and they operate in a society where most people are as deprived as themselves. They and their readers have intellectual and spiritual rickets" (p. 344). Where MacLennan rebukes Hemingway for mere sensualism, Davies rebukes Hemingway's followers for carrying romantic attitudes to excess: "well-educated people could not think or write so sentimentally. Sentimentalism is the philosophy of boobs" (p. 344). Davies is much more approving towards modern British writing. In British fiction, he argues, "there is a tradition of classicism ... which has never been entirely submerged, and, perhaps more important and significant for the writing of fiction, a classical restraint in the expression of romantic feeling" (p. 343). For "classicism" in this passage we could equally well read "education"; and Davies would have that education worn on the writer's sleeve.

Davies does not feel that a writer should attempt to ingratiate himself with his readers by aping the bumbling verbal ineptitude of the common man. He strongly disapproves of the efforts made by many well-educated American writers to keep their education from showing in their fiction. Users of the colloquial style frequently give us the mind in undress. Even American protagonists with pretensions to be intellectuals – think of Bellow's Moses Herzog and Mailer's Stephen Rojack – present themselves as erratic and driven men, not as careful, analytic reasoners. On the other hand, *A Voice from the Attic* is devoted to urging educated readers to cease hiding their intellects under a basket. The intelligent readers whom Davies likes to call the "clerisy" should assert their right to determine standards of good taste. Davies surely believes that writers too should cease being ashamed of their intellectual propensities. As he puts it, "If you are an intellectual, your best course is to relax and enjoy it" (p. 36).

For a writer to hide his intelligence and education is a needless act of desperation. Davies laments that "Virtuosity, so much admired in some of the other arts, is at present unfashionable in literature" (p. 245). In his most explicit comment on the colloquial style, he scornfully remarks: "Many authors, on the North American continent, write as if they were apprentice blacksmiths making their first horseshoe; the clank of the anvil, the stench of the scorched leather apron, the sparks and the cursing are palpable, and this appeals to those who equate sincerity with sweating ineptitude" (p. 245). Davies, however, considers such deliberate bluntness a "fake sincerity which springs from clumsy craftsmanship and a shared loutishness between writer and reader" (p. 245).

Yet the colloquial style is far from being the limited medium Davies describes. As a counter-example, here is the opening paragraph of Morley Callaghan's first published story, "A Girl with Ambition":

After leaving public school when she was sixteen Mary Ross worked for two weeks with a cheap chorus at the old La Plaza, quitting when her stepmother heard the girls were a lot of toughs. Mary was a neat clean girl with short fair curls and blue eyes, looking more than her age because she had very good legs, and knew it. She got another job as cashier in the shoe department of Eaton's Store, after a row with her father and a slap on the ear from her stepmother. [1]

Certainly the passage is marked by colloquial diction: the chorus girls are "cheap" and "a lot of toughs"; Mary has a "row" with her father rather than a quarrel; and by way of discipline she receives a distinctly unrefined "slap on the ear." Readers are assumed to share the cultural and linguistic norms of the narrator and his society, so that much can be inferred from Mary's decision to leave school at the minimum age and from her dubious choice of employment. We also draw conclusions from the vulgar level on which family discussions are apparently conducted.

Let me pay closer attention to just one sentence from Callaghan's paragraph: "Mary was a neat clean girl with short fair curls and blue eyes, looking more than her age because she had very good legs, and knew it." The first half of the sentence is primarily a vehicle for applying five monosyllabic adjectives to Mary. These words present Mary as she appears to others. Considered one at a time, the five adjectives simply describe Mary's physical appearance as pleasing. But collectively they carry a connotation of innocence. For example, the double adjective "neat clean" – when either word alone might have carried the literal meaning – suggests an appearance of careful grooming. Mary is "fair" and has "blue" eyes, both details suggesting conventional good looks. Mary's "short" hair may seem to imply practicality – not the sensual freedom that would be implied by long, loosely flowing hair. The word "girl" in the phrase "a neat clean girl" is redundant, for femininity is implicit in Mary's

---

[1] Morley Callaghan, "A Girl with Ambition," in *Morley Callaghan's Stories*, Laurentian Library, No. 5 (Toronto: Macmillan, 1967), p. 238.

name. The word's function is not semantic but rhythmic; the phrases "neat clean girl" and "short fair curls" are rhythmically parallel, in deliberate contrast with the concluding element in the series, the shorter phrase "blue eyes."

The first half of Callaghan's sentence, then, seems to describe a sensible, wholesome, no-nonsense young lady. The second half of the sentence, however, creates quite another impression. Mary's "very good legs" give her a sophistication and even sensuality that alters the reader's assessment of her. Moreover, the sentence's last three words make it clear that Mary is well aware of the impression she creates; and in all likelihood she deliberately exploits her appearance. The sentence starts with a physical description, dispassionately offered; but it concludes with the narrator quietly reproving Mary's vulgarity. Mary starts the sentence as the girl next door, but she ends as a flirt or worse – perhaps as someone willing to exploit her body to influence men in her favour. The passage gives us a glimpse inside Mary's materialistic calculating mind, but without describing her thoughts directly.

In *Strange Fugitive* (1928), as well, Callaghan effectively uses the colloquial style. The following speech, for example, in which Harry Trotter harangues Isaac Pimblett, makes it clear without any authorial comment that Harry's aggressive bravado masks a deep insecurity:

> "Is that so, eh? Well, if you think I'm doing any fitting you got another think comin'. You think I'm just one of the guys that go the same old way home, eh. Yeah, like hell I am. See. Settled down, eh. You're all wrong. Married? Sure, but just let me get the breaks and I'll have everybody eating out of my hand. Get that straight."[1]

The mannerisms of vernacular speech – the fragments, the profanity, the interjections, the repeated "eh," the belligerent "See" – are thrust obtrusively at the reader, just as Harry thrusts them at Isaac Pimblett. Despite Harry's vehemence, we feel that he lacks any real ideas or goals. However, the

---

[1] Callaghan, *Strange Fugitive*, p. 75.

passage just misses real effectiveness. Too many of the colloquialisms are lifeless cliches ("got another think comin'," "get the breaks," "eating out of my hand"). The final effect is overdone, a bit heavy-handed. Nonetheless, in Callaghan's early stories and novels, the colloquial style, working by indirection and implication, sometimes achieves effects of considerable subtlety. In his later work, the urgency of his moral message often seems to overwhelm his faith in his own style. Too often Callaghan treats his characters like idiot children, whose rudimentary actions and thoughts must be interpreted for readers by the omniscient narrator.

Mordecai Richler, on the other hand, seldom overtly intrudes into his novels. As an additional example of the colloquial style in operation, here is a passage from *The Apprenticeship of Duddy Kravitz*:

> To a middle-class stranger, it's true, one street would have seemed as squalid as the next. On each corner a cigar store, a grocery, and a fruit man. Outside staircases everywhere. Winding one, wooden ones, rusty and risky ones. Here a prized plot of grass splendidly barbered, there a spitefully weedy patch. An endless repetition of precious peeling balconies and waste lots making the occasional gap here and there. But, as the boys knew, each street between St Dominique and Park Avenue represented subtle differences in income. No two cold-water flats were alike. Here was the house where the fabulous Jerry Dingleman was born. A few doors away lived Duddy Ash, who ran for alderman each election on a one-plank platform: provincial speedcops were anti-semites. No two stores were the same, either. Best Fruit gypped on the scales, but Smiley's didn't give credit. (pp. 13-14)

Some of the most obvious grammatical features of the colloquial style are prominent here: contractions and sentence fragments. But the passage's omissions are perhaps as significant as what is actually said. The narrator catalogues physical details of the neighbourhood, but offers a minimum of interpretive commentary. The most important general

212

statement is that each street "represented subtle differences in income." However, the narrator does not give an explanation of the gradations in social status that these differences imply. Instead, the reader is left to make inferences for himself. The narrator's overall thesis is that life in the Jewish ghetto offers more variety than a casual observer would expect. But this thesis is never explicitly stated. As in Callaghan's writing, great reliance is placed on the reader's ability to hear the proper tone and make the correct inferences.

If the colloquial style can be a rich and subtle literary medium, why do MacLennan and Davies reject it? Part of the answer is that the colloquial style uses a limited viewpoint. Often, the colloquial voice belongs to a first-person narrator, speaking within the limitations imposed by human subjectivity. Even when the colloquial style is used in third-person narration, the language of everyday life encourages a limitation of the narrative to the thoughts and experiences of ordinary life. Davies, in particular, objects to "the convention (so dear to one school of modern criticism) which demands that a writer should conceal himself, should pretend that he does not exist . . ." (p. 148). The pedagogue in Davies does not wish to be misunderstood. He is unwilling to allow the scope for private interpretation that characterizes the colloquial style. Perhaps Davies also senses that he is simply not very good at capturing vernacular speech. Certainly, the rather clumsy dialogue of *Overlaid* reveals his difficulties in handling the speech of uneducated characters. Pop, in particular, sounds like one of the country bumpkins found in so many comic plays and movies. His speeches embody a dramatic convention that signifies rusticity; they are not an authentic recreation of actual rural speech.

Fundamentally, however, Davies eschews the colloquial style because it is intrinsically modern, aggressively up-to-date. Using such a colloquial style would imply a commitment to immediate experience in the ever-moving present. But in *A Voice from the Attic* Davies imperiously warns against placing too great an emphasis on today's standards: "to do that would be to commit ourself to what is merely contemporaneous, which is a pitiful slavery, unworthy of anyone who pretends to any taste in literature,

however humble, or understanding of life, however small"
(p. 203). As this attempt to browbeat his readers shows,
Davies is committed not only to traditional values but to
explicitness and didacticism in his prose. He believes in a
hierarchy of ideas, which it is his duty to promulgate. And
there is a corresponding hierarchy of styles, which he
likewise must endorse through both precept and practice.

Scrutiny of a few sample passages will illustrate the
alignment of theory and practice in MacLennan and Davies's
work. For instance, here is the opening of Davies's *Fifth
Business*:

> My lifelong involvement with Mrs. Dempster began
> at 5:58 o'clock p.m. on the 27th of December, 1908, at
> which time I was ten years and seven months old.
>
> I am able to date the occasion with complete
> certainty because that afternoon I had been sledding
> with my lifelong friend and enemy Percy Boyd
> Staunton, and we had quarrelled, because his fine
> new Christmas sled would not go as fast as my old
> one. Snow was never heavy in our part of the world,
> but this Christmas it had been plentiful enough
> almost to cover the tallest spears of dried grass in the
> fields; in such snow his sled with its tall runners and
> foolish steering apparatus was clumsy and apt to
> stick, whereas my low-slung old affair would almost
> have slid on grass without snow. (pp. 1-2)

Dunstan is a precise and confident speaker. His diction and
syntax mark him as educated, as does the way he generalizes
and uses abstractions. For example, he speaks of his "complete certainty" and talks about being "able to date the
occasion," when a colloquial speaker would say something
like: "I know for sure when it happened."

Just a few pages into Davies's novel we find Dunstan's
carefully phrased account of his home village, which is the
setting for the early part of the story:

> Village life has been so extensively explored by
> movies and television during recent years that you
> may shrink from hearing more about it. I shall be as

214

brief as I can, for it is not by piling up detail that I hope to achieve my picture, but by putting the emphasis where I think it belongs.

Once it was the fashion to represent villages as places inhabited by laughable, lovable simpletons, unspotted by the worldliness of city life, though occasionally shrewd in rural concerns. Later it was the popular thing to show villages as rotten with vice, and especially such sexual vice as Krafft-Ebing might have been surprised to uncover in Vienna; incest, sodomy, bestiality, sadism, and masochism were supposed to rage behind the lace curtains and in the haylofts, while a rigid piety was professed in the streets. Our village never seemed to me to be like that. It was more varied in what it offered to the observer than people from bigger and more sophisticated places generally think, and if it had sins and follies and roughnesses, it also had much to show of virtue, dignity, and even of nobility. (p. 10)

Dunstan's education is evident here, both in the reference to Krafft-Ebing and in the catalogue of abstractions that concludes the passage. Dunstan cannot resist generalizing his opinions into universal truths. He deliberately organizes the passage to highlight a thesis: his village offered a wide variety of experience. On the surface, the thesis is similar to the argument of the Richler passage quoted earlier. But Dunstan is aware of writing on what traditional rhetoric terms a *topos*, a conventional topic previously treated by many other writers. Dunstan is aware of what is new and what is old in his account of village life. He also is open about his intention to instruct his readers. Dunstan the schoolmaster has turned this description of his village into an informal lecture on village life in general.

A didactic purpose also animates MacLennan's George Stewart, as he introduces himself near the beginning of *The Watch that Ends the Night*:

I have never felt safe. Who of my age could, unless he was stupid? Quite a few people thought me successful, but in my own eyes I was no more successful than the old Greek who pushed boulders up the hill knowing they would tumble down the moment they reached the top. Some people thought me calm, but inside I knew I was not. I have often heard myself described as a "mature" commentator, but I have never seemed mature to myself. The young seem more so because they know nothing of the 1930s. The young have the necessary self-confidence and ignorance to feel mature, and that is why I like them so much better than I like my own generation. Was there ever a crowd like ours? Was there ever a time when so many people tried, so pathetically, to feel responsible for all mankind? Was there ever a generation which yearned to belong, so unsuccessfully, to something larger than themselves? (pp. 3-4)

George not only delivers generalizations about society, as Dunstan does; he also turns himself into a generalization when he presents himself as the embodiment of an entire generation. The diction of the passage stresses abstractions; there is a classical reference, which rather awkwardly tries to appear informal by avoiding the direct naming of Sisyphus. The passage is organized by the skilful management of antithesis. The first half of the paragraph contains three consecutive statements of the contrast between George's "mature" external appearance and his internal insecurity. Thus, George begins by giving us three antitheses that stress his own insecurity; then he provides the antithesis to himself, when he contrasts his insecurity with the apparent self-assurance of the younger generation. The passage, then, is filled with devices that heighten its formal tone. In addition to the antitheses already mentioned, it concludes with a series of three rhetorical questions. And throughout the passage there is an effective use of parallel constructions.

Plainly the colloquial style is an inappropriate vehicle for the moral and intellectual instruction that MacLennan and Davies wish to impart. The colloquial style is a no-nonsense, pragmatic manner, tending towards informality and even chattiness. It is suited to convey transitory emotions, immediate physical sensations, and spontaneous thoughts. In contrast, the Tory mode, with its formal, educated, and precise tone, is a good vehicle for considered reflections. It specializes in elaborate descriptions, rational syntheses, and qualified generalizations. The Tory mode does not capture the mind in action, but presents the carefully arranged results of prolonged cogitation.

Davies and MacLennan are not the whole of Canadian fiction, as the very different practice of Callaghan and Richler demonstrates. But until recently the Tory mode, as exemplified by the work of MacLennan and Davies, has been the most common manner in Canadian fiction. As a result, the most memorable characters in Canadian fiction are cultivated, reflective, and polished talkers like George Stewart and Dunstan Ramsay. There has been a dearth of those protagonists the critic Walker Gibson labels "Tough Talkers." [1] Most of the Canadian modernists are reluctant to entrust their books to the limited perspective of a first-person narrator. MacLennan and Davies did not give up the omniscient viewpoint until late in their careers, when they had acquired considerable self-confidence as writers – and, not incidentally, when they had acquired a sense of the mutability of the world. Even then, the narrators created by MacLennan and Davies are fictional versions of the didactic *persona* each author uses in his discursive essays.

Today, the state of Canadian fiction has greatly altered from what it was only twenty years ago. A majority of younger writers have adopted some version of the colloquial style. In addition to Richler, obvious examples are Margaret Laurence, Robert Kroetsch, Alice Munro, and Margaret Atwood. In Laurence's novels, for example, the narrator's conversational voice becomes a primary means of characterization. All of Atwood's narrators speak with a version of her own flat and ironic voice. Many younger authors write in a manner that is influenced by oral style. In other words, despite the critical industry that is growing up around Davies' Deptford trilogy, the Tory mode appears to be on the wane. But there remain a handful of writers who have vigorously argued for the continuing value of the Tory

---

[1] Walker Gibson, *Tough, Sweet and Stuffy: An Essay on Modern American Prose Styles* (Bloomington: Indiana Univ. Press, 1966), pp. 40-41.

outlook.

By far the most prominent advocate of the conservative viewpoint in recent years has been George Grant. Grant's view of Canada, expressed so memorably in *Lament for a Nation* (1965), has given a renewed impetus to the notion that Canada's *raison d'être* is to provide an alternative to the American political and social model. Historically, Grant argues, English Canadians have been trying "to build, along with the French, a more ordered and stable society than the liberal experiment in the United States."[1] Grant fears, however, that in the modern world this idea of Canada is no longer sustainable. He contends: "In no society is it possible for many men to live outside the dominant assumptions of their world for very long" (p. 42). But the liberal ideology that dominates the modern world locates man's essence in his freedom, not in his capacity for making moral choices. Hence, Grant offers his lament, a lament for the passing of a Canada based on the notion that the collective good ought to come before the desires of the individual.

Early in Scott Symons's *Place d'Armes* (1967), the narrator, Hugh Anderson, refers explicitly to Grant's book: "there's that new book on Canada ...lamenting our dead nation. Well, I've never dared read it. Because I'm simply a result of what it diagnosed. Why read it anyway? I know it all by heart already!".[2] Like George Grant, Symons has impeccable credentials as a member of the Canadian Establishment. But in his two unusual works of confessional "fiction" Symons has stridently announced his rebellion against his background. Moreover, according to Charles Taylor, Symons' own personal life has confirmed his rejection of Rosedale respectability, for he has literally enacted the scenes and images that function as metaphors in his "fiction."[3] Symons' protagonist

---

[1] George Grant, *Lament for a Nation: The Defeat of Canadian Nationalism*, Carleton Library, No. 50 (Toronto: McClelland and Stewart, 1970), p. 4. All further references to this work appear in the text.

[2] Scott Symons, *Combat Journal for Place d'Armes* (Toronto: McClelland and Stewart, 1967), p. 48. Subsequent page references are given in the text.

[3] Charles Taylor, *Six Journeys: A Canadian Pattern* (Toronto: Anansi, 1977), pp. 189-243.

in *Place d'Armes* describes himself as by family heritage a *"Legitimist, Establishment, Hereditary, Infeodated, Loyalist, Christian Canadian Tory"* (p. 140). *"Our Toryism is our culture as Canadians"* (p. 14), Hugh Anderson remarks, and he casts himself as the "bad conscience" (p. 46) of English Canada. That is, he speaks – as does George Grant – for those values that English-Canadian life has abandoned to go whoring after the liberal gods of progress and comfort.

Hugh Anderson accuses English Canadians of an extreme self-repression amounting to a kind of psychological self-castration. The first step in freeing himself from this repressive mindset is to accept his own emotions and impulses. His quest leads him to Montreal, where he hopes to find the antidote to his own Protestant heritage in the Catholic ethos of French Canada. In fact, these two cultures become metaphors for aspects of Hugh Anderson's psyche. He speaks of the need to placate "the Protestant Gods in me ...so that I can allow me to write, to rejoice, to procreate ... to achieve the commanded Grace of the Catholic God me" (p. 268). The most striking aspect of Hugh Anderson's adventures in Montreal is his homosexual relationship with several French-Canadian male prostitutes. Indeed, Hugh Anderson's initiation into a new way of being is not completed until he allows one of the male prostitutes to penetrate what he terms, with playful obscenity, his "assoul." The outrageous imagery of Symons's book likens Hugh Anderson's recognition of his sexual preferences to a religious awakening. This linking of sacred and profane motifs suggests that self-fulfillment can only be reached when there are no more dualisms, when the sacred and secular realms are united, and body and spirit are no longer thought of as separate.

In style as well as in content, Symons' book is a rebellion against genteel norms. Throughout *Place d'Armes*, Symons offers his readers a formless outpouring of words and feelings, a flow of language that is abundant and often nearly incoherent – everything that the classically controlled Tory mode is not. Symons also rejects the idea of a well-made plot. His apparently chaotic manner is designed to promote immediacy. He wants to present a series of spontaneous, immediately apprehended experiences. Whatever his private

219

idiosyncrasies may be, Symons does join MacLennan and Davies in rejecting the American way of being. All three writers desire what Symons calls "presence." That is, they want experience to be luminous with otherworldly significance. But in Symons's exuberant prose, the romanticism that MacLennan and Davies are at pains to tame and civilize is allowed free rein. Only in this way, Symons feels, can he express what his culture has conspired to repress and deny. Yet it may be that Symons' extravagant mannerisms achieve the opposite effect to the one he strives to attain. For many readers, Symons' self-indulgent manner enacts the breakup of those Tory values that Grant laments to greater effect in his more measured cadences.

Symons shares with the other Tory writers a desperate need for coherence. One indication of the desperation underlying the work of these writers is found in their use of a meretricious or sentimental symbol as the principal embodiment of their meaning. Dunstan Ramsay sees a madwoman as a saint; George Stewart sees his wife's suffering as part of a divine plan to further his personal psychomachia; John Diefenbaker becomes a tragic hero in Grant's version of Canadian history; and Hugh Anderson's encounters with male prostitutes take on spiritual significance in Symons' book. The sense of strain that these images create betrays the difficulty the Tory writers find in their endeavour to work against the dominant flow of North American thought.

There is, however, one writer whose work shows that adherence to the conservative outlook is not inevitably accompanied by desperation and strain. That writer is Hugh Hood, and Hood's serenity is most apparent in his work-in-progress, the cycle of novels known collectively as *The New Age/Le nouveau siècle*. Hood's ease with the world is explained, at least in part, by his Catholicism. Davies, MacLennan, Grant, and Symons are all Protestants who long for the inter-penetration of the secular and the divine that Hood, a Catholic, finds it easy to take for granted. George Grant contends that Catholics have not staked everything on private experience, as have Protestants. The Church's authority ensures that the pursuit of goodness will be given precedence over the pursuit of personal freedom. "To Catholics who remain Catholics, whatever their level of sophistication," Grant writes, "virtue must be prior to free-dom" (pp. 75-76).

In "The Governor's Bridge Is Closed," an early essay that is also a trial run at the kind of narration used in *The New Age*, Hood makes some remarks that are pertinent to the present discussion. He writes:

> Many modern writers have executed variations on the theme "You can't go home again." And they're wrong, I think. Of course you *can* go home again, and again, and find the place essentially the same as it was before you went away. The man who denies that you can go home is making a metaphor for what he considers the fatal impermanence of life. Thomas Wolfe and the members of his school may not exactly prefer change to permanence; hardly anybody does, I find. But they find it more striking, more impressive. They think with Heraclitus that everything is chang-ing all the time. This is what I wish to deny.[1]

Hood here aligns himself with those who see an unchanging essence at the heart of things. Like George Grant, he questions whether the liberal or "progressive" ideology of change is an accurate description of the immutable nature of the universe.

Throughout *The New Age* Hood's narrator, Matt Goderich, is a voluble and opinionated talker. However, Matt has none of Dunstan Ramsay's asperity; in fact, he seldom criticizes anyone. Forbearance and tolerance are his watch-words. Matt is more like George Stewart, though he shows none of George's insecurity and self-pity. Matt has opinions – an abundance of opinions, in fact – but his personality is bland, and he blunts the force of his judgments by embedding them in lengthy analyses. Technically speaking, he is not a professional academic, but he definitely has the academic temperament. Just like Symons's narrator, Matt Goderich is a historian of Canadian art and architecture. In fact, like Hugh Anderson, Matt interprets Canadian architecture as

---

[1] Hugh Hood, "The Governor's Bridge Is Closed," in *The Governor's Bridge Is Closed* (Ottawa: Oberon, 1973), pp. 14-15.

an index of the development of the Canadian character, though he avoids the embarrassing excesses of Symons' self-indulgently emotional narrator. A deliberate comparison to Symons may even be intended when Matt calls himself "the first prophet of the Canadian style" (p. 120), and announces that he is working on a massive study of the Canadian character as revealed through the nation's architectural history.

Hood's purpose in *The New Age* is not simply documentary; rather, he wants to express the nation's invisible essence, the "moral imagination" that he sees as a distinctive attribute of Canadian society.[1] His twelve-volume cycle of novels is meant to do for twentieth-century Canada what Proust's *A la recherche du temps perdu* does for *fin de siècle* France. Hood's view of Canada is inextricably embedded in his conception of *The New Age*. Hood has argued that Canada was fortunate to escape the excesses of the Romantic movement. In the nineteenth century, Canadians "were all poor and we had no time for ideas. But we did what we could ... to lay the foundations of a civilized society" (p. 90). Hood admits that much of Canadian life has been dominated by rather narrow and intolerant religious attitudes. But much of value has also been retained, he feels. As a result, the characters in *The New Age* experience Canadian society as a network of those invisible relationships and traditions that give richness and depth to everyday experience. In other words, Hood's novels suggest that Canadian culture is richer, more varied, and more sophisticated than most people think.

It is time to ask whether the prominence of the Tory mode has helped or hindered the development of Canadian fiction. Have some of our writers barricaded themselves within a sort of garrison style, long after such a course of action was necessary? Have some of our writers weakened their work by turning away from the rhythms of vernacular speech? Certainly, to cavil at the specific accomplishments of the Tory mode would be churlish and illogical. In *Fifth Business* and *The Watch That Ends the Night* the Tory mode

---

[1] Hood, "Moral Imagination: Canadian Thing," in *The Governor's Bridge Is Closed*, pp. 87-102. All further references to this work appear in the text.

splendidly justifies itself. And *The New Age* is probably the most ambitious project a Canadian novelist has ever undertaken. It seems clear, then, that the future of the Tory mode rests with Hood. Whether Hood can successfully complete his magnum opus remains to be seen, but among our contemporary writers he is the outstanding spokesman for the idea that Canadian society represents a positive alternative to the American way of life. Yet a suspicion lingers that figures such as George Stewart, Dunstan Ramsay, and Matt Goderich, however entertaining they may be, are anachronisms in twentieth-century North American writing. And a literature that turns its back on the present is probably, in the long run, doomed to become overly introverted and precious; eventually, it must become irrelevant. Whatever its virtues in the abstract, then, I can see little future in our literature for the Tory mode.

CHAPTER NINE

Contemporary Fiction
and the Art Novel

> If I describe my house
> I may at last describe my self
> but I will surely lie
> about the house.
>
>   – George Bowering, "The House"

By now, the label modernism is firmly attached to the literary mode that prevailed during the first half of the twentieth century. The label that shows definite signs of becoming equally firmly linked to the literature of the century's second half is postmodernism. In both Europe and North America, a vigorous branch of the critical industry is engaged in defining the nature of the literature that marches under the new banner, and the contemporary literary scene is often viewed as a struggle between these two competing literary ideologies. In this chapter, however, I want to suggest that the quarrel between the modernists and the postmodernists is not the most signficant aspect of the current literary scene. In fact, the advocates of post-modernism may actually have a great deal in common with those they are attacking. It is possible that our highly polarized way of seeing current literary developments has distracted us from examining other, more fundamental changes that are now occuring in our literature.

Since World War II, Canadian writers have belatedly begun to follow British and American writers in moving away from straightforward documentary realism. Novels such as Sheila Watson's *The Double Hook* (1959) and A.M. Klein's *The Second Scroll* (1951) mingle snippets of poetry into the flow of their prose narratives. These books show that Canadian authors have at last discovered the structural use of myth that T.S. Eliot described in his review of *Ulysses*. The "inward turning"[1] towards psychological realism that marks so much of twentieth-century fiction is also present in many Canadian novels of the sixties and seventies, notably in sensitive character studies by writers such as Margaret Laurence, Margaret Atwood, and Alice Munro. More recently, in works such as Robert Kroetsch's *What the Crow Said* (1978), Jack Hodgins' *The Invention of the World* (1977) and *The Resurrection of Joseph Bourne* (1980), and Timothy Findley's *Not Wanted on the Voyage* (1984), Canadian writers have moved away from the documentary or sociological realism that until recently has characterized our fiction.

In an article that surveys the fiction of the sixties and the early seventies, Donald Cameron announces: "The realistic novel, which has dominated Canadian writing for decades, has largely fallen out of favour."[2] Of course, Cameron exaggerates the decline of the traditional kind of fiction. But he exaggerates in order to make a valid point. Striking changes *are* taking place in contemporary Canadian fiction, as our writers respond to the same literary forces that are transforming fiction elsewhere in the Western world. Today, many of our most interesting novelists and story writers are turning away from traditional modes of fiction and are turning instead to various kinds of experimental writing, including fantasy and the sort of self-referential writing called metafiction. As a result, in the work of some writers traditional realism has been supplanted by a realism that is somehow "magic."

The precise meaning of postmodernism is a vexed question, but most often it is defined in opposition to modernism – a literary term whose meaning is assumed to be familiar and

---

[1] Edel, *The Psychological Novel 1900-1950*, p. 27.

[2] Donald Cameron, "The Bizarre and the Freaky in Recent Canadian Fiction," in Carl F. Klinck and Reginald E. Watters, eds., *Canadian Anthology*, 3rd ed. (Toronto: Gage, 1974), p. 640.

well-understood. Literary modernism is frequently interpreted as a strategy by which writers seek to impose an intelligible order on a world from which the old absolute standards have vanished. Postmodernists, on the other hand, frequently claim to relish the uncertainty which characterizes most aspects of contemporary life and thought. Thus, the modernists are sometimes depicted as anti-life reactionaries, the enemies of spontaneity. Frank Davey, in his polemical handbook *From There to Here*, tells us: "the modernists sought to control both their world and their art; the post-modernists seek to participate in anarchic cooperation with the elements of an environment in which no one element fully controls any other." The objective of the postmodernist writer, Davey says, "has been no longer to retreat from the experiential world [as the modernists did] but to embody – and thus make intelligible to his readers – its rapidly increasing variety, fragmentation, non-linearity, and unpredictability."[1]

Davey represents a viewpoint that seems to be gaining ground in Canadian literary circles. There are several prominent authors and critics who habitually speak slightingly of conventional realistic fiction, and draw a sharp line between traditional modes of fiction and the newer fictional modes. According to them, our contemporary novelists can be split into two opposing groups: the reactionary realists, and the up-to-date postmodernists. "For years," says George Bowering, "I have been wondering why it is that in Canada we hold with such tenacity to realism & naturalism in our fiction."[2] He patronizingly describes Alice Munro, Margaret Laurence, and Margaret Atwood as "good writers all, who tell the normal realist story of sensitive child growing up to be disillusioned but wisely maladjusted adult" (p. 77). Robert Kroetsch has voiced the exasperated complaint: "For the moment, there is so much half-assed prose in Canadian

---

[1] Frank Davey, *From There to Here: A Guide to English-Canadian Literature Since 1960*, Our Nature-Our Voices, II (Erin, Ont.: Porcépic, 1974), pp. 20, 21.

[2] George Bowering, *The Mask in Place: Essays on Fiction in North America* (Winnipeg: Turnstone, 1982), p. 77. All further references to this work appear in the text.

writing, so much surrender to subject matter. There are writers for whom it would be an embarrassment, even a disgrace, to write an interesting sentence. There is something in our literature that is a linguistic equivalent to the national crossing of the legs."[1] Geoff Hancock has argued that the avant garde stories he likes to anthologize "return to the sources of story telling, to the impulses that generate fables, fantasies, and metafictions within us."[2] He flatly asserts: "This is the real literary tradition; the other was an illusion" (p. 12).

Bowering, Hancock, and Kroetsch habitually equate the techniques of modernist fiction with the techniques of realism. Bowering, for example, identifies modernist fiction with realism when he explains the difference between the modernist novel and the innovative work of contemporary writers:

> A realist fiction was intended to produce a window on the world. Hence the value of invisibility, or more properly of transparency. One did not so much read the novel as read through it to the world. Post-modern novels, on the other hand, are in a way decorative. If they are windows they are stained-glass windows or cut-glass windows that divert light waves & restructure the world outside. (p. 25)

Hancock also uses a visual image in order to discredit traditional or realistic fiction. "Once, writing represented what was optical," he writes. "The story writer imitated visual sensations, and the images did not go past the limits of sight."[3] Kroetsch remarks succinctly: "The whole realistic

---

[1] Robert Kroetsch, "Contemporary Standards in the Canadian Novel," in Charles R. Steele, ed., *Taking Stock: The Calgary Conference on the Canadian Novel* (Downsview: ECW, 1982), pp. 17-18.

[2] Geoff Hancock, "Introduction," *Illusion One: Fables, Fantasies and Metafictions* (Toronto: Aya, 1983), p. 7. All further references to this work appear in the text.

[3] Geoff Hancock, "Introduction," *Metavisions* (Montreal: Quadrant, 1983), p. 5.

movement was based on the notion of language as picture."[1]

It is worth asking why Bowering and Hancock – and to a lesser extent Kroetsch as well – offer such a hostile portrait of modernist fiction. The answer is implicit in some remarks offered by Bowering. "In most countries of the technological world," says Bowering, "the writer of post-realist fiction is no longer in the avant-garde, but is rather the prime product for export" (p. 78). This is not an appeal to logic, but an appeal to literary fashion. At bottom, I think, the postmodernists are really saying that our writers should adopt the new modes because everyone else has done so – and we don't want to be left behind, do we?

The same attitude is also present in much of the criticism that deals with contemporary Canadian writing. For example, in 1981 Stan Fogel published a controversial article titled "Lost in the Canadian Funhouse." Fogel begins by comparing contemporary Canadian fiction with the contemporary fiction of the United States, and then he asks some pointed questions. He writes: "The formalist or metafictive concerns that have dominated the pages of *Tri-Quarterly* and *American Review* and the novels of Barth, Barthelme, Coover, Gass, Pynchon, et al are almost non-existent in Canadian journals and in the novels of prominent Canadian novelists. Why is this the case? Is it a salutary thing?"[2] The main purpose of Fogel's article is to answer the last question with a resounding "No!" and to urge Canadian authors and critics to mend their ways. In fact, Fogel seems to regard most of our leading novelists and critics as literary dinosaurs, who have remained faithful to modes of fiction that are hopelessly passé in more civilized places. I think the weakness of Fogel's logic will quickly become obvious. His article is a manifesto, not a cautiously argued and thoroughly documented scholarly exposition. Its polemical intent, however, makes it a revealing summary of attitudes that

---

[1] Russell M. Brown, "An Interview with Robert Kroetsch," *University of Windsor Review*, 7 (Spring, 1972), 16.

[2] Stan Fogel, "Lost in the Canadian Funhouse," *Queen's Quarterly*, 88 (1981), 690. All further references to this work appear in the text. Fogel has subsequently incorporated much of this article into his book *A Tale of Two Countries: Contemporary Fiction in English Canada and the United States* (Toronto: ECW, 1984).

often underlie the advocacy of avant garde writing.

Fogel complains that most Canadian critics still accept "the now challenged premise that the language of fiction is, in Ortega y Gasset's metaphor, a window onto the world, instead of writing *on* the window which retards mimetic and referential entrees" (p. 691). Fogel is particularly hard on those critics who still insist on scrutinizing our literature for evidence of a maturing national identity. Their work "perpetuates the claustrophobic context in which contemporary Canadian literature is read and studied" (p. 693). In the era of structuralism and deconstruction, critics such as Roland Barthes and Jacques Derrida and their followers have made "insistence on the anti-referential nature of literary language" into "the prevailing critical fashion." Against this critical background Fogel remarks, the views of Canadian literary nationalists seem "fusty to an extreme" (p. 694). Indeed, Fogel confidently announces: "the idea that there is a national character to enunciate in literature and that that identity has the kind of ontological certitude devalued by the contemporary critical theory of Derrida and Barthes, among others, can only distort the shape of literature in Canada" (p. 696).

But what is the proper shape of Canadian literature? For Fogel, as for Bowering and Hancock, it is a shape that is determined by the example of the literary avant garde in other countries. In fact, for properly initiated readers, the title of Fogel's article telegraphs this message in advance. The title is borrowed from John Barth's book of experimental stories, *Lost in the Funhouse.* And readers who recognize this allusion are probably also aware that Barth's essay "The Literature of Exhaustion" is one of the most influential apologies for the new fiction.[1] Fogel wants his essay to carve a niche in Canadian letters for the new fiction, in the same way that Barth's essay helped to legitimize the new fiction in the United States.

---

[1] John Barth, "The Literature of Exhaustion," *Atlantic Monthly*, Aug. 1967, pp. 29-34.

Fogel's chief positive examples are two relatively unheralded works, Martin Myers's novel *The Assignment* (1971) and Ray Smith's collection of stories *Cape Breton Is the Thought Control Centre of Canada* (1969). He likes these works because they "constitute a challenge to mimetic notions of fiction, to verisimilitude and other shibboleths of the traditional novel" (p. 697). Fogel admits that both *The Assignment* and *Cape Breton Is the Thought Control Centre of Canada* have conspicuous weaknesses, but he thinks their authors are headed in the right direction. For example, he likes Smith's stories because "they constitute an attempt to engage prose fiction in a manner vital in other parts of the world – not only the United States, but also France (the *nouveau roman* of Robbe-Grillet, Butor, Sarraute) and South America (the Borgesian fictions of Donoso, Puig, Cortazar) – but mostly neglected in Canada" (p. 701). That is, Fogel likes Smith's stories because they ape the manner of writers who are fashionable in the larger world of the international avant garde. This is equally true of the other texts he mentions with approval.

What should we make of this quarrel between modernism and postmodernism? Perhaps not very much. In the first place, the claim that postmodern writers are somehow closer to the essence of literature than the modernists is pure nonsense. In the second place, the quarrel is, to a considerable extent, based on a false dichotomy. The seeds of postmodernism are present in the work of some writers from the modernist period, for example in the work of Gertrude Stein. The postmodernists' account of modernist fiction is a tactical over-simplification – perhaps even an outright distortion of the principles of modernism. In fact, I think the quarrel between modernists and postmodernists is a sort of family argument within the literary fraternity, an argument whose vehemence conceals a considerable degree of underlying unity. The combatants may irritate each other – as family members with divergent personalities often do – but they are tied together by their common allegiance to certain fundamental values. Both groups view literature as an activity that is carried out by highly qualified specialists. Both groups feel that literary texts benefit from undergoing a microscopic examination at the hands of expert critics. In short, both groups view literature as the preserve of an educated elite. Their agreement about this point outweighs their disagreements about details of literary theory.

I want to suggest that modernists and postmodernists agree in regarding a particular form of fiction, which I have previously called the art novel, as the highest reach of the twentieth-century novel. I must immediately point out that the art novel is not a genre in the usual sense of that term, for it has no distinguishing group of conventions that sets it unmistakably apart from other kinds of fiction. Rather, the art novel comes into being when novelists think of themselves as the producers of high art. This way of understanding the novel represents a shift away from the nineteenth-century's view of the novel as entertainment, social history, or fictionalized sermon. And the notion of the novelist as an artist is far removed from the roles of story-teller, historian, reporter, or moralist that formerly served as the paradigms of the novelist's function.

Harry Levin has pointed out: "The thought that a man of letters should consider himself a practitioner of the fine arts, or that he should be designated professionally as an artist, is a legacy from Flaubert's generation. . . ." Levin goes on to link Flaubert with his most important English-speaking disciple, James Joyce. "The cult of intransigent artistry," he continues, "which both men practised as devoutly as if it were their religious vocation, is embodied in and elucidated by the latter's *Portrait of the Artist as a Young Man.* . . ."[1] Perhaps Levin's comments do not apply to poetry, for historically poets have often claimed an exalted status, even a semi-divine inspiration. But Levin is quite right to argue that novelists before Flaubert were considered to be somewhat déclassé. Indeed, from its association with the middle classes, the novel was often regarded as a distinctly ungenteel form, and viewed with distaste or suspicion. Flaubert, however, placed the novel on a par with the work of the most serious artists in any medium. In the English-speaking world, the transformation of the novel into high art did not

---

[1] Harry Levin, "What Was Modernism?" in Stanley Burnshaw, ed., *Varieties of Literary Experience: Eighteen Essays in World Literature* (New York: New York Univ. Press, 1962), p. 325.

definitively take place until the early years of this century. The later novels of Henry James and then the novels of James Joyce announced the formulation of an artistic conception of the novelist's vocation. The status of the novel as a form of "high" art was confirmed during the 1920s, when the literary mode we now know as modernism firmly established itself in Europe and the United States as the principal vehicle for serious writing.

Although the art novel is not a genre in the usual sense, there are nonetheless certain motifs that are recurrent in many art novels: the use of artists as protagonists; the use of symbols and learned allusions; the artful manipulation of narrative point of view; the disruption of conventional patterns of plot and character. But these motifs are not the infallible badges of the form. The art novel is produced because writers take a certain view of literature, not because they use a specific group of conventions. In practice, the distinguishing mark of the art novel is its "difficulty." The writer of an art novel usually makes considerable demands on the reader's interpretive skills – skills that can be acquired only through an extensive literary education. In other words, the art novel requires a reader who is both educated enough and patient enough to puzzle out the author's meaning.

George Bowering has made some comments that are pertinent at this point. In the introduction to *The Mask in Place* Bowering tells us: "though I gobble up every book produced by Philip Roth, I don't find his work as interesting as, say, Raymond Federman's, which I can hardly stand reading" (p. 2). I find this a peculiar outlook. Apparently Bowering enjoys Roth's fiction, and he doesn't enjoy Federman's writing. Then why is Federman's work more "interesting?" The answer is connected with Bowering's literary ideology. Federman eschews conventional realism, and Bowering is committed on theoretical grounds to the idea that realism is intrinsically dishonest. In effect, I suggest, Bowering is praising Federman because Federman is a "difficult" writer. The "difficultness" of a literary text is also used as an index of worth by two other contemporary writers, Robert Kroetsch and Hugh Hood. Kroetsch has said: "I like difficult texts – that's really what it comes down to, texts that demand a lot from the reader."[1] Hood has written: "My work demands to be read silently and with close attention by mature men and women – there is nothing I could do to change this, even if I wished to – and a single reading won't do."[3]

But the great modernists are notoriously "difficult" writers – the cries of pain that their works regularly produce from novice students of literature furnish ample proof. Therefore, if the writer's demands on the reader become the criterion of evaluation, modernist fiction is not distinguishable from postmodernist fiction. Examined closely, the works of the great modernists are just as subtle and complex – and just as problematical – as are the works of the contemporary fabulists or metafictionists. Leon Edel has astutely said about one of the acknowledged classics of modernist fiction: "what he [the ordinary reader] must discover, above all, in such a book as *The Sound and the Fury*, is a new way of reading fiction."[4] The interpretive habits that Edel advises Faulkner's readers to adopt are also applicable with little change to most postmodernist fiction. In this respect the modernists are not the enemies of the postmodernists, but their allies. They share the aim of redeeming literature from the unimaginative hands of the bourgeoisie, those readers who, as Bowering insultingly says, demand novels that "run easily along the tracks laid by literary artists in the early days of realism" (p. 77).

I now want to turn away from the manifestoes of Fogel, Bowering, and Hancock, and look directly at the practice of contemporary fiction writers. If we look at what is actually being written and published, the situation is not as clearly polarized as the advocates of postmodernism have painted it. Moreover, the writers who use traditional fictional modes are still more numerous and more accomplished than are the writers who adopt some variant of the postmodernist man-

---

[1] Shirley Neuman and Robert Wilson, eds., *Labyrinths of Voice: Conversations with Robert Kroetsch, Western Canadian Literary Documents Series, 3* (Edmonton: NeWest, 1982), p. 162.

[2] Hugh Hood, *Trusting the Tale* (Toronto: ECW, 1983), p. 129.

[3] Leon Edel, "How to Read *The Sound and the Fury*," in Burnshaw, ed., *Varieties of Literary Experience*, p. 242.

ner. What a scrutiny of today's fiction does make clear, however, is that more and more writers – both modernists and postmodernists – are producing examples of the art novel. This is true not only of newer writers such as Timothy Findley, Jack Hodgins, and Chris Scott, but also of established figures such as Sinclair Ross, Mordecai Richler, and Margaret Laurence.

The first art novel to be written by a Canadian is probably Howard O'Hagan's remarkable *Tay John* (1939). But O'Hagan's novel was published in New York, and made little impression in Canada until it was rediscovered by D.G. Jones, who gave it a prominent place in his influential study *Butterfly on Rock*. Likewise, Elizabeth Smart's *By Grand Central Station I Sat Down and Wept* (1945) has until very recently been little read in Canada. And I can see no legitimate reason for claiming Malcolm Lowry's *Under the Volcano* as a Canadian novel. Thus, the first significant Canadian art novel, and still the most Joycean of our novels, is A.M. Klein's *The Second Scroll*.

Klein became fascinated with Joyce's *Ulysses* during his undergraduate days at McGill. When he decided to turn the journal of his 1948 visit to Israel into a novel, Klein adopted the method of Joyce's novel. Joyce had drawn his mythic parallel from the principal literary monument of classical culture, and his avoidance of Christianity as a paradigm was certainly in some measure a value judgment. Klein, on the other hand, looks to a text that is central to both Jewish and Christian traditions, the Pentateuch or first five books of the Old Testament. Although Klein's method is borrowed from Joyce, his mood is very different. Klein does not use his mythic substructure as an ironic counterpoint to the present age, but as a pointer to the deeper significance of his contemporary story. He does not portray contemporary history as a panorama of anarchy and futility. As Leon Edel puts it: "Joyce was a chronic belittler and Klein was, in my opinion – and I do not exaggerate – an eternal exalter of human spirit and the human spirit of survival."[1]

---

[1] Leon Edel, "Marginal *Keri* and Textual *Chetiv*: The Mythic Novel of A. M. Klein," in Seymour Mayne, ed., *The A. M. Klein Symposium* (Ottawa: Univ. of Ottawa Press, 1975), p. 27.

Klein saw a parallel between twentieth-century history and the events narrated in the Pentateuch. According to the scriptural narrative, the prolonged wanderings of the ancient Hebrews were ended by their belated arrival in the promised land. That ancient period of exile resembles the modern diaspora, which ended with the formation of the new state of Israel and the return of the widely scattered Jewish people to their ancient homeland. The mission of Klein's protagonist is to compile an anthology of modern Israeli poetry. Much of his time, however, is spent in an unsuccessful pursuit of a mysterious relative, Uncle Melech. This obsessive quest symbolizes the pursuit of an elusive divinity by humanity.[6] Although the narrator does not find Uncle Melech, he does read Uncle Melech's remarkable commentary on Michelangelo's paintings in the Sistine Chapel. Uncle Melech presents Michelangelo's paintings as a synthesis of pagan and Christian mythologies, a prophetic vision of a harmony that transcends earthly divisions. Klein's message seems clear. Art provides the strongest evidence of divinity's presence in everyday life. Even more important is the narrator's realization that the most authentic expression of Israeli life can be found not in the nation's formal poetry but in the daily speech of ordinary Israelis. Klein is saying that divinity should not be sought in any transcendent form, but in the texture of ordinary life. Ultimately, Klein's art novel expresses the desire that everyday life should become as shapely and joyous as art.

When it first appeared, Klein's novel was a puzzling anomaly in our fiction. So was Sheila Watson's *The Double Hook*, which burst on the literary scene in 1959 as a striking departure from the conventional form of most Canadian fiction. Bowering has called Watson's novel "the watershed of contemporary Canadian fiction" (p. 97) and it remains one of our leading examples of "experimental" fiction. At the time she wrote *The Double Hook*, Watson was a graduate student at the University of Toronto, working on a thesis that dealt with the works of Wyndham Lewis. This circumstance is

---

[1]This point is made by Solomon J. Spiro, *Tapestry for Designs: Judaic Allusions in The Second Scroll and the Collected Poems of A. M. Klein* (Vancouver: Univ. of British Columbia Press, 1984), pp. 185-93.

significant, for it makes her one of the first important Canadian authors who was committed to a full-time career as a university teacher of literature. Today, it is common for our poets and novelists to be employed in university departments of literature, but this was not always the case. Of the major novelists from what I have called our "classical" period, only MacLennan and Davies have pursued careers in the university. The other members of this literary generation conducted their careers essentially outside the academy.

Over the past twenty or thirty years, however, the academic writer has emerged as a mainstay of Canadian letters. This development represents a significant change in the make-up of our literary community. I am well aware that some earlier writers also taught in our universities. But writers such as Edward McCourt, Philip Child, and Hugh MacLennan habitually kept a certain distance between their vocation as writers and their academic careers. And when they thought about their own writing, they retained something of the outlook of the educated layman, the common reader. Just think of the difference between the informal essays of Hugh MacLennan and the academic essays of such contemporary university-based writers as Frank Davey, Eli Mandel, George Bowering, or Robert Kroetsch. MacLennan writes about many subjects besides literature; moreover, he was educated as a classical scholar rather than as a literary critic, and he came to the teaching of literature after ten years of schoolteaching and a fling at earning his living as a full-time writer. Even Robertson Davies, though he was latterly an academic at one of our most prestigious universities, was an actor and newspaper editor before he became a university professor. When he writes and speaks about literature, Davies never presents himself as a professional scholar, but always assumes the persona of a gentleman amateur. On the other hand, today's academic writers publish articles in learned journals, present papers at academic gatherings, and write about little else but literature. Above all, they speak of their own creative writing in the light of current academic theorizing about literature.

Today, not only do writers habitually work in universities, but the academy seems to have taken virtual custody of our literature. After decades of being neglected, Canadian literature has become over the past quarter century or so the focus of a great deal of scholarly attention, both in the classroom and in the pages of several critical journals devoted exclusively to the discussion of Canadian letters. In consequence, the primary audience for much of today's fiction is made up of university teachers of literature and their students. Surely the academy's sponsorship of our literature has greatly encouraged the writing of the art novel, which is designed for a readership that possesses an extensive literary education.

Our contemporary novelists, like writers the world over, place an increasing emphasis on seeing themselves in aesthetic terms. As a result, artistic self-consciousness is a prominent feature of a large number of recent Canadian novels. The artist-novel or *Kunstlerroman* – the portrait of the artist as a young man or woman – is a common sub-genre of the twentieth-century novel, and the most outstanding Canadian examples are probably Alice Munro's *Lives of Girls and Women* (1971) and Margaret Laurence's *The Diviners* (1974). Writers of various kinds are also the protagonists of Margaret Atwood's *Lady Oracle* (1976), Robert Harlow's *Scann* (1972), Norman Levine's *From a Seaside Town* (1970), John Metcalf's *General Ludd* (1980), and Timothy Findley's *Famous Last Words* (1981). Other kinds of artists – a film director, a painter, a musician, and an actress – are portrayed in Mordecai Richler's *St. Urbain's Horseman* (1971), Hugh Hood's *White Figure, White Ground* (1964), Michael Ondaatje's *Coming Through Slaughter* (1976), and Munro's *Who Do You Think You Are?* (1978). Well-educated and introspective figures – historians who are linked closely with our cultural heritage – are central to Robertson Davies' *Fifth Business* (1970) and Rudy Wiebe's *My Lovely Enemy* (1983). The nature of art is an important theme in Robert Kroetsch's *The Studhorse Man* (1969) and in his subsequent novels. In other words, there is a pervasive artistic self-consciousness in contemporary fiction.

But self-conscious artistry need not lead to fiction that is obscure or difficult. Sinclair Ross's *As for Me and My House* (1941) and Margaret Laurence's *The Stone Angel* (1964) are usually viewed as the leading examples of prairie realism. These novels are known above all for their portraits of the constricting condition of life in small prairie towns. Although both novels contain elaborate systems of symbols, the reader is not forced to think of the stories as "art." The books can be read simply as transcriptions of life, in the manner of naive realism. In subsequent novels, both Ross and Laurence have drawn greater attention to the literary artifice with which they present their stories. In *Sawbones Memorial* (1974) Ross's acknowledgment of his own artistry is indirect. The reader cannot avoid noticing that the novel is a tour de force of narrative technique, in which Ross manipulates the events of a few hours in order to make his characters' conversations reveal the life story of Doc Hunter, the retiring town doctor. This virtuoso performance was inspired by Ross's acquaintance with a French *nouveau roman*, Claude Mauriac's *Dîner en ville*.[1] Laurence's *The Diviners* is a more openly self-conscious novel, for Laurence's protagonist becomes a writer, and the novel is almost a textbook study of how to use a variety of narrative viewpoints and styles to tell a story. Yet neither of these novels abandons its writer's usual subject-matter. Ross and Laurence write art novels, but they still use the materials of bourgeois fiction that Canadian readers have come to expect from them.

The Diviners, by its preoccupation with Morag's creative processes, proclaims itself a work of art as well as a study of Canadian life. Laurence pays considerable attention to the artistic process itself, and to the artistic growth of her artist-protagonist. We are not just told that Morag is a writer; on several occasions we see her at work, and we are given summaries of her novels. Moreover, we watch Morag growing up, and can understand some of the ways in which her life has generated emotions and situations that she projects into her art. This aspect of *The Diviners* illustrates the extent to which our contemporary fiction has turned introspective, inspecting its own origins in Canadian experience, and even examining the peculiar epistemological status of fiction itself – those self-confessed lies that somehow speak truth. Laurence's novel joins in the exploration of the Canadian past that many other recent novelists have been

---

[1] Lorraine McMullen, *Sinclair Ross*, Twayne's World Authors Series, No. 504 (Boston: Twayne, 1979), p. 119.

conducting – most notably, Rudy Wiebe in *The Temptations of Big Bear* (1973) and *The Scorched-Wood People* (1977) and Graeme Gibson in *Perpetual Motion* (1982). But Laurence also follows the example set by many recent works of fiction that acknowledge their own fictionality – for Morag at the novel's end goes into her house to write the last words of the very novel we have been reading.

The artistic self-consciousness of *The Diviners* is by no means unusual in our recent fiction. But there is one respect in which Laurence's novel does not mirror the way most current Canadian novelists think of themselves. This is Morag's isolation as an artist. Like Laurence herself, and like many of Laurence's immediate forerunners, Morag for a long time works at her writing almost totally in isolation. Her community gives her no support in her artistic ambitions; she is not even allowed to improve the style of the local Reports from South Wachakwa and Freehold that she edits for the *Manawaka Banner*. Morag has only one literary friend, her college classmate Ella, and she knows only one other artist, the painter Daniel McRaith, her friend and sometime lover. She has to master her art in private; she is not even taken seriously as a writer by her husband. And in her artistic isolation, Morag resembles most Canadian writers of her own and earlier generations.

Laurence's portrayal of the artist's place in Canadian society, however, does not represent the view of many contemporary writers who are now conducting their careers within the university environment. To illustrate how these writers view their vocation, I will turn to another fictional character, namely Matt Goderich, the garrulous narrator of Hugh Hood's cycle of novels known collectively as *The New Age / Le nouveau siècle*. True, Matt is not himself a novelist. But he is a writer – specifically, he is a historian of Canada's artistic and social development. In his examination of the Canadian past, Matt goes far beyond Morag Gunn's recognition of her personal roots. Indeed, he builds his career out of his knowledge of the Canadian cultural tradition. Matt also experiences a far greater sense of community with his contemporaries than Morag does, for his cultural interests do not isolate him from his society. In fact, Matt grows up with several people who also become involved with the arts.

Maura Boston becomes a noted poet; Edie Codrington, later his wife, becomes a painter; Valerie Sherbourne becomes a pillar of the local theatre group; and Matt's brother, as we learn in *The Scenic Art* (1985), becomes a successful novelist and playwright. "In Canada," Matt remarks to his wife at one point in *A New Athens* (1977), "we've expected our artists to do it *all by themselves*, without a milieu" (p. 205). In Matt's own time, however, this deficiency is being rectified. As Matt says: "everything was coming together and preparing us to have trained artists in this country, with the gifts and the visionary power *and* professionalism" (p. 204). Matt himself eventually presides over an endowed foundation, the Codrington Colony for the Encouragement of Visionary Art, that is meant to provide a supportive environment for artists. According to Matt Goderich, then, the Canadian artist now has a supportive cultural milieu in which to work.

Hood is, by training and by profession, an academic student of literature, and he enters wholeheartedly into the era of the art novel. His major inspirations or precedents for *The New Age* appear to be the work of James Joyce and Marcel Proust's massive novel *Remembrance of Things Past*. "I think it would be marvellous for Canada," Hood has said, "if we had one artist who could move easily and in a familiar converse with Joyce, and Tolstoy, and Proust; and I intend to be that artist if I possibly can; and I am willing to give the rest of my life to it."[1] He has also said:

> I really want to endow the country with a great imperishable work of art. If I do, it will be the first one that we have. I think it would make an enormous difference to the confidence of this country if we did have one thing like the plays of Shakespeare or *War and Peace* or *A la recherche du temps perdu*, and we knew it, and were sure of it. *Jalna*, ha, ha, won't do. It isn't good enough. I think that *The New Age* and the works of mine which go with it and around it *will*

---

[1] J.R. (Tim) Struthers, "An Interview with Hugh Hood," *Essays on Canadian Writing*, Nos. 13/14 (Winter/Spring 1978-79), p. 61. All further references to this work appear in the text.

be good enough, and I think it will do a lot for the country. I would even go so far as to say I feel as though this were a mission given to me. (pp. 85-86)

Whether Hood's abilities can measure up to his ambitions remains to be seen. But one thing is clear. If the twentieth century is the age of the art novel, then Hood is among its leading prophets in Canada.

Like Laurence, Hood combines the outlook of an art novelist with the subject-matter of a bourgeois novelist. His work remains accessible to the ordinary reader, though perhaps barely so. In some other recent fiction, however, artistic self-consciousness takes an even more extreme form. The novelist becomes the acknowledged creator of his fiction, an overt story-teller. This sort of novelist is not creating a nineteenth-century omniscient narrator, who relates a tale that supposedly exists outside the novelist's control; instead, these postmodernist writers become god-like creators of a wholly private and fictional world, where the only rules are determined by the writer's whims. George Bowering, for example, intrudes himself, as the twentieth-century author of *Burning Water* (1980), into his retelling of the story of Captain George Vancouver's eighteenth-century voyage of exploration to Canada's west coast. Now, there is certainly no fixed rule that compels Bowering to emulate Rudy Wiebe's approach to history. But *The Temptations of Big Bear* is, in my judgment, a much better book than *Burning Water*.

Perhaps the most extravagantly self-conscious Canadian novel of all, however, is Chris Scott's *Bartleby* (1971). Like John Barth's *The Sot-Weed Factor*, *Bartleby* pays homage to the eighteenth-century picaresque fiction from which the modern novel descends. In particular, he honours that most self-conscious of picaresque fictions, *Tristram Shandy*. The reader of *Bartleby* is led on an eclectic chase through the conventions of fiction from the eighteenth century to the present, from the most highly regarded classics to the farthest reaches of pornography. In a sense, Scott's novel is an education in the nature of reading. The reader is repeatedly reminded that nothing is *really* happening; the reader is just encountering words on the page. "Follow the MS," Scott's narrator is urged by his "fantastical friend," "as you would follow life. Read, read where it is written and begin at the beginning."[1] Yet in *Bartleby* this self-consciousness is pushed to a laboured extreme. Certainly, the novel is an exuberant performance. A celebration of the power of both language and fiction. But many readers don't like to have their experience of fiction interfered with in this way. I wonder how many readers think that *Bartleby* is worth the considerable effort it demands? It does not offer the more conventional consolations that other highly regarded contemporary novels, such as *The Sot-Weed Factor* or John Fowles' *The French Lieutenant's Woman*, offer even a relatively untrained reader. Scott, I fear, has created a book that only a demented professor of literature could love without reservations.

Fogel remarks that "most Canadian prose fictions of the seventies are not structurally innovative" (p. 697). As a description of our fiction, this is a fair comment. It is Fogel's interpretation of this situation that I want to question. Certainly, formal innovation has never been a leading feature of Canadian writing. With the notable exceptions of the poets bpNichol and bill bissett, Canadian writers have seldom pursued technical experiment for its own sake. Even when their themes are rebellious or critical, our writers have relied heavily on inherited literary tradition: the fathers they repudiate are personal and societal, not literary. Except for the work of Robert Kroetsch, recent Canadian writing contains little of the masturbatory self-celebration found in the work of some American "fabulators." Perhaps Leonard Cohen's *Beautiful Losers* (1966) is an exception to the last statement. But Cohen's book, and for that matter Scott Symons' eccentric *Place d'Armes* (1967) and *Civic Square* (1969), may be more significant as symptoms of a widespread cultural malaise than as attempts to introduce a new aesthetic into Canadian letters. Moreover, Symons' fiction is actually just as didactic in intention as the work of many earlier Canadian preachers-in-novelists'-clothing, such as Ralph Connor. Indeed, one of the most persistent features of the Canadian literary tradition is its didactic tone.

---

[1] Chris Scott, *Bartleby* (Toronto: Anansi, 1971), p. 9.

The formal conservatism of Canadian fiction, then, does not result simply from a head-in-the-sand refusal to emulate the avant garde, but occurs because our combination of literary and social conditions have demanded this sort of writing. Our writers are still engaged in the task that was performed for the United States by the American critical realists: they are still revealing the vitality and variety of Canadian life; they are still creating for Canadians the imaginative geography of their country. At the present time, literary and social forces may be demanding another sort of literature from Canadian writers. The current drift towards the art novel and towards postmodernism may prove to be irreversible. But I'm still not convinced that the change is either an inevitable or a desirable event.

I can explain some of my reservations by again referring to Stan Fogel's deprecating assessment of contemporary Canadian fiction. When Fogel decries the conservatism of Canadian writing, he pays attention to the formal features of literature but neglects its thematic content. The foreign writers he holds up as models are not simply playing games with fictional technique. Robert Coover's *The Public Burning*, which he praises, is an attack on the American national myth that presents the United States as the home of liberty, the apogee of free enterprise, and the defender of the free world. Fogel also praises the magic realism of South American writers, but does not acknowledge that these writers use their fantastic stories to offer critiques of the authoritarian regimes under which they live. However, for a Canadian writer to unthinkingly ape the formal innovations of *The Public Burning*, as Fogel recommends, would be, in cultural terms, a surrender of identity – merely the aping of American avant garde mannerisms. Fogel ends up recommending a variant of the cultural colonialism that he decries. Canadian writers need to deal with their own surroundings, both personal and political, in their own way. For good reasons, Canadian writers have usually dealt with the American cultural impact on Canada by exploring their own alternate cultural identity.

I have previously argued that the Canadian tradition in fiction took shape out of the bourgeois or realistic novel. It was, in spirit if not always in fact, a "popular" literature. At least, it was "popular" writing in the sense that it was accessible to relatively untrained readers. If the postmodernist writers and their critical accomplices have their way with our literature, the future will be quite different. For postmodernist writing does not rest on a broad cultural consensus. Instead, it is the private preserve of a trained literary elite, and the move towards postmodernism is being promoted largely by a vocal minority within the academy. Outside the academy, the conventions of realism are still the assumptions that most readers bring to fiction. As a result, the further our writers move away from realism, the smaller the audience they can expect to reach.

Lest my concern for the common reader be thought a personal eccentricity, an outburst of pure philistinism, I hasten to bring Fogel's implied master, John Barth, to my support. In a subsequent article, Barth has expanded, clarified – and perhaps to some extent recanted – the opinions expressed in "The Literature of Exhaustion." In his later article Barth displays a surprising degree of concern for the ordinary reader. Modernism, he suggests, went too far when it ceased criticizing the values of the bourgeoisie, and instead turned inward, becoming a private playing for the literary elite. Barth describes the novel as "a genre whose historical roots are famously and honorably in middle-class popular culture." The contemporary novelist, he urges, "*should* hope to reach and delight, at least part of the time, beyond the circle of what [Thomas] Mann used to call the Early Christians: professional devotees of high art." Barth concludes, with good-humoured eclecticism: "The ideal postmodernist novel will somehow rise above the quarrel between realism and irrealism, formalism and 'contentism,' pure and committed literature, coterie fiction and junk fiction."[1] Barth, then, espouses a marriage of popular fiction and the art novel. This is also the course that I would like Canadian authors to pursue.

----

[1] John Barth, "The Literature of Replenishment: Postmodernist Fiction," *Atlantic Monthly,* Jan. 1980, p. 70.

The Academy and the Canadian Tradition

"Amcan's the coming thing, and particularly the Canadian end
of it."

— Robertson Davies, *Leaven of Malice*

We are sometimes told that we are now living in the heyday
of Canadian letters. In the second edition of the *Literary
History of Canada*, for example, Northrop Frye speaks
admiringly of "the colossal verbal explosion that has taken
place in Canada since 1960."[1] In the *Oxford Companion to
Canadian Literature* Sam Solecki has written: "With a
handful of exceptions Canada's best novels and stories have
been written in the past two decades."[2] The Canadian writer
no longer resembles the unhappy figure A.M. Klein describes
in "Portrait of the Poet as Landscape." Klein's poet, you will
remember,

---

[1] Northrop Frye, "Conclusion," in Carl F. Klinck, gen. ed., *Literary History of Canada: Canadian Literature in English*, 2nd ed. (Toronto: Univ. of Toronto Press, 1976), III, 318.

[2] Sam Solecki, "Novels in English: 1960 to 1982," in Toye, ed., *The Oxford Companion to Canadian Literature*, p. 576.

245

makes of his status as zero a rich garland,
a halo of his anonymity,
and lives alone, and in his secret shines
like phosphorus. At the bottom of the sea.[1]

Today, having surfaced to breath the common air, the
Canadian writer seems certain to obtain a hearing.

During the past quarter of a century, there has been a
profound alteration in the conditions under which our
literature is being produced. Above all, we have seen the
acceptance of Canadian Literature as a respectable academic
field of study. Today, courses in Canadian Literature are
given at nearly every university and community college in
the nation, and the criticism of Canadian writing is now a
full-scale branch of the academic industry. Journals are
edited, articles and books are published, annual meetings of
learned associations are held, promotions are obtained, and
tenure is granted – all for the greater glory of Canadian
letters. In other words, since about 1960 an entire new
gallery, labelled Canadian Literature, has been added to the
literary museum presided over by our university departments of English Language and Literature.

The academy's involvement with our literature has had
important consequences. Increasingly, specialists in Canadian Literature are forsaking the academy's traditional
custodial role to comment on the latest works produced by
established authors or to tout the work of new authors. That
is, academics who once contented themselves with monitor-
ing the progress of our literature have begun to exert a
significant influence on its development. This change of
attitude on the academy's part has generally been ap-
plauded. But I think that the implications of the academy's
love affair with Canadian writing deserve a closer examination. My conviction is that there has existed, and exists now,
a distinctive northern segment of North American literature.
But its continued distinctiveness is seriously threatened.
And I find myself suspecting that one of the agencies now
abetting the erosion of a distinctive Canadian literature is

---

[1] A.M. Klein, "Portrait of the Poet as Landscape," in *The Collected
Poems of A.M. Klein* (Toronto: McGraw-Hill Ryerson, 1974), p. 335.

the university, particularly those within the university who militantly profess a sophisticated, avant-garde view of our literature. In fact, our literature is in danger of being taken over by a small academic minority.

Just consider some of the developments that have flowed from the creation of the Canada Council in 1957. A small change, but a symptomatic one, saw the Governor General's Awards taken out of the hands of the Canadian Authors' Association and put in the Council's charge. This transfer indicated that a new management team, composed of professionals rather than amateurs, was taking control of our literature. The Canada Council soon began to sponsor public readings by Canadian writers, and a programme for funding writers-in-residence was also created, though it later fell victim to one of the early rounds of governmental budget restraints. The end result was that a serious and committed writer could think of living exclusively by writing, provided he or she could endure a rather spartan and nomadic way of life.

The formation of the Canada Council indirectly reinforced the academy's growing influence. The actual dispensing of money was controlled by the Council's cadre of bureaucrats. But the bureaucrats, in their turn, usually sought advice from recognized "experts" in the various branches of the arts. When it came to giving grants either to publishers or writers, many of the expert advisors were drawn from university circles. Specifically, when the money was going to support Canadian writers or to support the publication of Canadian books, the advisors often came from among those professionally committed to the study of Canadian literature.

Several other developments have played an even larger part in helping the academy to consolidate its substantial and growing power over the course of Canadian letters. One development is the hiring by our universities of an increasing number of creative writers. Canadian writers have always experienced difficulty in supporting themselves by their writing. In the past, they have often pursued careers in the churches, in government service, or in journalism, while turning out their creative work on the side. The growth of our university system during the late fifties and sixties, together with the recognition now extended to Canadian writing, has made the academy a very congenial refuge for many poets and novelists. A related development is the proliferation of creative writing programmes within our universities. Therefore, in many of our classrooms the writers of the present are instructing the writers of the future.

All of these developments add up to a significant shift in the functioning of the entire literary institution in Canada, a shift whose end result amounts to something approaching an academic takeover. For good or ill, the health of our literature has been committed to the stewardship of an alliance between academics and the government functionaries who hold the pursestrings of the Canada Council. The shift has very significant consequences. Above all, the divorce between the writing and publishing of "serious" literature and the writing and publishing of all other forms of literature has been confirmed. That is, the elite or minority forms of literature have been definitively hived off from writing done for a larger public.

Formal instruction in Canadian literature is now the single most important factor in shaping the future readership for Canadian writing. Such teaching cannot be a neutral act. Students must study the texts their instructors select, and their knowledge of Canadian writing will usually become a lesser version of their teachers' knowledge. Students will – if they develop literary tastes at all – often develop tastes that reflect their instructors' preferences. But there is a very special set of values governing the literary opinions that many academics hold. The writing studied in university classrooms is almost exclusively poetry, fiction, and drama that can be certified by academic standards as "serious" art: that is, writing that pleases a small group of highly educated and specially trained readers. However, this academic bias excludes some authors who form a significant part of the Canadian literary tradition. Authors who have appealed conspicuously to the commercial marketplace are seldom studied, partly because their very popularity is construed as evidence of vulgarity. Yet figures such as Ralph Connor, L.M. Montgomery, and Mazo de la Roche have a legitimate place in any historical survey of our literature.

The academic approach to Canadian writing also suffers from other serious limitations. Some academic critics are unselective antiquarians: they collect, preserve, and annotate the works of third-rate writers in the same ponderous solemnity that they would bring to the preparation of a new edition of Shakespeare's plays. Other academic critics are overly exclusive: in the name of maintaining standards they summarily dismiss the vast majority of a culture's creative efforts. Applying the first approach to Canadian writing results in the absurd inflation of even the most mediocre nineteenth-century books into major "classics" of the Canadian tradition. Applying the second approach results in the contention that a Canadian literature worthy of serious critical attention has appeared only in the past two decades or so. Both approaches create a serious distortion of our literary history.

At the present time, however, a new threat to a balanced view of Canadian writing is gaining strength. Many of the leading younger critics of Canadian writing are advocates of the contemporary modes of literature that are variously described as experimental, avant garde, or postmodern. These instructors introduce students to works that satisfy the latest dictates of literary fashion; but they may show less sympathy for authors who continue, however skilfully, to practise traditional modes. Too often, such teaching can create a small group of enthusiasts whose tastes are narrowly avant garde, at the same time as it alienates many students whose tastes are more orthodox.

What should we make of the widening split between popular and serious literature? Is this development necessarily conducive to the health of our literature? Especially, is it conducive to the health of our fiction? Today, the common run of readers is catered to by specialists in mass market fiction. Fewer and fewer writers can appeal to both the elite and the mass audiences. For the novel, above all other literary forms, this seems a disaster. If not a disaster, then certainly it represents a highly significant transformation in its nature. For the novel, by historical origin, is a bourgeois art form. It presents images of the everyday life of everyday people. Just as important, it presents itself in an apparently straightforward manner, as an accurate transcription of a

249

social and emotional world the reader can imagine existing out there somewhere in the "real" world. Of course this picture is too simple. The conventions of realism, we are rightly told by many critics, are just as intricate as the conventions of the other literary genres and modes. But it remains true that writing based on the conventions of realism is accessible to a large potential readership, including many who are untrained in formal literary analysis. Consigning literature to the academy, however, will encourage the production in increasing numbers of contemporary forms of the art novel.

Like so much of contemporary art, the art novel is intended to pass directly from the artist's workroom to the museum's display gallery. This represents an important departure from the way most art was created in the past. Most of the objects displayed as "art" in conventional museums of the fine arts were intended to serve a social function in their cultures of origination: religious art acted as an aid to worship; prephotographic portraits provided flattering likenesses or suitably dignified images of the artist's clients; and so on. Today, the sole purpose of much art is to become part of a museum collection. Art has thus lost its social function, save in the eyes of those who have a vested interest in the idea of "pure" art – namely, artists and critics. This analysis, I suggest, is as valid for literature as for most other forms of contemporary artistic activity. And when the creation of art becomes introverted and self-serving to this extent, when art serves the needs of so narrowly defined a group of specialists, who are far removed from the centre of their society, we may well wonder if such art any longer fills a meaningful social niche.

My real purpose here is not to impugn all experimental fiction. Rather, I want to raise some questions about the general direction in which Canadian fiction is being steered, under the enthusiastic guidance of the academy. When there is an emphasis on technical innovation in fiction – and a concurrent denigration of the straightforward mimetic possibilities of fiction – then our fiction may lose its capacity to mirror the particularities of culture and personality. Our writers may lose their desire to examine specific social conditions and particular backgrounds – whether ethnic, religious, or regional. Under these conditions, the Canadian novel, as we have known it, may cease to be written by our most talented writers. The Canadian tradition in fiction has been established above all by the bourgeois novel with a Canadian setting. Today, this sort of fiction is an endangered species, squeezed ever tighter between, on the one hand, the burgeoning Americanism of the popular entertainment available through film and television and, on the other hand, the mid-Atlantic rootlessness of the international style of high art.

Let me immediately make one thing clear: I am not predicting the imminent demise of literary activity in Canada. Novels and other forms of literature will continue to be written, perhaps in increasing numbers. It is the nature of our future literary productions that concerns me. Our literature may increasingly be written in conformity with an intricate set of conventions that are of interest only to a small group of specially trained readers. Our fiction, in particular, may increasingly lose contact with the social realities experienced by the majority of Canadians. The upshot will be not the cessation of literature in Canada, but rather the assimilation of our literature to the style of the international avant garde. That is, the trendier forms of the art novel would decisively become the chief form of Canadian fiction. And if this were to happen, a distinctively Canadian fiction would continue to exist only as an exhibit in the literary museum. Our fiction would change direction with the latest winds of avant-garde literary fashion, or rely on superficially clever tricks played with narrative point of view. But, in literature at any rate, novelty for its own sake often leads merely to eccentricity or triviality. Many contemporary writers, I have reluctantly concluded, are in danger of falling into just such triviality.

I offer this conclusion hesitantly. But it seems to be the logical upshot of the line of reasoning I have followed. In the twentieth century, writers have increasingly adopted a view of art that has alienated them from the social consensus. This was all very well when writers responded to their isolation by attacking the meannesses and the hypocrisy of bourgeois society. Writers who are social critics at least remain involved with their society. However, if a writer's

251

preoccupations are not shared by other members of the community, then the writer's work will probably occupy at best a marginal status in the community's literary tradition.

Today, our writers increasingly speak for no-one but themselves and a few like-minded readers. This makes me uneasy. I suspect that a healthy and vibrant literary tradition cannot sustain itself for long if the majority of writers try to stand apart from the central values of their society. I do not mean that literature should be overtly didactic, or that writers should crudely seize contemporary social issues by the throat. Rather, my point is that a writer's skill and ingenuity will be wasted if the resulting literature does not somehow grapple with issues that concern a large number of the people around him. If literary works do not arise from concerns that have engaged the interest of a substantial number of people, those works will somehow be hollow at the core. For surely indifference to the community's major preoccupations amounts to little less than indifference to most human concerns.

Until very recently, as I have argued earlier in this study, the central tradition of our fiction could be found in the work of writers such as Grove, Callaghan, MacLennan, Buckler, Ross, Mitchell, Wilson, Laurence, Richler, Davies, and Munro. (These writers use the conventions of the bourgeois novel to make statements about the life that is lived in particular parts of our country, at particular times.)They do not pander to the mass market, yet their fiction exists in a fruitful tension with more popular kinds of storytelling. For they use the same realistic techniques as popular or mass-market writers, but they put these techniques to a more critical use. As a result, they write books that are accessible to a wide readership, and they do so without sacrificing their private visions. Our universities should be encouraging such writing, rather than calling for experimental or language-centred fiction. After all, what will we get if Canadian fiction wholeheartedly adopts the international style? At best, we will see more incarnations of *The Studhorse Man* (1969). At worst – and this is a more likely result – we will get more works like Chris Scott's *Bartleby* (1971) or George Bowering's *A Short Sad Book* (1977) and *Burning Water* (1980). The games these works play with

Canadian themes may not announce the health of a national tradition, but may predict its death, crushed by the weight of excessive self-consciousness.

Now, I will readily admit that I may be hasty in my lament for the death of our fiction as a distinctive expression of our collective life. I'd like to think so. Cultural survival is surely a matter of collective social will, as well as the expression of brute economic and political forces. In spite of the thrust of my own argument, therefore, I retain a desire for the survival of the Canadian cultural identity. And I remain convinced that, whatever its eventual fate, the Canadian experiment was worth attempting.

But I wonder if I have anticipated the mark by much. Perhaps at most by a few decades. At any rate, premature laments are not without precedent in Canadian letters. For example, George Grant's *Lament for a Nation* (1965) incongruously sounded a national threnody just as the patriotic choruses were tuning up for our centennial year festivities. Grant complained that Canada has never brought into concrete social being the Platonic ideal upon which its national existence was originally based. Canada, Grant mourned, has not achieved an incarnation of the good, but only a lesser imitation of the meretricious culture that exists to the south. The disappearance of Canadian literature, which I am tentatively lamenting, is hardly equivalent to the disappearance of the entire nation. Yet if our literature cannot keep its distinctiveness, then one more reason for the country's continued existence as an independent nation will have vanished.

Some ideas that have been expounded by Northrop Frye are relevant to my discussion at this point. As far as Canadian writing goes, Frye is usually seen as a muted nationalist. His well-known essays "Preface to an Uncollected Anthology" and "The Narrative Tradition in English-Canadian Poetry" and above all his "Conclusion" to the *Literary History of Canada* are devoted to defining the distinctive quality of Canadian letters. Particularly in the "Conclusion" he draws a contrast between Canadian and American literatures that is based on their expression of divergent national ideals. But in *The Modern Century* (1967), a small book that prints three lectures Frye delivered two years after the *Literary History* was published, Frye's assessment of the future of Canadian letters takes another direction.

Frye's ideas might well be considered a literary corollary to Grant's view of Canada, although Frye's equanimity in the face of the cultural transformation sweeping over the contemporary world makes him sound more like Marshall McLuhan than George Grant. In *The Modern Century* Frye seeks to explain how Canada's cultural situation is affected by social forces that are at work throughout the modern industrialized world. "It seems to me," Frye says, "quite clear that we are moving towards a post-national world, and that Canada has moved further in that direction than most of the smaller nations."[1] He announces his purpose as "neither to eulogize nor to elegize Canadian nationality, neither to celebrate its survival nor to lament its passage, but to consider what kinds of social context are appropriate for a world in which the nation is rapidly ceasing to be the real defining unit of society" (pp. 17-18). There has appeared in the arts, Frye contends, an international style, a style that is common to all the industrialized democracies. He says of the arts in Canada: "Complete immersion in the international style is a primary cultural requirement, especially for countries whose cultural traditions have been formed since 1867, like ours" (p. 57).

Frye adds an optimistic rider to this last statement: "Anything distinctive that develops within the Canadian environment can only grow out of participation in this style" (p. 57). I'm not so sure about the possibility of distinctiveness appearing at some future time. Instead, I fear that Canadian literature is moving inexorably towards an international style, in which characteristics arising from the idiosyncrasies of our history will become vanishingly small. I am suggesting that the future of the Canadian literary tradition is inextricably bound up with the vexed question of Canada's overall cultural autonomy. It is uncertain whether the majority of Canadians have any desire to keep Canada's cultural identity separate from that of the United States. And how can the

---

[1] Northrop Frye, *The Modern Century* (Toronto: Oxford Univ. Press, 1967), p. 17. All further references to this work appear in the text.

Canadian literary tradition survive when our writers no longer have a distinctive culture to write about?

The conservatism of the Canadian temperament is one more example of the outlook that, according to George Grant, "has made us a society of greater simplicity, formality, and perhaps even innocence than the people to the south" (p. 70). As Grant points out: "The belief in Canada's continued existence has always appealed against universalism. It appealed to particularity against the wider loyalty to the continent" (p. 85). Canadian fiction has provided some of the most eloquent expressions of our devotion to such particularity, and our rejection of continentalism. The question now is: How long will it continue to do so?

INDEX